Problem solving
stuff on p 137 and
after

The

Intelligence

of

Democracy

CHARLES E. LINDBLOM

The
Intelligence
of
Democracy

DECISION MAKING THROUGH MUTUAL ADJUSTMENT

The Free Press, New York
Collier-Macmillan Limited, London

To my wife

Collier-Macmillan Canada, Ltd., Toronto, Ontario

Library of Congress Catalog Card Number: 65-16269

printing number
3   4   5   6   7   8   9   10

Contents

Part 5
Comparative Analysis
of Central Coordination and
Mutual Adjustment

Part 6
Policy Toward
Mutual Adjustment

PREFACE

       INSOFAR AS I CAN SORT
out—and I do not wholly trust either my memory or percept
this point—the origins of this study are threefold. First is
adequacy, relative to the rest of the book, of the section on b
ing in R. A. Dahl's and my *Politics, Economics and Welfare* (New
York: Harper, 1953). At the time we sent the book to press we
were both less satisfied with that section than with any other, and
I looked forward to investigating the subject further. Second, as a
consultant to the RAND Corporation in the summer of 1954, I was
involved in some problems of an appraisal of defense policy against
a background of rivalry among the military services. The stimulating environment of RAND greatly advanced my interests in mutual adjustment processes. Third, I am an economist whose stock in
trade is supposed to be competence on mutual adjustment processes
as they appear in markets; I thought I could perhaps apply that
competence to a study of political bargaining and other marketlike
mutual adjustment processes in government.

From these origins, this book—but only slowly. Along the way I have worked out pieces of the analysis in journal articles; recently David Braybrooke and I combined in *A Strategy of Decision* (New York: Free Press, 1963) his philosophy and my social science in an exposition of a kind of decision making that appears prominently in the present study.

Central to this study is a comparison of coordination through a central coordinator and through mutual adjustment. In making this comparison I comment on various scholars whose writings indicate that they simply do not grasp the possibilities of coordination by mutual adjustment. A reader of the manuscript has suggested to me that these scholars know more than they write. On many topics, he says, there is a kind of professional wisdom that social scientists draw on when they face practical problems even if they lose it when they write their theoretical works. My critic is correct. The works whose shortcomings I display for heuristic purposes are often written by men who smuggle into their less formal thinking elements missed in their articles and books. I want, of course, to get the missing elements into the literature of social science; hence it is fair game to draw attention to what is presently missing from that literature, even if what is missing is not wholly unknown.

I have pursued this study at Yale and at the Center for Advanced Study in the Behavioral Sciences with the assistance of the Social Science Research Council and the Ford Foundation. To these institutions my thanks, to which I append the customary assurance that they are not responsible for anything I say.

One way or another, often without their knowing it, I have tapped the intelligence and skills of several hundred colleagues while working on this study. Although it would be foolish to list them, I wish to thank them and acknowledge my very great obligation to them.

Part
I

Introduction

RATIONAL POLICY

THROUGH

MUTUAL ADJUSTMENT

Coordination through Mutual Adjustment

A SIMPLE IDEA IS ELABORATED in this book: that people can coordinate with each other without anyone's coordinating them, without a dominant common purpose, and without rules that fully prescribe their relations to each other. For example, any small number of people can through a series of two-person communications arrange a meeting of them all; no central management is required, nor need they all have originally wanted to organize or attend the meeting. When two masses of pedestrians cross an intersection against each other they will slip through each other, each pedestrian making such threatening, adaptive, or deferential moves as will permit him to cross, despite the number of bodies apparently in his way. Similarly, the representatives of a dozen unions and the management of an enterprise can coordinate with each other on wages and working conditions through negotiation.

On an immensely larger scale coordination also is often achieved through mutual adjustment of persons not ordered by rule, central management, or dominant common purpose. An American consumer of coffee and a Brazilian supplier are so coordinated. The market mechanism is, both within many countries and among them, a large-scale, highly developed process for coordinating millions of economically interdependent persons without their being deliberately coordinated by a central coordinator, without rules that assign to each person his position relative to all others, and without a dominant common purpose. Market coordination is powered by diverse self-interests. Scholars can hardly fail to note the possibilities of coordination through mutual adjustment of partisans* in the market, for a long tradition of theory has produced an increasingly refined explanation of the process.

Development of common law may be another example. The law as laid down by different judges is coordinated, at least in part if not entirely, because the judges have an eye on each other. They are, of course, bound greatly by rules, but on those points at which new law is required, one cannot wholly explain its coordination as no more than a result of rule observance. As to whether judges hold to a dominant purpose or, on the other hand, to diverse purposes hidden under abstract language is a matter of dispute. In any case common law development, like the other examples, suggests possibilities for coordination through mutual adjustment.

Similarly, to speak a language is to follow rules. But innovations in language—usages that depart from existing rules—are coordinated by mutual adjustment among persons who have no necessary common interest, not even in the improvement of the language. Each person on his own reacts in one way or another to an innovation; the result is that the innovation either fails or is given an agreed meaning or use. It has then been made a coordinate part of a complex system for communication.

The first striking fact about this simple idea is that although significant examples of coordination through mutual adjustment

* In this chapter "partisans" are persons without a dominant common purpose.

are easy to find and coordination through mutual adjustment is the subject of a body of theory in economics, many informed persons either in effect deny that it is possible or treat it as of little consequence. Although no one who once reflects on it will explicitly deny the possibility, habits of thought inhibit the reflection. Gulick has, for example, found only two primary means of coordination in public administration: central direction and common purpose. Mutual adjustment is denied or reduced to triviality simply by its omission from his list.[1] Thompson finds four approaches to coordination: command, routines, group identification, and cooperation based on recognized interdependence. Command and routines correspond to central management and rules; group identification and cooperation based on recognized interdependence are two forms, he says, of employing common goals. Again the mutual adjustment of partisans is by-passed.[2]

The pedestrian of our example and the coffee consumer or supplier play their coordinating roles in mutual adjustment without being aware of it; that is, they do not ordinarily see their problem as one of coordination and in any case do not deliberately discharge a coordinating function. What coordination is achieved is not in their minds, nor governed by their minds' concern with coordination. Yet William Yandell Elliott has written, "If a government is ever to be coordinated, it must be coordinated in the minds of the people who authorize it and those who operate it, from the top to the bottom of the structure."[3] The statement comes close to denying the fact of coordination through mutual adjustment—at least in government.

Reinhold Niebuhr has said:

Human society therefore requires a conscious control and manipulation of the various equilibria which exist in it. There must be an organizing centre within a given field of social vitalities. This centre must arbitrate conflicts from a more impartial perspective than is available to any party of a given conflict. . . .[4]

That society requires conscious control and manipulation is one assertion; that an "organizing centre" is required is quite another. To be sure, Niebuhr may have meant no more than that government is necessary to discipline the "balance of forces" that he recognizes as an alternative form of organization; if so, it is significant that his concept of government is that of a central managing competence. Mutual adjustment he recognizes as a possibility, but an unsatisfactory one unless subordinated to an "organizing centre."

It appears that for some reason, despite the obvious usefulness of mutual adjustment elsewhere, it is its coordinating role in politics that is doubted—doubted even in a pluralist society with a pluralist theme in much of its political philosophy and science. Dahl and Lindblom, for example, acknowledge bargaining among leaders (which, given their use of the term, can be taken as approximating what is here being called mutual adjustment among partisans) to be a major method of political organization. They go so far as to specify forms of reciprocal control as methods of at least small-group coordination. On the other hand, their extended discussion of how to remedy problems of malcoordination in American government locates the source of the problem in bargaining and the possible cures in development of various methods for bringing more central coordination to bear.[5] Moreover, they are more interested in bargaining among leaders as a control device; its merits for rational calculation and coordination are less sympathetically dealt with.

For an example from public administration, Pfiffner and Presthus, in an extended discussion of the interrelationships between top administrator, legislator, and interest group, display an appreciation of the fact of and usefulness of mutual adjustment. They too, however, declare that mutual adjustment aggravates the problem of coordination, as though it had not occurred to them that it might do the job of coordination; they then go on to discuss methods of coordination other than mutual adjustment among partisans.[6]

A major contemporary work in the pluralist tradition is, of course, David Truman's *The Governmental Process*. Although deferring extended comment on it, we take note that whatever its benefits in the representation of interests, mutual adjustment is there regarded as posing, not solving, coordination problems.[7] And Arthur Bentley's *Process of Government*,[8] it is probably correct to say, simply does not raise the question of whether his interplay of group pressures can serve a coordinating role.

A curious feature of some common views on mutual adjustment

among partisans in politics is the distinction implicitly drawn between organization and coordination. Not that such a distinction is odd, only that the difficulties of drawing it might have been expected to have provoked a reconsideration of mutual adjustment. For, on the one hand, mutual adjustment is recognized as a fundamentally useful feature of social organization as, for example, in Truman; yet, on the other hand, it is doubted as a fundamental coordinating process. Can it be the one and not the other? If one's view of governmental policy machinery is that somehow parts usually fall into place but sometimes do not (and only then is it necessary to coordinate), one can hardly escape asking how it is that usually the parts do fall into place. If the answer is that they do so with the aid of mutual adjustment, it is then incumbent on us to ask whether some improvement or reconstruction of mutual adjustment in trouble spots might serve to get all the parts into place—that is, to coordinate. That they do generally fall into place only with the aid of mutual adjustment seems to be the belief of all those who assert the general utility of mutual adjustment while still shrinking from conceding it a significant coordinating role.

To be sure, one might believe that failures in coordination, examples of which are painfully plentiful in American government, are themselves evidence of the limitations of mutual adjustment, hence *prima facie* a case for coordination by central direction. Such an appraisal of a situation is hardly profound: malcoordination may be the result of either defective mutual adjustment or defective central direction, and presumably its cure could lie in either.

Heightened attention in recent years to bargaining and related phenomena, as in game theory or as in the work of Schelling,[9] indicates that the coordinating possibilities of mutual adjustment among partisans are now being more fully explored. Game theory itself, however, has not come to grips with the possibility of political coordination through mutual adjustment except in very simple situations; and even for these, the formal relation of a "solution" to the phenomenon of coordination remains unspecified, lying as it does beyond the bounds of mathematics. Insofar as Schelling has explored the strategies appropriate to "winning" in various kinds of mutual adjustment, his work does not bear directly on the possibility of coordination, but the indirect bearing is fruitful. Moreover, some of his investigation does ask directly about features of outcomes of mutual adjustment relevant to co-ordination. It is no objection to any of this work, though important to note, that none of it undertakes sustained comparative analysis or evaluation of central and noncentral coordination or decision making.

From a variety of quarters, in fact, come insights into the possibility of exploiting mutual adjustment for rational calculation and coordination, all of which can be more fully developed. Polanyi, for example, has in three different ways explored the role of non-partisan mutual adjustment, that is, adjustment responsive to a common goal though independent of central direction: first, ab-stractly; second, as a phenomenon in the coordination of science; and third, as a method outside the market for reducing the burdens of central direction of the Soviet economy.[10] March and Simon have discussed the role of bargaining to resolve conflict, comparing it with "analytical" methods.[11] Years ago Follett enthusiastically ex-plored the virtues of reciprocity rather than central direction for coordination;[12] but her arguments have apparently been either forgotten, taken to be applicable only to small-group situations, or neglected because unsystematic. And although the pluralist tradi-tion has not, as we have said, looked very far into the specific question of coordination through mutual adjustment, there is much to be tapped on the question in Bentley, Truman, Latham, and Herring, among others.[13]

Symptomatic of growing interest in noncentral governmental systems is a study of government in metropolitan areas by Ostrom, Tiebout, and Warren.[14] Reacting to allegations that metropolitan political organization is a "crazy quilt," they found a "system" in it. For Los Angeles County and the municipalities within it they found an elaborate system of contracting—between county and municipality for specific services, between municipality and munici-pality, and between municipality and private firms—that accounts for a good deal more organization than would at first appear. And for political conflicts among the governmental members of the metro-politan area they found "a rich and intricate 'framework' for negotiating, adjudicating and deciding questions that affect their diverse public interests." The specific methods of noncentral coordination they explore are, however, limited to the market and to negotiation.

New Inquiries

Among other possibilities, what remains to be done is to undertake a more or less *systematic comparison of central coordination and mutual adjustment* in which such claims for centrality as the claim that it achieves a rational adjustment of decisions or policies to each other are appraised for mutual adjustment as well. Doubts stir, it was noted, in the minds of those who do not believe it can coordinate the governmental process; its coordinating potential is elsewhere conceded. Hence, the comparison should be *limited to the coordination of political leaders and their decisions.* In the existing literature, "bargaining" sometimes appears as a fairly precisely defined form of adjustment, sometimes as a general name for undifferentiated types of mutual adjustment which now require differentiation. Hence, the analysis should *specify the various kinds of partisan mutual adjustment.*

This, then, is the proposal of this book: To undertake a systematic comparative analysis of centrality and partisan mutual adjustment among various kinds of political officials and leaders as competing methods for rational coordination of governmental decisions, mutual adjustment denoting a group of devices to be classified.

There is more in such a proposal than meets the eye. Although one can draw a distinction between ordinary decisions and coordinating decisions in central coordination, in partisan mutual adjustment, one cannot. There are no coordinators in partisan mutual adjustment; such coordination as is achieved is a by-product of ordinary decisions, that is, of decisions not specifically intended to coordinate. *For partisan mutual adjustment, therefore, to study coordination is to study decision making generally.*

Moreover, what meaning is to be given to "coordination"? "Balance" or "adjustment" is not enough. One wants to know whether, through mutual adjustment, decisions can be brought into the kind of relation with each other that in central adjustment leads one to say that they are rationally, or efficiently, or intelligently, or wisely related. But then the question of whether mutual adjustment is capable of coordinating governmental decisions is hardly distinguishable from the question of whether mutual adjustment produces rational decisions. In central systems one can imagine rational ordinary decisions being poorly coordinated. In mutual adjustment, however, where all decisions are ordinary, it would be hard to imagine calling a decision coordinated if it had not in some sense been rationally adapted to other decisions to which it is a response. In a simple case we coordinate each new decision with past decisions of ourselves and others to the extent that we take the status quo, which is the product of past decisions, as the real world to which our decision has to be adapted. But to adapt a decision to the real world is to practice at least an elementary form of rationality. Hence coordination and rationality tend to fuse. *For partisan mutual adjustment, therefore, to study coordination is to study rationality.*

Thus the proposal of this book becomes: To undertake a systematic comparison of centrally directed decision making and of partisan mutual adjustment as processes for rational decision making by political leaders.

There is, of course, a great deal more to political coordination than coordination of decisions of political leaders. Although it would be one of the tasks of a study of political coordination to specify how much the term embraces, it is clear that it might refer to all those processes by which diverse interests or values are aggregated in the making of public policy. If so, it would embrace those processes that create and maintain a common culture, including common language and common historical experience, but especially those that maintain common standards of evaluation, common moral rules, and other dispositions toward procedural agreement. It would include also personal influence and the variety of value-forming relations within small groups, as well as indoctrination through the schools and the mass media;[15] also processes that maintain coordinating subcultures, like those that have been said to explain coordination of decision making within professional groups within the political process;[16] in addition, elections, party competition, representation and delegation; various forms of mutual adjustment among officials, interest group and opinion leaders; and, finally, deliberate central coordination of sets of decisions.

Out of all this we select for study only those aspects of coordination or decision making in which it is possible to conceive of centrality and mutual adjustment among political leaders as possible alternatives: for example, in policy making by administrative agencies or in Congressional policy making, where one can imagine some central coordination by party leadership on the one hand, and mutual adjustment among legislators on the other. We exclude, for example, mutual adjustment among citizens. Moreover, we shall be almost entirely concerned with these two alternative processes as they do or might operate within a more or less democratic or polyarchal political system; that implies specifically that we are not considering either of them as possible substitutes for, say, elections or any other essential feature of polyarchal politics.

Against a background of coordination in the large the fruitfulness of comparative analysis of centrality and mutual adjustment is more apparent. For against that background it appears that central coordination is a highly specialized process resting lightly on more pervasive social processes. On the other hand, it is at least possible that mutual adjustment among partisan political leaders, being ubiquitous, may turn out to be a more fundamental political coordinating process than centrality.

Our inquiry will take us beyond the boundaries of the decision-making approach to governmental phenomena. For it becomes clear that government acts or policies are not simply decisions, nor do they stand in any one-to-one relation with decisions. An act or policy is sometimes a decision or, to state it better, directly the product of a decision. But it is sometimes a resultant, in ways to be explored in this study, of conflicting or at least diverse decisions. The focus of inquiry must often be not the decisions, but their complex consequences for each other.

Mindful of this we shall hereafter call a system of mutual adjustment a policy-making system, not a decision-making system, intending by that to draw a distinction between decisions made and governmental actions actually taken. (In introducing the term "policy" we are not referring to a continuing line of decisions or set of constraints on individual decisions, although elsewhere in the literature the term is sometimes so employed.) A central system is, however, appropriately called a decision-making system, as well as a policy-making system. For in centralized systems relations of one decision to another are, roughly speaking, regulated by a co-ordinating decision rather than by their consequences for each other. Hence, in a sense not true for mutual adjustment, policy in a central system is what decisions directly make it, even if, of course, central decisions are not always wholly effective.

Pluralist Thought

Alternatively, this book can be described as attending to some unfinished business in pluralist thought in response to widespread dissatisfaction with conspicuous lacunae in group theories of politics. Where group and pluralist theory says that conflicting "forces" achieve "adjustment" or "balance" or perhaps even "equilibrium," many students of government have understandably wondered whether a satisfying content could be pumped into such abstractions.

A good deal of English pluralist thought can be represented in several summary propositions that are either not employed or are denied in the present study; and their rejection is an economical way of saying that the present study, if taken as an attempt to fill in lacunae, both challenges and supplements the pluralist tradition. Although it is not accurate to attribute precisely the following views to any one English pluralist or antecedent, a legacy from Figgis, Maitland, Laski, Cole, and others is a set of beliefs that (1) the state is only one of many associations and is without any moral or legal priority; (2) the state is not sovereign; (3) individual loyalty to an association, and involvement and satisfaction in it are less marked than for smaller associations; (4) the state is primarily a coordinating apparatus for the other associations; and (5) associations have or ought to have individual-like rights.[17]

It will become clear in succeeding chapters that a special role is indeed conceded to the state and that, although sovereignty is a troublesome concept not necessary to employ in this study, the special authority of the state takes a prominent place in the exposition of mutual adjustment. Nor does the study play down the pervasiveness and force of citizenship as against membership in other associations. And the state's role is a good deal more complex than that of a coordinating mechanism for other associations. On the rights of associations the question simply does not arise.

American pluralist doctrine is unacceptable on many counts. The emphasis that Bentley and others give to the interest group goes too far. Interest groups are of course major participants in partisan mutual adjustment, but Bentley carries this concept too far when he says: "The whole social life in all its phases can be stated in such groups of active men, indeed must be stated in that way if a useful analysis is to be had." Or when he says, "Indeed the only reality of the ideas is their reflection of the groups, only that and nothing more."[18]

Nor should common national interests and values be denied.[19] Mutual adjustment of partisans within constraints of common values and—what is more—adjustment of partisans that produces a national convergence of interest or value will be examined. Then, too, mutual adjustment sometimes takes the form of conflict among officials or group leaders who sponsor different versions of a common or public interest; in an important sense groups do not always sponsor group interests, nor do public officials.

Bentley, Truman, Latham, and Herring, to mention a representative sample, all recognize that public agencies or groups of public officials can themselves constitute interest groups, although official groups are accorded much more prominence in Latham than in Truman. For the most part, however, the prime movers in mutual adjustment in the pluralist tradition are private groups; state groups are often cast in a more passive role. In Latham, for example, the legislature "referees" the group struggle.[20] In fact, however, governmental participants in mutual adjustment often play no less an entrepreneurial or activating role than do private group leaders.

Moreover, insofar as pluralist thought generally endorses as well as describes the interaction of groups, the endorsement is often overgeneralized. Partisan mutual adjustment, as seen here, is useful in some situations and not in others; a general endorsement of it seems as misplaced as a general condemnation.

A most unsatisfactory feature of pluralist thought has been its failure to describe with some precision what might be taken as the purposes of or appropriate consequences for group interplay. In Bentley the purpose or desirable consequence is "balance" or "adjustment;" but the difference between balance and imbalance, between adjustment and maladjustment, is never clear; nor does he explain in any systematic way why balance or adjustment is a significant concept. Sometimes balance and adjustment refer to those conditions that keep the peace; his examples of adjustment often slide over into examples of how social peace is maintained.[21] More generally, in Bentley, the terms refer to the representation of interests: groups are in adjustment or are balanced when interests are represented. But then is any pattern of representation balanced or adjusted? Truman's concept of what group interplay achieves is perhaps also fairly described by "representation of interests"; but he also puts almost no content into the term, although he specifies, to be sure, some possible unacceptable outcomes of group interplay; such as "chaos and indecision."[22]

Now just what does one say when he declares that group interplay represents interests? Does one say that they are represented "democratically?" Bentley dismisses the question as not essential[23] Does one say that interests are "fairly" represented? His reference to such a question is casual.[24] Does one say that the reconciliation is "controlled" by the people? It is a kind of myth, a "matter of speech alone."[25] Does one say that interplay brings reason to bear on policy making? "Argument pure and simple," he says, "holds a very subordinate position," and reason generally is of small weight.[26]

If I say that groups interact but then refuse to specify any consequences of their action, other than that in unspecified ways interaction represents interests, I have said nothing of importance. Other pluralists manage to say more than Bentley. Consider for the moment the Founding Fathers as pluralists. They were concerned with the consequences of "faction" and of Constitutionally sponsored interplay of governmental groups both for minority rights and for the representation of the will of acceptable kinds of minorities. The pluralist tradition is generally strong in its concern for safeguarding democracy through dispersing power. Thus at least some pluralists can specify features of mutual adjustment that they wish to understand, often as a basis of subsequent evaluation of the process. They will ask whether the character of interplay and of its results is such as to protect minorities or, more generally, to inhibit a concentration of power.

These questions, however, are by no means all that can be asked about the mutual adjustment of officials, private individuals, and groups in governmental affairs. One can, for example, ask, does the process result in a representation of uninformed or informed interests? Does it result in a representation of values other than anyone's perceived interests? What consequence does the process itself have for forming and reforming—perhaps for inventing or discovering—interests or values? What is the role of information, of analysis, of "reason" as a force or pressure in the interplay? Are interests drawn toward each other in the process? Or are they driven apart? Do participants become intransigent? Are reconciliations of conflicting values mere compromises or are mutually satisfying adjustments achieved? What kinds of values yield other values? Do the results conform to any standards, even if only roughly stated, of intelligence or reason? Are the results in any meaningful sense efficient? Or are they wasteful of values? It is to these kinds of questions, largely neglected by the pluralist school, that this study is directed.

Not only have pluralists generally bypassed questions turning on the rationality of policy making through mutual adjustment, but they have taken the irrationality of the process for granted, then accepted irrationality as the necessary cost of a system that has the essential virtue of dispersing power. In this respect they have followed a long-standing belief in the United States, that social and constitutional checks and balances serve, as Justice Brandeis said, "not to promote efficiency but to preclude the exercise of arbitrary power."[27]

That some pluralists passed by not only questions of efficiency but also all other questions that might bear on an appraisal of group interplay is to be expected from their extreme pluralist conviction. Bentley, for example, believed he could not ask such questions because he looked upon the questions themselves as mere products of group interplay, and therefore apparently not appropriate to his research. On the subject of whether he could evaluate the group process of government, he in effect demurred: "It is these group pressures, indeed, that not only make but also maintain in value the very standards of justice, truth, or what not that reason may claim to use as guides."[28]

Pluralist disinclinations to examine the social rationality of group interplay, as well as Bentley's even more extreme reduction of human interchange to "force" and "pressure," as though minds were among the most trivial of resources available to the group, are elements of a kind of clumsy realism. The role of reason in politics is now generally obscured by the popularity in our time of the concept of political science as the study of power. But there are both very old and very new views of politics as much more than the play of power. Plato thought a fundamental problem in politics was posed by the difficulty of locating power and wisdom in the same place. They could be combined only in a philosopher-king. In partisan mutual adjustment there is at least a suggestion of how they can be brought closer together, although on terms that Plato would deplore.

Implications

Clarification of partisan mutual adjustment has more implications than can be spelled out in the study itself. Some practical implications will be illustrated in the closing chapters: specifically those for administrative organization, for the budgetary process, and for party organization. Moreover, during the course of the analysis its implications, for example, for customary appraisals of the virtue of consistency in policy making, for a reconsideration of the case— somewhat weakened under recent attacks—for constitutional checks and balances, and for the possibility of achieving important policy objectives epiphenomenonally rather than directly will be considered.

The analysis may also throw some small light on a venerable question in political philosophy, the role of common values in government, especially in democratic government. The pluralist skepticism of the existence of common values is not here shared; nor is politics viewed generally as a Hobbesian–Lasswellian process deciding "who gets what, when, how."[29] But the governmental process is not, on the other hand, seen in Rousseau's terms. And yet, again, the analysis finds a place for a great national leader like Lincoln whose synthesizing role in American history would seem to be foreign to politics through partisan mutual adjustment.

Part
2

Elements of the Process of Partisan Mutual Adjustment

Chapter

2

THE PARTICIPANTS

AND THE

PROCESS

Interdependent Decision Makers

CONSIDER A GROUP OF GOVERN-
ment policy makers, or for that matter, decision makers generally.
For the moment it is not necessary to define decision maker; the
term can be taken in any ordinary meaning. Postulate, however, that
the group is large enough to give rise to some complex problems in
the adjustment of members to each other. Postulate, in addition,
that the group is not so large as to include all or nearly all people
in the society in which the group makes decisions. Because one can
view each and every person in a society as a decision maker, a
decision-making group identical with the whole society is a logical
possibility; but it is one to be discarded both for simplicity and
because the governmental decision makers on whom the study is
focused are not so inclusive a class.

Assume the decision makers to be interdependent. Interdependence among any set of decision makers is defined in this way:
Within the set, each decision maker is in such a relation to each

• *other decision maker that, unless he deliberately avoids doing so (which may or may not be possible), he interferes with or contributes to the goal achievement of each other decision maker, either by direct impact or through a chain of effects that reach any* • *given decision maker only through effects on others.*

Thus, by definition, every decision maker is directly consequential for at least one other, and all are related indirectly through at least one chain whose links are composed of direct relations. A is directly consequential for B, for C, for D, and so on; or A is directly consequential for B, B for C, C for D, and so on until all are included.

Coordination Tentatively Defined

The question to be asked is how might such a group of decision makers be brought into coordination with one another. But coordination is in itself an elusive concept; it requires some specification even if it is not, at this point, either precisely defined or elaborated. In some usage "coordination" denotes the actions of a central decision maker who controls subordinates; that is, it is a term applied to a specific supervising process. Clearly, a different notion of coordination is called for here, for if coordination is defined as certain acts of a central decision maker, then there is no possibility of noncentral coordination; and the investigation of this book is finished at this point.

But to refuse to define coordination as a process suggests that it might be defined as results; that is, as the relationships existing among policies or decisions regardless of how these relationships are achieved. What relationships are the mark or test of coordination? • Where everyone agrees on a set of values sufficiently complete and well-structured to provide adequate criteria for decisions, one could simply say that the decisions are coordinated whenever their relationships are such as to satisfy the agreed criteria. "Coordination" would then denote desired or valued relationships among policies. Where, however, agreement is not to be had or is incomplete; or where, as is almost always the case for complex policy problems, not even one person can formulate his values so that they conclusively point to one rather than another set of policies; or where various kinds of uncertainty must be coped with, the desired or valued relationship among policies is subject to controversy, both in principle and in practice. Whether policies are or are not co-ordinated would then be disputed.

It would be premature to specify a desired relation among policies, or, for that matter, to beg the question whether such a specification is always possible even in principle. It is important to hold open a wide variety of possibilities. In later chapters, in discussing the differences in the ways in which central coordination, on the one hand, and noncentral coordination, on the other hand, achieve various relations among policy decisions, it will be important that the difference in results not be prejudged. Differences in method of coordination will throw light on what relations among policies are or are not to be desired, or valued; and what is desirable or valuable, or whether the valuable can be specified, is not to be decided upon *a priori*.

Coordination conceived of as the achievement of a desired or valued set of relations among policies is furthermore objectionable because such a concept makes it impossible to say of a set of policies that they are coordinated but badly, or coordinated and well.

For present purposes it would be helpful to have a concept of coordination that in some way denoted more or less systematic relationships among decisions and not much more. A preliminary concept suitable for this chapter can be found by asking how a set of policy decisions might, aside from luck, be brought into a valued relationship, whatever the relationship might be. The answer is, of course, that there must exist some methods of response among decision makers such that each policy is somehow adapted to the others, not merely randomly related. By this notion coordination can be said to exist whenever policies respond to, or are adapted to, other policies in the set; and it is possible to say of a set of policies that they are coordinated—because responsive or adaptive to each other—even if one cannot specify the character of a valued or desired relationship among them.

This is a weak rather than highly constraining definition of coordination, as is appropriate at this stage of the analysis; but it is sufficient to distinguish a phenomenon from its absence. It is not so weak as to sweep under the definition of coordination all possible relationships among policies. Uncoordinated decisions are those not adapted to each other. The maker of an uncoordinated decision gives no thought to the decision of any other decision maker; he enters into no communication with other decision makers; and he does not allow his decision to be altered by what another decision maker has already decided. There is simply no influence or effect from another decision to his or, turning the case around, from his to another.

By this definition a set of interdependent decisions is coordinated whenever each decision is adjusted to the others; that is, whenever any one decision is changed from what it would otherwise have been because of the direct or indirect influence of other decisions. If X can order Y to do as X wishes, or if X and Y come to terms with each other by reciprocal adaptations, or if X takes account of Y's decision in making his own, their decisions are coordinated in the elementary sense of the term "coordination."

The concept can now be strengthened slightly by further definition: the adjustment or influence of one policy to or on another is such that in the eyes of at least one decision maker the resulting situation is better than it would have been without the adaptation or influence. We cannot specify that the adjusted situation is valued by all, for by any reasonable notion of coordination, coordination is often achieved by thwarting some decision makers in the set.

The tentative definition of coordination, then is: *A set of interdependent decisions is coordinated if each decision is adapted to the others in such a way that for each adjusted decision, the adjustment is thought to be better than no adjustment in the eyes of at least one decision maker.*

One is tempted to add that coordination exists *to the degree* that each decision responds to the others. Even this modest amendment would go too far. For it would imply the greater the response, the more the coordination; and it would strongly suggest the more response, the better the coordination. Again, it is important not to foreclose possible lines of analysis prematurely. Let us leave untouched the purely definitional question whether the heavier the influence, the more the coordination; and let us even doubt that the heavier the influence, the better the coordination. All that the term "coordination" needs to do in this chapter is to denote a situation in which each decision in a set is somehow adjusted, to a degree unspecified, to other decisions in the set rather than standing without any influence from the others.

If such a concept of coordination strongly hints that there are elements of coordination in almost every set of decisions worth investigating, the hint should be no ground for disqualifying the concept as excessively broad. Perhaps there are in fact significant processes for the adaptation of decisions to one another in almost every significant kind of circumstances. If so, wholly uncoordinated decisions are a limiting case rather than a broad category. For the moment, such a possibility is quite acceptable.

General Types of Coordination Processes

With this definition, one can now attack the earlier question: In what various ways might coordination of interdependent decisions be achieved?

At one extreme is the familiar case of central coordination: decision makers adapt to one another on instruction from a central decision maker. Only rarely, of course, are all of a large number of decision makers subject directly to a central regulator. More typically, only some small number of decision makers are subject to coordinating decisions immediately central to them. That is, decision makers *a, b, c, d* and *e* are regulated by another decision maker L, whose duties include and are perhaps limited to the supervision of them. But L is brought into relationship with M, N, and O, each of whom is, like L, a coordinator for some number of decision makers "under" him, through the decisions of T, who is a coordinator at a higher level, and so on. Everyone is familiar with the pyramidal model of coordinated decision making in which coordination is central even if indirectly so. For the moment, the familiar model will do.

At the other extreme, one can imagine decisions to be governed by a process of mutual adjustment, in which no central mind or decision maker exercises any coordinating responsibility. The most familiar mutual adjustment process is negotiation, even if it is only one of a number of possibilities. Negotiation can sometimes achieve a very nicely adjusted relationship. This one example is sufficient to show the possibility of noncentral coordination through mutual adjustment, even before other kinds of partisan mutual adjustment are introduced into the discussion.

Diagrammatically, decision making centrally regulated is characterized in its purest form by adjustments of the pattern represented in Diagram 1a. Decision making through mutual adjustment is characterized by the variety of relationships in Diagram 1b.

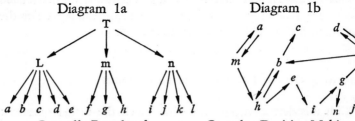

Diagram 1a

Diagram 1b

Centrally Regulated
Complex Decision Making

Complex Decision Making
through Mutual Adjustment

(1) Each letter indicates a decision maker.
(2) $x \rightarrow y$ means y's decisions are adjusted to x's decisions

Notice that in Diagram 1b, decision making through mutual adjustment, not every decision maker is adjusted directly to every other decision maker. That one or more decision makers might directly adjust to every other decision maker in mutual adjustment is only a remote possibility. Note also that among pairs of decision makers in mutual adjustment, their control relations can be either formally symmetric, as in bargaining, or not. In this diagram, note that a and m are in a symmetric relation with each other, and so are b and h. But m and h are not. Although it is not uncommon to identify mutual adjustment with symmetric control relationships, the decision-making possibilities to be explored in this study go well beyond that restricted possibility.

The diagrams fall short, however, of adequately distinguishing between central and noncentral coordination. In Diagram 1b note that l might be argued to be central with respect to d and k and b, or *h* central for *b* and *e*. This is a possibility to be ruled out by postulating that, in mutual adjustment no decision maker acknowledges a supervisory responsibility or role for himself while, on the other hand, some decision makers do so in central coordination. In Diagram 1a, in the cases of T, L, M, and N, each explicitly plays a supervisory role and, what is more, will typically exercise control actively over their "subordinates." By contrast, in Diagram 1b, *l* and *h* will not play a supervisory role even with respect to *d, k* and *b*, in the one case, and *b* and *e*, in the other case (we shall shortly specify what they do do positively instead of supervise). Moreover, they may or may not be able to exercise power actively over *d, k,* and *b,* and *e;* instead, *d, k,* and *b,* or *b* and *e* may be, for example, deferentially adapting to *l* or *h* while *l* and *h* remain in ignorance of their relations with *d, k,* and *b,* or with *b* and *e*.

What of the possibility that *l* and *h* do play an explicit and active supervisory role while at the same time participating in a mutual adjustment process, as in Diagram 1b? Such a possibility will be considered a mixed system rather than still another pure type. Mixed systems are in fact common, and diagrammatically can be represented as in Diagram 2, where we make L both a central supervisor to a degree (of *d, b,* and *k*) and a mutual adjuster.

Diagram 2

Mixed Central and Noncentral Coordination

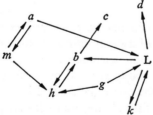

There is a third kind of coordination: coordination through agreed acceptance of rules of behavior sufficient to specify how, in any case of interdependence, each decision in a set is to be adjusted to each other. How important such a method of coordination is, is a question on which opinions will differ. Coordination by agreed rules is at least sufficiently important to require that some attention be given to it when it is intermixed with mutual adjustment, even if it is not a kind of coordination that this study will explore beyond that. Insofar as adequate rules are laid down by a central coordinator, the case is subsumed under central coordination.

There would appear to be still one final closely related alternative method by which coordination among political leaders could be achieved. In the face of conflicts among their actual or intended decisions, decision makers might enter into a cooperative discussion of their common problems on the supposition that there are agreed criteria sufficient to determine upon investigation the proper course of action for each of them. This is a kind of coordination meant to be excluded from mutual adjustment as shown in Diagram 1b. It is a kind of coordination strikingly like central coordination in its simplest nonhierarchical or nonpyramidal form, for the group of decision makers in effect plays the role of the central coordinating mind. Given the assumption that there is an agreed criterion sufficient for the resolution of their problem, it is clear that they cooperatively investigate their problem rather than bargain or negotiate with one another or employ any of the other techniques of mutual adjustment. We can, however, more carefully distinguish coordination through cooperative discussion from mutual adjustment by introducing the concept of the partisan.

Partisans

Diagram 1b should not be construed as picturing the adjustments to each other of a group of cooperative problem solvers who as a collectivity deliberately assume a task of coordination. To make certain that this possibility is ruled out—ruled out as a phenomenon different from the one to be studied in this book—it will now further be specified that all the mutually adapting participants in the decision making are, in a special sense to be defined, partisans.

A partisan decision maker is defined in the following way: *In a group of decision makers a decision maker is partisan with respect to the others if (a) he does not assume that there exists some knowable criteria acceptable to him and all the other decision makers that is sufficient, if applied, to govern adjustments among them; and (b) he therefore does not move toward coordination by a cooperative and deliberate search for and/or application of such criteria or by an appeal for adjudication to those who do so search and apply.*

A partisan decision maker is therefore one who makes decisions calculated to serve his own goals, not goals presumably shared by all other decision makers with whom he is interdependent, except as he is controlled by other partisans or by central supervision.

One kind of partisan decision maker is familiar. He assumes that the interests of the various interdependent decision makers are seriously in conflict; he therefore openly seeks to prevail over the others, and he is overtly hostile to the others. Another type is the decision maker who doubts the existence of agreed criteria adequate to govern his interrelationships with other decision makers, who in any case does not believe that a cooperative search for such criteria will be fruitful, but who is reluctant to play the role of the avowed partisan. He does what he must to pursue his own objectives, but often with an overlay of the rhetoric of harmony and cooperation. Still another kind of partisan decision maker is one who makes his decisions in the "public interest" but whose concept of the public interest, he well understands, is not shared by those with whom his decisions are interdependent. All decisions makers who pursue their own conceptions of the public interest, general welfare, or public good in relations with others who have different conceptions are partisans.*

One should be careful not to lapse into an identification of partisanship exclusively with the avowed partisanship of a decision maker responsive to no more than a narrow clientele. In the present meaning of the term, all decision makers are partisan much of the

---

* For example, of the OPA gasoline eligibility committee in World War II, Victor A. Thompson writes: "The committee clearly regarded itself as the interpreter of the 'public interest' within its special field of competence. To the committee, this involved insisting on a rule even though nearly everyone else disagreed with it. It meant protecting the 'real' interests of the people against strong public pressure, a pressure from within the OPA, to recognize actual and immediate interests, until it was overruled or 'forced' to change." (*The Regulatory Process in OPA Rationing* [New York: Columbia University Press, 1950], p. 84).

time. Nor, on the other hand, should one assume that the avowed partisan, because of his narrow-mindedness, is less likely to play an important role in effective mutual adjustment. The avowed partisan is often a more conciliatory adjuster than the covert partisan who thinks of himself as responsible for the public interest. Where the former expects to concede something in the light of the claims of others, the latter is sometimes godlike in his intolerance. In any case, however, a wide range of attitudes toward decision making is embraced under partisanship.

Notice that by the present conception, partisanship is not always of one's choosing. If other decision makers with whom one is interdependent choose to be partisan, one is forced into partisanship because a cooperative search for and / or application of common criteria is of course impossible without cooperation.

It is immediately apparent that partisan decision makers in American governmental processes include all the recognized pressure groups. But the President sometimes chooses to be and is sometimes forced to be a partisan, as are all members of Congress and all administrators. Also partisan are all groups who espouse, as do the American Civil Liberties Union and the League of Women Voters, a public good that though broad in conception is nevertheless not a conception agreed to by other decision makers.

The theory-of-games counterpart to some forms of partisan mutual adjustment is not, as might appear, the zero-sum game; it may be either zero or nonzero sum. Partisans engage in mutual adjustment in the pursuit of their own perceived interests, which are not assumed to be either the same as, or harmonious in some sense with, the interests of others. As they play out their moves in partisan mutual adjustment, however, it may turn out either that what one gains another loses, that everyone gains, that everyone loses, that some gain more than others, or that some lose more than others gain. As will often be the case, a "solution" reached is to the advantage of all participants, yet the distribution of the advantages is a point of conflict in the settlement. Although the partisan is defined as one who does not assume that an adequate agreed criterion is discoverable and that it should be found and applied, there will nevertheless sometimes exist such a criterion in a partisan mutual adjustment situation; and it will sometimes be found and applied as the result of the partisan moves of the participant decision makers.

So that it will not be forgotten that the mutual adjustment processes to be studied are those in which the participant decision makers are partisan, the processes will repeatedly be referred to as partisan mutual adjustment.

But having identified partisanship with the mutual adjustment processes to be studied, one must not, by contrast, identify centrally coordinated decision making with nonpartisanship. The decision makers to be coordinated in centrally regulated decision making are themselves often, perhaps typically, partisan. Mutual adjustment is defined as partisan not to contrast it with the ordinary case of central coordination of subordinate decision makers by a coordinating and separate decision maker such as L or T, but specifically to contrast it with the case of decision makers who cooperatively (in a nonpartisan way) constitute themselves collectively a coordinating decision maker.

In many circumstances what appears to be a case of central coordination is, of course, in fact a case of partisan mutual adjustment. In centrally coordinated decision making, defined as a pure type and illustrated in Diagram 1a, decision makers are assumed to accept the decisions of coordinators as governing their adaptations to each other, for otherwise their decisions could not accurately be described as centrally coordinated. Suppose, however, that in fact they do not wholly obey. Suppose each partisan tries to go his own way unmindful of the others. Or suppose that some scheme to cripple certain others, mutually threaten each other, cajole each other through an exchange of promised benefits, and so on. If, in what appears on its face to be a centrally coordinated decision-making process, displaying perhaps the familiar pyramidal form of control, decision makers in fact indulge in such tactics as these, the process is in actual fact one of partisan mutual adjustment, or is at least a mixture of partisan mutual adjustment and central coordination.

Everyone knows that these adjustment tactics are to be found behind almost every pyramidal facade. Looked at this way, the present project is to investigate and formalize our knowledge both of certain of those methods of decision making that are sometimes swept under the rug of the "informal organization," and of these same methods when they are part of the formal organization, even the constitutionally prescribed organization. Partisan mutual adjustment appears in a variety of degrees of formality.

For centrally coordinated decisions one can distinguish between the decisions to be coordinated, on the one hand, and the coordinating decisions, on the other; hence one might study coordination processes as distinct from decision processes taken generally. For partisan mutual adjustment, however, *every decision is itself part of the coordinating process;* there exists no separate set of coordinating decisions. In bargaining, for example, decision and the coordination of decisions of the participants are indistinguishable. If the term "coordination" is central to these introductory pages, the process to be studied turns out, as already noted, to be the decision-making process as a whole.

Possible Methods of Partisan Mutual Adjustment

To the extent that partisan decision makers are not centrally directed in their relationships with one another, what are the logically possible ways in which each might independently adjust to the others or effect others' adjustments to him? It will be desirable to use a method of classification that while accommodating familiar forms of mutual adjustment like negotiation, will also point up other possibilities corresponding to real-world situations. But it is further desirable that the system of classification also identify hypothetical limiting types analytically useful for displaying the full range of possibilities.

In any specific real-world decision situation in which a number of decision makers are interdependent, any one decision maker A is in one relation with another decision maker B, another relation with C, another with D, and so on. He may of course be in the same relation with B as with C; but, taking all other decision makers with whom he is in some direct relation in the given decision situation into account, it is likely that at any one time, his relations with the others encompass many, even all, of the relations that we shall identify. We shall explore the various possible methods of partisan mutual adjustment in a given situation as two-party relations; this makes it possible for us, for any given decision maker X, to specify the variety of relations with other decision makers as some combination of two-party relations. Even in a given decision situation X may, with respect to Y alone, practice more than one method of partisan mutual adjustment, for although some forms are mutually exclusive, some are not. Moreover, considering that X makes many decisions over time in many different situations, sooner or later he is almost certain to try all the possible methods of partisan mutual adjustment, even if he does not do so in any one decision situation.

The procedure to be followed for exploring possible types of partisan mutual adjustment is one designed to achieve an exhaustive list. If one considers the range of possibilities, two large categories are apparent: first, *adaptive adjustments,* in which a decision maker simply adapts to decisions around him, that is, makes those decisions that he can make without first enlisting, as in negotiation, a response from another decision maker; and second, *manipulated adjustments,* in which he seeks to enlist a response desired from the other decision maker.

Roughly and briefly, the range of possibilities includes the following methods of adjustment:

I. Adaptive (X seeks no response from Y.)
   A. *Parametric,* in which the decision maker, X, adapts to Y's decisions without regard to consequences for Y.
   B. *Deferential,* in which X seeks to avoid adverse consequences for Y.
   C. *Calculated,* in which X does not wholly avoid adverse consequences for Y but nevertheless adjusts his decision out of consideration for adverse effects for Y.
II. Manipulated (X, as a condition of making his decision, induces a response from Y.)
   A. *Negotiation,* in which X and Y, in a variety of ways, induce responses from each other.
   B. *Bargaining* (a form of negotiation), in which X and Y induce responses from each other by conditional threats and promises.

C. *Partisan discussion* (a form of negotiation), in which X and Y induce responses from each other by effecting a reappraisal of each other's assessment of the objective consequences of various courses of action. (Where bargaining alters the consequences, partisan discussion exchanges information about unaltered consequences.)

D. *Compensation,* in which X induces a response from Y by a conditional promise of benefit; and *bargained compensation* (a form of bargaining), in which X and Y make conditional promises to each other.

E. *Reciprocity,* in which X unilaterally, or X and Y symmetrically, in negotiation or otherwise, induce a response by calling in an existing obligation or acknowledging a new one.

F. *Authoritative prescription,* in which X prescribes a response to Y, who concedes X's authority.

G. *Unconditional manipulation,* in which X induces a response from Y by unconditionally altering the advantages or disadvantages to Y of various responses.

H. *Prior decision,* in which X takes a prior decision to induce Y to respond rather than forego the advantages of coordination with X.

I. *Indirect manipulation,* in which X uses any of the above forms of manipulation to induce a third decision maker to induce Y to make the desired response.

The following three chapters explain the derivation of this list, at the same time outlining, illustrating, and more precisely defining each of these forms of adjustment.* How they play their parts in the governmental process is then taken up again in Chapter 6.

* For another summary of manipulated adjustment, see especially Table I, p. 63 below.

Chapter

3

ADAPTIVE

ADJUSTMENTS

IN CONSIDERING THE DECISION maker X, who acts without requiring, as a recognized condition of making his decision effective, a response from another decision maker Y, let us take him to be an initiator of a decision. That is, postulate that X's decision is not a response to the attempt of any decision maker Y to control him as a condition of Y's making his own decision effective. X may be responding to a new situation resulting from a move of Y; but he is not responding to Y's deliberate attempt to control where X's response is a condition of Y's making his own decision effective.

Parametric Adjustment

Every such decision maker who is not wildly irrational will take account of a prevailing state of affairs in making his decisions. It is in fact difficult to imagine a decision maker who acts without any regard for the circumstances around him. Since among the prevailing conditions to which he adapts are past decisions still operative as well as roughly contemporary decisions, every such decision maker will adapt at least to these past and contemporary decisions. If, for example, the budgetary appropriations of a municipal government are made, as they will ordinarily be, in light of available funds, on the one hand, and public needs, on the other, they are in fact adapted to those past revenue and expenditure decisions that account for whatever funds are available and for whatever public demands are yet unsatisfied. In referring to such an obvious method of adaptation of decisions to other decisions as this we move to identify the first simple building block in the structure of coordination.

When a decision maker adapts to the circumstances in which he finds himself he adapts both to decisions firmly made in the past, to decisions roughly contemporary with his own, and to expected decisions. In sizing up the prevailing state of affairs he may seek to manipulate another decision maker to bring him into coordination with his own decision. Or he may decide, after appraising the situation, to make a decision only after considering its consequences for the other decision maker, thus achieving some coordination in that way. These methods of adjustment we put aside at this point in order to see clearly that the mere response to an existing state of affairs in which one does not consider the consequences of his decision for another decision maker is itself an adaptation of the decision to other decisions.

This most simple form of adjustment we shall define as parametric adjustment. It is adjustment by a decision maker who does not try to control another decision maker, does not defer to the other decision maker, does not allow the possible reactions of the other decision maker to his decision to influence the decision he makes. Whatever adjustment he achieves is due to his accommodating himself to a state of affairs without contemplating what he might do to the other decision maker. A traffic officer, for example, achieves coordination with another traffic officer a few intersections to his north whose presence is unknown to him simply by following a policy of temporarily stopping north-south traffic and opening east-west traffic whenever north-south traffic through his intersection becomes slow or vanishes, indicative of blockage to the north. He does not try to manipulate the other officer; but not even knowing that there is another officer whose signals cause northbound traffic to slow or stop, neither does he consider his effect on the other officer.

In all the forms of adaptive adjustment discussed in this chapter the decision maker X treats another decision maker Y as not subject to his control in the sense that he is not enlisted as an aide; and, if Y's decision constitutes an obstruction, X does not, as a condition of making his own decision, induce him to remove the obstruction. But in this simplest form of adaptive adjustment the decision maker is defined as acting as though the subsequent consequences of his decision were without effect on the other decision maker, hence without even unintended control over him. Whether X in fact believes his decision to be without consequence for Y, he acts without regard for the consequences, acting as though the consequences did not exist. He may, in fact, in contemplating a course of parametric adjustment, first raise with himself the question whether he will thereafter disregard the consequences of his decisions for the other decision maker, in which case he is concerned with those consequences only long enough to decide not to be thereafter concerned. Or he may unthinkingly, blindly ignore the consequences of his decisions for Y. It is because the other interdependent decision is viewed simply as a parameter in X's problem solving that this simple type of adjustment is called parametric.

The first method of partisan mutual adjustment, *parametric adjustment*, is, then, defined as follows: *In a decision situation, a decision maker X adjusts his decision to Y's decisions already made and to Y's expected decisions; but he does not seek, as a recognized condition of making his own decision effective, to induce a response from Y; nor does he allow the choice of his decision to be influenced by any consideration of the consequences of his decision for Y.*

To recognize such an apparently simple process as a method of coordination is to see at once that complex tasks of central coordination of multiple concurrent decisions can be and are in some circumstances transformed into relatively simple series of tasks of adjustment of each decision in a series to the given state of affairs existing at the moment of decision. The seating of a hundred people, many of whom care about whom they sit with, can be solved either as a problem in central coordination of concurrent or sequential decisions or, as is more often actually the case, easily arranged, once a few persons first seat themselves, through a rapid sequence of adaptive decisions, in which each party in turn makes what appears to be a desirable choice in the light of the location of persons already seated. Neither method will necessarily produce ideal results; the point here is only that the second, as well as the first, will produce a coordinated set of decisions.

In public affairs state income taxes are in this way coordinated with the federal income tax because decisions of the states take as given existing federal tax decisions. Similarly, when new decisions on the federal tax are contemplated, they take account of existing state and local decisions on local property taxation; and, in turn, when the local property rates are raised or lowered the discussion of changes is mindful of the burden of federal taxation carried by property owners as a result of federal decisions.

The apparent simplicity of the method is deceptive. It is, indeed, relatively simple in its least interesting form, when, for example, a decision maker finds a course of action wholly satisfactory to himself and so well adapted to past decisions that the new decision does not in the least disturb the other decisions. A municipal government, for example, finds it possible to impose a sales tax that is adequate for the revenue required and yet is without adverse consequences for other tax decisions bearing on the same taxpayers. Taxpayers pay with no more than the usual protest, and no other taxing unit has to revise its tax decisions as a result of the new sales tax. Or certain commanding officers of United States military posts in the South, faced with conflict between their own desires to avoid racial discrimination against Negroes under their command and local government decisions that maintained discriminatory practices, once adopted a policy of transferring Negroes to other areas.[1] The simplicity of this kind of coordination does not, however, deny its significance and its usefulness; it is fundamental and ubiquitous.

Parametric adjustment is more complex when it becomes a method of adjustment not merely to past decisions but to other present and expected decisions. If, for example, each House appropriations subcommittee adapts its appropriations decisions to its expectations of the decisions of the others, their decisions will be by our definition coordinated (to be sure, there are other coordinating mechanisms at work in this case). But there is still another important sense in which adaptation to contemporary decisions is made parametrically, leaving expectations aside. Consider again the example of seating a hundred people. The problem is a here-and-now problem, and the relevant present is the time required to make and implement the decision, say, from two or three minutes to ten or fifteen, which is the time required regardless of the method of coordination employed. If the problem of coordinating the seating is attacked through parametric adjustment, only in a very formal sense is each succeeding decision adapted only to past decisions. For a more meaningful description of the process one would say that a set of simultaneously pending decisions were coordinated by making them in very rapid succession. What coordination is achieved is not simply the adaptation of pending decisions to a historical past but the adaptation of pending decisions to one another by creating in the "present" a rapid succession of "pasts" to which each rapidly succeeding decision can be adapted. Similarly, when the President sends his Budget Message to Congress the task of coordinating the decisions of the various appropriations subcommittees is a task in the adjustment of pending decisions to one another, not merely the adaptation of new decisions to those still operative from an earlier period. If the appropriations subcommittees report their decisions in turn over a period of six months, and each successive report represents decisions adapted to the decisions of the subcommittees that have already reported, there is an important sense in which we can still speak of the coordination of contemporary decisions.

Parametric adjustment becomes even more complex through still another feature for adapting contemporary decisions one to another. Suppose, to continue the example of coordinated seating, that Jones decides to sit by Smith. This suits Jones but not Smith, who now decides to move to another seat. Jones's decision was first adapted to Smith's, then Smith's to Jones's. Whether the first adaptation represents better or worse coordination than the second is, for the moment, irrelevant; what is important is that Jones's decision led Smith to reopen his decision problem; and, although Smith's decision was "past" to Jones, it is now again pending. Similarly, the decisions of state or local governments on taxation, which decisions take federal decisions as given, may lead the federal government to reopen its tax decisions. Although the state and local governments may act as though without consequence for federal tax decisions, their decisions do in fact sometimes have effects on the federal decisions. The consequent variety of adaptations includes, then, not simply the state and local adaptations to historically earlier federal decisions but present or near future adaptations of federal to current state and local decisions.

There are two important "theoretical" points here. The first is that when X adapts to the existing state of affairs, that state of affairs includes decisions of others just made, decisions that have thrown new problems onto X. Hence X is adapting, not simply to a stabilized past, but to a continuing process of decision making. In that sense, he is adapting to contemporary decisions.

The second is that parametric adaptation often links together the adaptations of many decision makers, all adapting to each other. If every decision maker X simply adapts with those decisions on which he is able to act without help from Y, letting the chips fall where they may, chaos is not the only possible consequence. What may ensue is a kind of process of successive approximation. If one were to imagine a number of decision makers all practicing this same kind of adjustment, each adversely affected decision maker Y would make appropriate parametric adjustments in his own decisions to meet the effects of X's decision, thus stimulating another round of adjustments, and so on. X may or may not be further involved in a long course of interaction in which he both stimulates others to adapt to adverse consequences he throws on them and at the same time adapts to adverse consequences thrown on him by certain others. At an extreme and in an especially favorable circumstance in a hypothetically static society, one could imagine a last round in which no further adjustment is required, every decision maker being satisfied. Similarly, one can imagine equilibrium tendencies in a much less static society. In any case, at any one point in the process, each decision maker makes adjustments in his own decisions, taking the decisions of all others as parameters in his own problem solving.

That rounds of adjustment may move further from a satisfactory form of coordination rather than closer to it is not left wholly to chance. Where parametric coordination "works" it tends to persist, as we shall later argue. Where it does not work the emerging problems it creates give rise to demands for the special attentions of other forms of adjustment, such as negotiation.

This last point is critical. The coordinating potential of the various partisan mutual adjustment processes may be greater than is at first supposed, since in these processes themselves are opportunities for participants to choose one or another of quite different methods, as circumstances require. If one can employ parametric or some alternative method of adjustment where it does in fact coordinate, dropping it in favor, say, of another form, or even in favor of central coordination where it does not coordinate, evidence on its contribution to coordination does not rest on any claim of its universal applicability.

There is, of course, one clear and well-known case of coordination through parametric adjustment that serves to suggest the possibilities of autonomous adjustment in government. It is the case of the price system or market system, in which, in a sufficiently competitive market, each policy maker, who there appears as a businessman, adaptively makes policies with total disregard for the consequences for his fellow policy makers, his competitors. The result of the parametric adjustment of many sellers in a market is that price and production decisions come to be coordinated; even more, price and production are systematically regulated with no disputes over them, and price and production do not randomly vary. The competitive market is held up as an example of what is possible, not what is certain; for, even within the domain of the market, partisan mutual adjustment of sellers is sometimes disorganized. And, in any case, one could not claim that partisan mutual adjustment in government can operate in such relatively favorable circumstances as in the market.

Still, this form of parametric adjustment sometimes works with enough speed and intricacy to make it evident that it can achieve coordination of a large number of contemporary governmental decisions. Consider, for example, coordination of such a variety of decisions as local decisions on the level of public education, local decisions on the level of public expenditure, federal decisions on the level of education to be provided for children of employees of large federal projects, local decisions on segregation in schools, and various conflicting federal decisions (of various federal agencies) on segregation. Central coordination is difficult; and, in the face of strong feeling on the issues, a high degree of consistency through a central decision might be beyond reach. Coordination of all these through partisan mutual adjustment, however, can be illustrated in the following decision steps, several of which are wholly parametric.

1. Local and state governments in the South decide on the level of public education they intend to support (parametric).
2. Finding these local decisions unsatisfactory, Congress, in 1950, acting through the Department of Health, Education, and Welfare, makes grants to "federally impacted" areas where large military or other federal installations give the federal government a degree of control over the level of educational expenditure and the distribution of costs between local and federal governments (parametric and other forms).
3. While to avoid paralyzing the federal aid to education decision, the grants to federally impacted areas do not specify nondiscriminatory provisions, subsequently (1954) the federal government promulgates nondiscriminatory provisions with respect to schools on military bases (parametric and other forms).
4. Some local governments, in order to reconcile their desire for aid with their desire to segregate, move local schools off military bases (parametric).
5. Some Army officers on the Southern bases and the Air Force as a whole adapt to some forms of off-base segregation by giving the men the option to transfer to nondiscriminatory areas, the Air Force specifying that no Negro need accept assignment to a training school that practices segregation [2] (parametric).

It is perhaps worth remarking that such a set of mutual adaptations is not to be deprecated as no more than a situation of continuing and unresolved conflict. Clearly, each policy is adapted to those that preceded it, which is all that needs to be demonstrated at this point. Moreover, the mutual adaptations in this case managed to achieve a kind of reconciliation of local demands for support of increased educational tasks, with federal demands for more adequate education, with some military demands, as well as with widespread demands for nondiscrimination, an achievement in coordination of no small consequence.

An example of parametric adjustment within an administrative organization shows how parametric adjustment can sometimes substitute for central coordination. In 1954 the chief of the tabulating section of the Department of Employment of the State of California made a study of the desirability of converting the section from conventional punch-card and electric accounting machine processes to electronic data processing. Faced with a very complex problem, pressed for time—and perhaps for other reasons—he gave little or no attention in his calculations to the adverse effects on morale and employment of the changeover, even though he had counted among its advantages the reduction of payroll by 170 jobs. He was not personally indifferent to these adverse consequences; he was in fact quick to admit they could not be disregarded by the department, but they did not influence his recommendation that the changeover be made.

From the department's point of view, and even in the chief's opinion when he had more time to think about these effects, maintaining morale and job security of his employees was a task that required coordination with the decision to change to electronic data processes. And we can imagine the question of the advantages of electronic processing being considered together with morale and employment problems as a problem for central coordination. In fact, the coordination was achieved by the parametric response of the department's personnel officer, who, taking the changeover decision as given, sought to amend employment, transfer, and separation policies in such a way to reconcile the switchover with employee morale and employment security. In so doing he subsequently enlisted the help of the chief of the tabulating section, who, unable to coordinate into his analysis a consideration for morale and employment, was however able to return to these problems to achieve a parametric adjustment to his own earlier decision on electronic processing. As it turned out the changeover was efficiently achieved without adverse effects on morale and without laying off a single employee, despite the earlier opinion of the personnel director that layoff was inevitable for some workers. We can even say, in view of his early opinion, that the two lines of policy—those on data processes and those on personnel—were better coordinated than he had thought possible when he first surveyed the problem. But the coordination was by the adaptation of a second step to a first, taken as given, not by an attempt to think through the relations between the two and centrally manage an adaptation of each to each.

Deferential Adjustment

To keep the first pure type of adjustment—parametric—as simple as possible, it is assumed that in adapting to past and expected decisions the decision maker does not adjust his decision in the light of his estimates of its effect on the other decision maker. What are the possibilities if that assumption is now removed? (We continue to hold to the assumption that the decision maker does not manipulate the other decision maker as a condition of making his own decisions.) How might a regard for the consequences of a decision on another decision maker influence the adjustment of the decision to the decision of the other?

A limiting case, and a revealing one for identifying an important component element in many mixed methods of coordination, is a policy of complete deference to the other decision maker. We can define deferential adjustment as the case in which, in a given decision situation, a decision maker takes care to make no demands on the other decision maker and to impose no losses or deprivations on him. He takes upon himself the entire burden of adjustment. X makes no moves designed to induce any response from Y, at the same time deliberately avoiding any disadvantage to Y as a consequence of X's decision. He may defer in this way because another decision maker has authority over him, because he fears retaliation, because he wishes to win specific favors. Or he may be pursuing a long-term strategy of identifying himself as loyal to some other decision maker in anticipation of unspecified advantages or virtues in such a course of action. (We later consider his manipulation of others in this way.) In any case, he coordinates by limiting his policy moves to those that adjust with no loss to the other decision maker.

Speaking very strictly, it is impossible for X to be sure that his decision is without adverse consequences for Y, because consequences can be both indirect and much delayed. For that reason we modify the case by envisaging X either as not knowingly impinging adversely, except trivially, on Y's values as Y perceives them at the time of X's decision, or as succeeding in not impinging adversely at all.

Deferential adjustment is clearly a limiting case, a pure type. In actual situations, where a decision maker considers the implication of his decision for another decision maker, he may be conciliatory without going so far as to avoid if possible any injury to the other decision maker. We shall refer to such a policy, less extreme than deferential adjustment, as calculated adjustment and discuss it below. The limiting case of deference is, however, well worth exploring first.

If deferential adjustment is a means whereby X avoids unfavorable consequences for Y, what shall we say about positively favorable consequences for Y? The case in which X *deliberately* does favors for Y beyond mere deference will be included below in the category of calculated adjustment; otherwise whether X's decision positively favors Y or not is immaterial to the definition.

The second method of partisan mutual adjustment, *deferential adjustment*, is, then, defined as follows: *In a decision situation a decision maker X does not seek, as a condition of making his own decision, to induce a response from another decision maker Y. He either deliberately avoids impinging adversely on Y's values or he takes care not knowingly to impinge adversely, except trivially, on Y's values as Y perceives them at the time of X's decision; nor does he tailor his decision to create a gain for Y.*

Deferential adjustment is, of course, a relation between policy makers. A relation like it can be found in central decision systems where Y is the hierarchical superior of X. For centrally regulated decision systems an approximation to a deferential relationship is often deliberately fostered. The decision system is often built on an exploitation of such an approximated relationship, participants are indoctrinated to accept it, and the task of ensuring acceptance of central coordinating authority is at the same time the task of ensuring that various X's willingly defer to some Y in the manner described. Thus, if central control is effective and not merely nominal, various subordinates of the President, each in X's role, defer to him in his Y role. Thus, also, colonels defer to generals; and, in some of their relations, administrative heads defer to the Bureau of the Budget.

The deference of subordinates to the authority of their superiors, is, however, different from deference in mutual adjustment. In centrally coordinated systems a deferential X, who is a subordinate in a hierarchy, typically defers to demands by his superiors made in the form of directives or instructions. He does not freely explore the array of deferential decisions through which he might pursue his interests, but instead contemplates deferential decisions that will accomplish the discharge of duties placed upon him by the demands of his superiors. Moreover, he is not necessarily a decision initiator, as the mutual adjuster is here assumed to be.

Furthermore, instructions given him are largely limited to those lying within the authority of his superior. Thus his deference is represented by acceptance of specific deference toward authority rather than by a much more general policy of avoiding any injury to his superior. Therefore he could be deferential in the common sense—he could obey all orders, yet not be deferential as defined here. On the other hand some idealized versions of hierarchical organization postulate such harmonious subordination of parts to the whole as would require deference in the stricter sense used here; in such a view of hierarchy no subordinate would ever make a decision counter to the interests of a superior.

Our present concern, of course, is in the role of deference in partisan mutual adjustment rather than in central systems. It is illustrated in the President's deference on some points to the wishes of his Secretary of the Treasury; on some points the President may be unwilling to make any demands on his Secretary or act in such a way as to impinge adversely on the Secretary's values. Or it is illustrated in a mixed form in the relations between two powerful Congressional leaders, each of whom defers to the other on certain kinds of issues. Or, again, it is illustrated in the Secretary of the Treasury's deference to the Federal Reserve Board in some policy areas. The ubiquity and coordinating potential of this fundamentally important relationship are both underrated so long as it is identified, as it has been, almost exclusively with centrally coordinated systems.

As one first conceives of the deferential relation in partisan mutual adjustment it may appear to be strikingly similar to a bargaining relationship in which one party finds that he must wholly surrender to his adversary. Because many people think bargaining is a useful relationship only if bargaining power is not too one-sided, they are tempted to dismiss the deferential relationship as a degenerate form of bargaining not relevant to an inquiry into coordinating relations among decision makers. But so might we also dismiss the deferential relation between a hierarchical superior and his subordinate in a centrally coordinated system as highly similar to a bargaining relation in which all bargaining power is on one side. We do not do so, however, because we are quick to see that there are many relations among policy makers in which equality of power between them is by no means desirable and, to make the point much stronger, we can think of many reasons for wishing control to be all on one side with nothing but deference on the other. If we can easily see the deferential relation in this light for centrally coordinated decision making, we cannot dismiss it in partisan mutual adjustment simply as a degenerate form of bargaining.

At the extreme—an extreme that serves only to indicate logical possibilities, not probabilities—one can imagine a complex decision-making situation in which, because every decision maker defers to all others, no decision maker is injured by any other. At the same time each decision maker nevertheless finds that adequate opportunities remain open for his own goal-achieving decisions. That is to say, in happy enough circumstances, it is logically possible that a universal policy of deference still leaves all decision makers in a position to attain their goals.

However, a case for deferential adjustment would not hinge on the demonstration that deference does not narrow the available range of decision for any X. To refer to the case of centrally coordinated decision making again as a point of reference, there the deferential relation is endorsed because it is an effective way to limit X's choices. Analogously, deferential adjustment in partisan mutual adjustment would be endorsed sometimes for the limitations it imposes on X as well as for the range of choice it leaves open to him. Whatever standard is brought to bear on the evaluation of a complex decision system, the standard must take account of the need both to confine in some directions and to liberate in others any given decision maker.

It has already been pointed out that deferential adjustment in partisan mutual adjustment is an adjustment made by an initiator, not, as is typically the case in hierarchy, by a decision maker responding to a manipulation. This point deserves emphasis. In the central system the relation is simply part of the linkage in a chain of command for permitting Ys actively to make demands on Xs, to which the Xs then defer. The emphasis is on each Y's intentions, functions, and demands, to which each X's interests are to be implemental. In partisan mutual adjustment, by contrast, X is not typically an implement for Y; the relation is given a much larger scope. In many cases one can envisage X and Y in such a relation that neither is an implement for the other. They may be relatively autonomous decision makers, each with decision-making responsibilities which can be discharged without calling on the cooperation of the other. Y is not actively demanding anything of X, as would a hierarchical superior. But X perceives conflicts between his decisions and those of Y; hence X sets out to explore imaginatively new ways of pursuing his goals which would not impose losses or make demands on Y.

Thus when the Tennessee Valley Authority first assumed responsibility for the encouragement of agriculture in its area, it found itself in conflict with the agencies already established there—the Extension Service of the Department of Agriculture and the land-grant colleges. It consequently adapted a policy ("a fixed administrative dogma," as one observer put it) of deferring to these agencies on policy matters of central concern to them. This is not to say that TVA was passively obedient as would be a hierarchical subordinate, but only that it adapted its policies to the other agencies, thus permitting them to pursue their objectives without obstacle while TVA found, within this limit, its own methods of achieving its own objectives.[4]

The generality of usage of deferential adjustment can be illustrated with an example of adjustment among individuals not playing what would ordinarily be called a decision-making role. For example, I want to plant a Norway maple in a certain location near my house for protection against the hot afternoon sun. But I know that the tree's shade will fall on my neighbor's windows in the morning hours; and although he will not mind this in midsummer, he will find it unpleasant in early and late season when morning sun will be welcome. I therefore decide to see if I can find a tree that will leaf out late in the season and will shed early. I find it and plant it, and my neighbor and I are both well satisfied. I did not bargain with him or even speak to him about the problem; nor did I disregard him, impose a loss on him, or make any demands on him. Our adjustment was achieved simply through my deference. Such employment of deferential adjustment as this is far removed from its employment in a chain of command.

For another example of deference, again not within a chain of command, some of the interests of the United States Army will be deferred to by the Air Force even where this deference is not prescribed by the Department of Defense or any other superior authority. The Air Force will forswear certain policies sometimes out of concern for predictable unfavorable consequences for the Army, sometimes out of concern for a convention that interprets a certain policy choice as a challenge to the Army, regardless of its specific consequences. In either case, incidentally, the Air Force's deference might be traceable to, though not precisely governed by, its respect for certain rules of the game thought good or to which it is profitable to adhere as a long-term strategy or traceable to a fear of immediate retaliation by the Army if the Air Force does not defer on these claims.

At an extreme, as already noted, one can imagine a situation in which each decision maker in a set finds a way to get what he wants without depriving any other decision maker of his interests. As an example in less utopian circumstances one can imagine such an intense search on the part of each decision maker for policies not adverse to the interests of others as to accomplish not harmony but a sufficient reconciliation or reduction of conflict as to justify describing the resultant policies as coordinated in terms of standards much more severe than those of this chapter. One can easily imagine, for example, pushing deference far enough to avoid the situation in which one decision maker simply undoes the work of another. Action at cross purposes would then be reduced to tolerable marginal discrepancies. If, for example, the Bureau of the Budget comes to understand and respect a set of claims that the House appropriations subcommittees wish to establish, its respect for them immediately achieves some degree of coordination between the Bureau and the subcommittees. There may be a great deal of conflict remaining, but deference has done part of the job.

Two aspects of coordination through deferential adjustment can be distinguished. If a decision maker decides to forego any policies that challenge the values of another decision maker, he has immediately achieved an adjustment of at least one policy to another. But if, in addition, the deferring decision maker sets himself the task of discovering new paths to the achievement of his goals, he will sometimes discover a policy no less satisfactory for his own goals than the policy rejected because of deference. In such a case deferential adjustment has achieved a further adaptation, and one that is satisfactory to both parties. A decision maker's motives to try imaginatively and diligently new deferential policies that are mutually satisfactory are, of course, in some circumstances very strong. Once he decides to defer to another's claims—and he may decide to do so for various reasons—his prospects for finding satisfactory policies depend entirely on the skill with which he can recombine variables in order to find means to his ends that do not challenge the claims to which he defers.

Deference displays what many people believe to be its worst form in log-rolling, where, for example, both among members of the House Appropriations Committee and among members of the House as a whole, one decision maker defers to another's request for funds for fear that his own requests will not be deferred to.[5] Deference appears in a perhaps indispensable form in international affairs where central coordination is simply out of the question. Writing of consideration given in the spring of 1941 to a rigid enforcement of a blockade against the U.S.S.R., Raymond H. Dawson said:

> The American policy-makers were reluctant to embark upon any such course as this, since it would have meant the imposition of an embargo against Russia. They were anxious, as Hull had remarked to

Lord Halifax, not to "tip the scales" at Moscow, to avoid any steps which might push Moscow closer to the Axis. They preferred, rather, to drift along on the route already being followed, marking time and watching developments. As long as it entailed no concessions that might touch upon major interests and vital principles, it was deemed more prudent to avoid giving offense to the Soviet Government.[6]

What is especially interesting about this example is the phrase "no concessions that might touch upon major interests and vital principles," in which the possibility of deferring yet holding to one's own values is illustrated.

These two extremes, log-rolling and international diplomacy, suggest the breadth of deferential adjustment; the two examples also indicate, of course, that methods of partisan mutual adjustment will vary from situation to situation in their efficacy, however judged.

Calculated Adjustment

The examples given above of deferential adjustment are, strictly speaking, examples of approximation to deferential adjustment, which is a limiting case. Although the examples serve well enough to illustrate deference, they fall, to speak very strictly, within, and at the edge of, a large classification already referred to as calculated adjustment. X, not ignoring the implications of his decision for another decision maker as he would in parametric adjustment, can nevertheless weigh these implications as a factor in making his decisions without going so far as to defer. A decision maker who does so will be said to be practicing calculated adjustment.

Calculated adjustment therefore covers the case, among others, of the decision maker who defers to another on some points but not all, or who concedes something to the interests of the other decision maker without accepting all his interest as constraints on the pursuit of his own. It covers the case in which X decides to undertake only those decisions in which any injuries to Y are expected not to provoke countermeasures more damaging to X than X is willing to bear. Also, it covers the case in which X decides to undertake only those decisions that, however damaging to Y, leave Y with no possibility of counterdamage to X.

Included also is the further possibility that X might adapt his decisions to favor Y, not because this is required as a condition of X's decision but simply because X sees an opportunity, in his own adaptive adjustments, to benefit Y at low enough cost to himself to make the opportunity attractive. In the dynamic processes of adjustment among decision makers it will often be the case that no decision is taken by any decision maker without regard to its long-term implications for his standing with other decision makers. Specifically, he will often want to create obligations on the part of other decision makers that he can cash in on later. In governing relations among men the sense of reciprocal obligation is a powerful one, about which more will be said later. It has been suggested that the norm of reciprocity is perhaps as important an element of culture as the incest taboo, although, as in the case of the incest taboo, it varies in concrete formulation.[7]

The third kind of partisan mutual adjustment, *calculated adjustment,* then, is defined as follows: *In a decision situation, a decision maker X does not seek, as a condition of making his own decision, to induce a response from another decision maker Y, nor does he defer to Y; but he does allow his decision to be influenced by his consideration of Y's preferences.*

This type of adaptive adjustment is called "calculated" to emphasize that when a decision maker neither avoids imposing losses, as in deference, nor ignores losses, as in parametric adjustment, but instead takes gains and losses into account, he is faced with special problems in calculation. His decisions call for weighing, among the other pros and cons, the expected short-term and long-term reactions of other decision makers, even if, to hold to the assumption underlying all types of adaptive adjustment, he does not seek to induce any response from the other decision makers as a condition of making his decision.

As an example of calculated adjustment imagine a park commissioner who wishes to lease municipal park land to a business firm that intends to operate a skating rink on it. He can act autonomously for he is legally empowered to lease the land for such a purpose. But the mayor, to whom he is not legally responsible, opposes the move; and the park commissioner must therefore, he feels, calculate the gains and losses of moving in opposition to the mayor. He may decide that the mayor's ill will on this issue is a price worth paying. Or he may decide to incorporate into the lease proposal other features designed to win the mayor's approval. Or he may decide to go ahead with the lease, while with another decision on another issue, appease, or even ingratiate himself with, the mayor.

Calculated adjustment is also illustrated by the practice of the Directors of TVA who, when the Authority was established in 1933, each took on responsibility for certain more or less independent aspects of the TVA program. Each director thereafter calculated his own intervention in a program assigned to another director.[8] Calculated adjustment is illustrated again in President Roosevelt's decision in 1943 and 1944 not to determine reconversion policy by executive order, as he was empowered to do. At that time Roosevelt apparently believed executive orders to be superior to legislation for reconversion; but, fearful of Congressional reaction to heavy reliance on executive orders, he made a calculated adaptation by asking Congress for legislation to convert the Office of War Mobilization into the Office of War Mobilization and Reconversion and by cooperating with Congress on other reconversion legislation.[9]

For still another example, when Roosevelt was developing a position on military aid to the Soviet Union in 1941, he became concerned about the acceptability of Soviet aid to Catholics; specifically, he was concerned about manifest disapproval from the Vatican or from the American hierarchy. While one course of action was to emphasize the antireligious tenets of Nazism, he undertook what would here be described as a calculated adaptation to Catholic leadership. He attempted to make Soviet aid contingent on some concession from the Soviet government on religious freedom, thus incorporating a new and palatable element into his decision on aid.[10]

The results of coordination through calculated adjustment can be seen in a preliminary way as parallel to those of deferential adjustment. That is to say, the consequence of X's calculating effects on Y as a factor in his own decision is to lead X to reduce the adverse effects, with results for coordination parallel to those in deference.

MANIPULATED

ADJUSTMENTS:

PRELIMINARY SURVEY

Manipulation for Coordination

REMOVE NOW THE ASSUMPTION
that X does not seek to induce a response from Y as a recognized
condition for making his own decision effective, an assumption not
relaxed for either parametric, deferential, or calculated adjustment.
X now wishes to move Y out of his way, to enlist the help of Y, or
perhaps to come to an agreement on a decision with Y. He will not
make his own decision without first or simultaneously manipulating Y.

Any method by which X can manipulate Y coordinates Y with
X and, depending on the relations of X and Y with still other
decision makers, coordinates others. To think of specific critical ways
in which a partisan decision maker might effect coordination by
manipulating another, however, is to think first of negotiation or

bargaining (the two terms being taken as synonymous for the moment). For in the absence of central coordination if X tries to manipulate Y, then Y often also tries to manipulate X even if only defensively; their attempts mutually to influence each other are then typically denoted by "negotiation" or "bargaining." For many observers of mutual adjustment "bargaining" or "negotiation" denotes all processes of mutual adjustment; as they see it, coordination is either centrally managed, on the one hand, or bargained or negotiated, on the other.[1]

We have already seen, in the preceding chapter, forms of coordination that are neither central nor bargained nor negotiated. We may wonder whether the remaining forms to be investigated—those in which X manipulates Y as a condition of making his own decision—do not include forms other than bargaining or negotiation. Let us therefore, in an exploratory frame of mind, examine the various facets of negotiation and bargaining to see what they suggest.

Negotiation and Closely Related Forms

In one of its simplest senses negotiation means discussion to reach an agreement. X talks over with Y their relation to, perhaps conflicts with, each other to see whether they can come to agreement on some decision of concern to both. The discussion might be nothing more than an exchange of information and appeals. But the discussion may be supplemented by conditional threats and promises, that is, by making advantages and disadvantages to Y a condition of what Y does. There is then some tendency to use the term "bargaining" rather than "negotiation." Whatever the terminology, negotiation wears a different aspect when the parties are able to say, "Do it, or else. . . ." or "If you will do it, I would be willing to. . . ." The concept of negotiation or bargaining is further extended by the notion of implicit bargaining, in which discussion disappears while threats and promises remain but are communicated by acts rather than words, as when a government threatens to use a missile not by saying so but by building it.

A moment's reflection will show that these manipulative devices

—information, appeals, spoken and unspoken threats and promises —can also be employed outside of any exchange that would ordinarily be called negotiation or bargaining. They then coordinate unilaterally; they induce Y to adapt to X. For example, the War Manpower Commission, notoriously lacking a position of strength in economic mobilization during World War II, "vigorously appealed" to the War Production Board for concentration of production of civilian goods within fewer plants and for direction of war production into areas where workers were already located. "Vigorous appeal" probably pretty well describes just what the Commission did. The War Production Board yielded to a degree to these appeals, but the decisions were for the WPB to make; if it listened to appeals from WMC, its independence and power relative to the WMC apparently spared it from the necessity of negotiating, let alone bargaining.[2] Moreover, the WPB wanted nothing from the WMC; on that count, too, there was nothing to negotiate or bargain over.

An even more striking illustration of unilateral coordination— in this case the employment of a threat without negotiation or bargaining—is successful union imposition, under threat of strike, of a wage scale voted by the union without any discussion with employers and with no attempt of the employers to open discussion.[3]

Take notice, however, of another element often present in exchanges called negotiation or bargaining: reciprocity. As noted in the preceding chapter, reciprocity is a powerful norm. It appears in negotiation when X makes a concession—a firm one, not merely an offer—in order to try to bind Y to make a counterconcession. It is a common tactic, yet clearly distinguishable from verbal appeal as well as from conditional promise and threat. Again, however, the exploitation of obligations arising from the norm of reciprocity is not limited to negotiation. X may cash in on an obligation incurred earlier by Y; when he calls for Y's response, Y gives it without discussion and even without tacit counterdemands. Or X may be able to induce a response from Y because Y, under no obligation to X, wants by his response to put X under obligation for the future. One might stretch the notion of tacit bargaining far enough to cover these last two examples of reciprocity. If so, bargaining no longer denotes only an interchange among participants in a decision in which each controls the other, but is extended in meaning to denote a sequence of decisions some of which are made by X, to whom Y adapts, and others of which are made by Y, to whom X adapts. For our present purposes terminology is not important; the variety of methods of adjustment is.

The intricacies of reciprocity are suggested in the following excerpt from a study of a decision on the location of a county hospital in Chicago.

> There were some who said that Ryan [Chairman of the Cook County Board] made Cunningham chairman [of a committee to choose a site] because Cunningham could be depended upon to bring in the recommendations that Ryan wanted. Cunningham's investment brokerage house, a politician said privately, did a big business in the county's bonds. . . .
> This was unfair. County bonds were always advertised and sold at competitive bidding. Cunningham's firm had only once, several years earlier, been a successful bidder "Frankly," Cunningham wrote, "I am not beholden to any public official. . . ."
> . . . That Cunningham may more or less consciously have wished to please his friend Dan [Ryan] is possible. Like almost everybody, Cunningham probably enjoyed being well regarded by people in power.[4]

That the excerpt shows some dispute over the extent of reciprocity does not reduce its value as an illustration of the possibilities.

With respect to all these methods of manipulative adjustment which can be employed both within or outside of negotiation or bargaining situations, a further distinction can be drawn. Leaving aside for the moment their unilateral use, their symmetric use, where X and Y manipulate each other, may lead to an "understanding," or it may not. That is to say, a contractual element may be present or absent in the adjustment achieved.

If two men discuss the height of a fence to separate their lots, the result of their interchange may be a commitment of each to the other not to build above a certain height. On the other hand, their discussion may satisfactorily terminate without an agreement, each confident that the other's views have been moved closer to his own. Neither feels that he has an understanding, an agreement, or a commitment with the other; neither wishes to persuade the other to accept any such understanding; each is satisfied, however, that the other will not offend him if and when he builds a fence.

The contractual element is essential in negotiation and bargaining as sometimes conceived. Again, terminology is unimportant; what is important is only that the distinction between the simple symmetrical employment of manipulative devices be distinguished from the symmetrical *cum* contractual adjustment process so that the variety of manipulative devices can be appreciated. In complex negotiations, it might be noted, the contractual element is often reduced to a minor role. The task as seen by each participating decision maker is to continue to influence his adversaries; there may be neither time nor staff to go so far as to arrange sets of mutual commitments, or it may be that no decision maker, in a rapidly changing situation, is willing to commit himself. In President Theodore Roosevelt's efforts to win Congress over to the regulation of railroads, and in the efforts of many legislators to resist him (which have been excellently chronicled as a sequence of partisan mutual adjustments, although not by that name), one sees Roosevelt holding the threat, among others, of tariff reform over the heads of recalcitrant legislators while they in turn try to hold over his head the threat, among others, of no railroad legislation at all if he does not accept their proposals for much weaker legislation than he wants. Roosevelt gets the Hepburn Act through the House by negotiations with Speaker Cannon, and the negotiations seem fairly clearly to result in a pact that trades railroad reform for tariff reform.[5]

In the Senate, however, where there was no figure of Cannon's power, the dispersion of influence over legislation made such a pact impossible. Senator Allison, as the President's unofficial representative, negotiated revisions in the bill attractive to a potential winning coalition. If there was any element of contract—any "understanding," in his attempts to win over various groups in the Senate—it was probably only with Senator Aldrich, one of the leaders of the opposition. Such a pact may have been decisive in bringing Aldrich around, but it seems clear—and this is the point—that Roosevelt's and Allison's bargaining with legislators embraced a wider variety of negotiations than those intending agreements or "understandings" among them.[6]

Look further now at that type of manipulated adjustment that consists of the employment of conditional threats and promises, whether unilateral or symmetrical. For coordination in the simple sense so far defined, adaptation through threats is quite as satisfactory as coordination through promises. But no one can miss the importance of the distinction between them. Where two decision makers are coordinated through threats at least one of them has adapted to the other to avoid worsening his situation. His adaptation may then represent, as he sees it, the lesser of two evils, as in the extreme case of "Your money or your life!" Where coordination is through promises, adaptation promises advantages to both parties: to X because if the adaptation of Y were not advantageous to him, he could not afford, aside from error or dishonesty, to promise Y anything; and to Y because he is moved to adapt only if he is adequately compensated for what is asked of him. The notion of compensation will turn out to be important in later chapters.

Exclusively Unilateral Forms

We have not yet distinguished all the identifiable types of adjustment that are sometimes lumped together as bargaining or negotiation. Suppose that X and Y can each make decisions "independently" of the other, but there are advantages to both if their decisions are not independent. X consequently tries to lure Y to his position by making his decision first, possibly altering his own position to make it more acceptable to Y. He addresses no words to Y, he neither conditionally threatens nor promises anything to Y, nor does he exploit reciprocity. Simply by making a decision first, he unconditionally increases the cost or disadvantages to Y of making any decision other than one adapted to X's.

One might wish on reflection to distinguish such a manipulated adjustment from negotiation or bargaining; but its close relation can be exposed by assuming that Y responds with a decision that, although not adapting to X's, is conciliatory in that it makes it easy for X now to adapt to Y's. Suppose as a result that X alters his decision once more, Y once more, and X adapts to Y's last decision. It would be difficult to deny that such a sequence of moves often takes on the character of threat and promise since there may be communicated a sense of "I've conceded again; if you don't concede again, I'll revert to my earlier decision."

On the other hand, in situations in which decisions cannot be sequentially altered as just illustrated, X's commitment to a decision leaves Y with no alternative but to adapt to it. He cannot counter with a decision of his own intended to influence X because X has already made a firm final decision. Such a state of affairs can hardly, in the ordinary meaning of the terms, be called negotiation or bargaining. Manipulation through a final prior decision is not even symmetric. It is so important a device for unilateral manipulation that it would be unfortunate to lose it under the rubric of negotiation or bargaining. We shall call it the method of prior decision.

In the struggle, for example, between the United States Treasury and the Federal Reserve Board over the short-term rate of interest in 1950 the Treasury's strategy was to head off the Board's attempts to increase the rate by Treasury advance announcements of the terms on which it would undertake new borrowing, leaving the Board in the position of going along with Treasury terms or facing Presidential, Congressional, and public criticism and weathering other disturbances of monetary policy if it failed to support the market for United States bonds on the Treasury's terms.[7]

The concept of bargaining or negotiation would have to be stretched beyond recognizable shape to include some remaining important types of manipulation. In a mistaken identification of authoritative prescription with central coordination, it is easy to miss its role in noncentral coordination. Clearly one of the principal means by which a partisan induces other partisans to adjust to him is to prescribe, where he has authority to do so, the required adjustment to them. In such cases he need not negotiate or bargain, he need neither promise nor threaten; he merely prescribes in a situation in which, because his authority is recognized, the other decision makers respond as requested. Thus the Port of New York Authority prescribes on some points to the legislature of the state of New Jersey; the legislature prescribes on some points to the New Jersey Highway Department; the Highway Department prescribes on some points to local police officers; and, finally, local police officers prescribe on some points to the Port of New York Authority. Such a system of linked authoritative prescription achieves coordination as defined, since on each critical relation calling for adjustment there is an established relation in which the one decision maker adjusts to another. The adjustments are not centrally managed; nor is the system of mutual noncentral adjustment one established by some authority or controller superior to them all and central in its views of their relationships to each other.

Then, too, there are still other ways beyond those already mentioned by which X can unconditionally alter the advantages or disadvantages attaching to any given course of action of Y. X can, for example, simply give money to Y to make it easier for Y to pursue a course of action Y had already resolved to decide upon. Or X might jam Y's communications in an attempt to obstruct some course of action unwanted by X.

Perhaps most of the methods by which X unconditionally creates disadvantages to Y in a course of action are only indirectly applied to Y by X. Consider, for example, this case: In December, 1959, there began an intense conflict between the Port of New York Authority, bent on constructing a new metropolitan jet airport in a partly residential area in Morris County, New Jersey, and the Jetport Action Association, a citizens' group organized to block the new airport at that site. Appeals from the Association to the Authority were unavailing, and apparently the Association lacked any strength or counters that it might move in a game of bargaining. Nor did it possess prescriptive authority. Lacking all these methods for inducing a response from the Authority, it nevertheless persevered. It appealed to the Governor of New Jersey, who did possess some authority to prescribe to the Port of New York Authority. Similarly, it appealed to the legislature, which likewise possessed certain authority. And it also sought to undermine support for the Port Authority by appeals to its political allies as well as by appeals to the voting public. Among other tactics it drummed up strong movement for a metropolitan jet airport not controlled by the Port Authority to be located in a nonresidential area in Burlington County.[8]

If this is not bargaining or negotiation, it is nevertheless an attempt at coordination through partisan mutual adjustment. The manipulative devices employed in this example turn out to include among other devices ones that have already been identified. They are not directed, however, at the Port Authority but at third parties who can then directly influence the Authority. The Association appealed to and bargained with the governor, the legislature, and other interest groups, hoping that subsequently they would be able to influence the Authority as the Association could not do directly. The possibilities of indirection open up a variety of means through which X can induce Y's response which would be missed in a preoccupation with negotiation between X and Y. Again, therefore, we miss the variety of relations between any X and Y if we try to conceptualize all of them as bargaining or negotiation.

Classification of Forms

By now the variety of forms of manipulation has become confusing. Let us therefore move to arrange the possibilities in tabular form. In doing so we can first group the various types into categories not wholly unfamiliar: (1) we can conceive of X's manipulating Y by altering Y's understanding or perception of the advantages and drawbacks, or costs, of a response that Y is contemplating; (2) on the other hand, we can imagine X's actually altering the advantages and costs. In the first case X calls Y's attention to an advantage to which Y had been oblivious; in the second case X may actually offer Y compensation for responding in the way X desires.

Given these two major categories, we can subdivide the second. For X can alter the advantages or costs to Y conditionally or unconditionally. X can offer Y compensation if and only if Y agrees to respond as X desires; or X can offer, say, funds to Y in the expectation that the funds will now make it possible for Y to do what X wants, which is what Y also wants to do but has been, for lack of funds, unable to do.[9]

Given these three categories we can, if we insist, cover every possibility, but some cases strain so simple a classification. Where X authoritatively prescribes a response to Y who concedes his authority to do so, Y is not responding because of advantages and costs attached to the response in question; advantages and costs may enter into the decision only in Y's calculation of whether he will generally

Table I. Types of Coordination Through Manipulated Adjustments
(The names to be given to certain critical types are indicated in capital letters.)

Abstract Categories of Types	Specific Types	Employed by X *directly* on Y or on third parties who in turn manipulate Y		
		Unilaterally?	Symmetrically, either with or without contractual element?	NEGOTIATION* symmetric only
X changes Y's perception of given advantages and costs of a course of action	X informs and appeals to Y	Yes	Yes	PARTISAN DISCUSSION
X alters advantages and costs to Y contingent on Y's response	X conditionally threatens and promises Y explicitly or tacitly	Yes	Yes	BARGAINING (symmetric only)
	X promises only	Yes COMPENSATION	Yes BARGAINED COMPENSATION	
X obligates Y to respond	X creates, then calls in an obligation	Yes	Yes	RECIPROCITY
	X calls in an already existing obligation	Yes	Yes if X and Y each already have standing obligations to the other	
	X requests a response where to do so implies a future obligation of X to Y	Yes	Yes	
X unconditionally alters advantages and costs to Y of a course of action of Y	Generally undifferentiated	Yes UNCONDITIONAL MANIPULATION	Unusual but possible	
	X makes a prior decision	Yes PRIOR DECISION	No	
X authoritatively prescribes to Y		Yes AUTHORITATIVE PRESCRIPTION	Unusual but possible	

* Negotiation will be defined to include also symmetric manipulation employing the specified devices without respect to whether X and Y employ the same device. For example, negotiation covers a case in which X promises and Y makes appeals.

concede X's authority. Consequently, we consider the case of authority as a fourth category. Similarly, decision makers obligated to each other by the norm of reciprocity can only with difficulty be conceived of as weighing the advantages and costs of each decision. Again, therefore, we make of reciprocity a separate category, our fifth and last.

These five categories appear in the first column of Table I; the specific types referred to in the discussion above appear in the second column.

If the exploratory discussion of various kinds of manipulated coordination in partisan mutual adjustment was confusing in its complexity, the table is itself complex. The following chapter will explore further and with more precision the various forms of manipulated coordination that appear in the table.

Responses to Manipulation

To relate the adaptive types of adjustment of the preceding chapter to the manipulative types of this chapter, let us ask how Y might react in the face of X's attempts to manipulate him.

First, he might not react at all in any way approximating that desired by X; he might in fact not react at all. He might be deaf to persuasion or, for example, invulnerable to threats, indifferent to promises, or resistant to authority. Second, Y might, as a response to X's attempts to manipulate him, set about manipulating X in the same decision situation. If so, his responses can range over the whole array of manipulative devices. Third, Y may adapt to X parametrically, deferentially, or in calculated adaptation.

To be sure, we defined adaptive adjustments to refer to decision makers who neither manipulate nor are manipulated. The definitions could, however, be rewritten to embrace the methods of adjustment both of Xs who initiate decisions without manipulation and of Ys who respond to the manipulations of others. But we do not need such an extension of the definitions for present purposes; in particular it is sufficient for our purposes that types of manipulation be identified by X's role in them, disregarding how Y might respond.

Speaking with the imprecision resulting from the definitions of adaptive adjustments, we will note that when Y responds to manipulation he chooses from combinations of parametric, deferential, and calculated forms of adjustment. There will always be a parametric element in his adaptation, since any adapter adapts to some past decisions. If X employs prior decision as a manipulative device, he has of course deliberately moved to force Y to adapt parametrically to his, X's, decision. If X employs threats and promises, he is at least inviting Y to adapt through what we have called calculated adaptation, since obviously he is asking Y to calculate the consequences for X of his, Y's, response; but he may get a deferential response. Similarly, when he employs the device of reciprocity the response can be either calculated or deferential, in addition to its parametric element characteristic of all responses. If X employs authoritative prescription, he is in effect counting on a response from Y that approaches closely to deference.

MANIPULATED

ADJUSTMENTS:

SPECIFIC FORMS

Negotiation, Partisan Discussion, Bargaining, and Compensation

NEGOTIATION

AS THE TABLE ON PAGE 63 IN-
dicates we have grouped together the usual symmetric forms of
manipulated adjustment under the heading of negotiation. Such a
concept of negotiation is common enough; it might appear too
broad only in its inclusion of tacit bargaining. It will serve our
purposes, however, to leave the concept broad.

By "symmetric" we mean to specify the decision situation in
which if X manipulates Y, Y also manipulates X. But what if X
this year induces a response from Y while Y next year induces a
response from X? We want symmetry to mean that X and Y

manipulated each other not alternatively over a period of time but more or less simultaneously. Strictly speaking, "simultaneously" is too strong a word, for we want to embrace situations in which the negotiation takes days, weeks, even months. We would not want to exclude the twenty-four-months prolonged negotiations at Kaesong and Panmunjom leading to a military armistice beween the United Nations and the Chinese and North Koreans. Symmetrical manipulation will therefore have to be considered as symmetrical not in a moment of time but with respect to an agenda. If two parties manipulate each other with respect to the same agenda, their manipulations are symmetrical.

Even this is not wholly satisfactory because in tacit bargaining there may be no sense of a common agenda. Preoccupied with his own agenda, X seeks to bring Y around; while Y, preoccupied with his own and different agenda, seeks to bring X around. This will be called symmetric if their respective efforts are locked into a sequence of moves and countermoves and the manipulations become highly interdependent, marked by a recognition on the part of X and Y of the interdependence of their moves. In a sense the resolution of the conflict at hand becomes the common agenda. For our present purposes such a concept of symmetry is precise enough.

We do not want to limit the notion of symmetry to the situation in which at the outset of negotiation both X and Y are on the point of trying to induce a response from the other. On the contrary, suppose X wants to induce a certain response from Y and Y thereupon, but only thereupon, seeks to induce a response from X in order to extract the most favorable terms from their negotiations. Until X began to manipulate Y, Y had nothing to ask of X. Such a possibility falls within the notion of symmetry, hence within the notion of negotiation; we follow customary usage in so defining negotiation.

If negotiation is defined to embrace the usual symmetric manipulations between any two decision makers, then it embraces situations in which the two parties do not use the same form of manipulation. X may simply try to persuade Y while Y threatens X; or X may threaten while Y promises; or X may try to call in an obligation owed by Y while Y counters with an attempt to persuade X that the obligation has already been discharged.

Negotiation is therefore defined as: *A form of partisan mutual adjustment in which in a symmetrical relation X and Y each, as a recognized condition of making effective his own decision, induces a response from the other, other than by unconditional manipulation or authoritative prescription.*

That negotiation is a method of coordination is obvious. Of all the methods of partisan mutual adjustment it is in the highest repute. Anyone can call up examples including cases in which, as in tripartite commissions, negotiation is very deliberately chosen as a decision making and coordinating process, as though it were obvious that for some circumstances there were no better way to take account of the complexities of the policy problem than to bring the various interested parties together, to let them explore each other's partisan views and to arrive at a settlement satisfactory to all concerned. One sees coordination, sometimes of a high order, emerging in such a situation because a wide variety of factors in the decision are brought into a considered relationship to each other and because the final settlement is not agreed to until the policy intentions of the various partisans are reconciled in some more or less satisfactory way.

The familiarity of coordination through negotiation, the variety of techniques subsumed by the term, the apparent equitableness of symmetry rather than unilateralness in manipulation, and, above all, the conspicuousness of talk in negotiation—all these combine to tempt one to believe that negotiation is, or perhaps ought to be, the dominant form of coordination by partisan mutual adjustment. Its actual restricted scope is therefore noteworthy. To be sure, we see it everywhere around us: one can define a politician as a full-time negotiator on governmental affairs. Still, the total number of other decision makers to whom any one decision maker can speak is quite limited relative to the total with whom he is coordinated in one way or another. Some are too distant; for the problem at hand, verbal negotiation is not worth arranging. Probably more important, no one decision maker has time to negotiate even tacitly with more than a few of the decision makers with whom he is interdependent. Then, too, at any given time any one decision maker will be unaware of many lines of interdependency; therefore, it will simply not occur to him to negotiate. If one could imagine a

frequency count of uses of negotiation and other adjustments, negotiation—for all its prominence—would certainly be found to be less
often turned to than parametric adjustment, which is a coordinating
element in every decision; and, as for manipulated adjustments, the
frequency of an X's negotiation with Y is much less than that of his
indirect manipulation of Y through third parties.

Negotiation, as well as each of its particular forms like bargaining, is easy to confuse with the kind of cooperative coordination through discussion that is to be left outside the scope of this
study. What begins, say, with an exchange of threats and promises
or with partisan appeals may, to be sure, turn into cooperative
nonpartisan pursuit of some common objective at any point at
which such an objective emerges, if it does. But "negotiation" is
limited to the exchanges that precede the arrival at such a point.

PARTISAN DISCUSSION AND BARGAINING

One of the tabulated forms of negotiation that will in subsequent chapters call for special attention is the mere exchange of
information and appeal. Assuming that two negotiators have no
power, in the ordinary sense of the word, over each other and can
merely talk over their problems, what is the character of their
interaction? By definition cooperative problem solving through
discussion in the light of adequate and agreed criteria is ruled out
as not belonging to the present category of *partisan* adjustment.

One possibility, we saw, is that one decision maker tries to bring
the other around to his preferred solution simply by attempting to
show the other how the proposed solution satisfies the other's partisan desires. In such a case nothing that could be called coercion is
employed: X neither threatens nor even promises, nor in any way
manipulates Y except by calling to Y's attention the ways in which
this or that policy does or does not serve Y's particular interests.
Often such a discussion identifies inconsistencies in the preferences
or preference statements of the participants, or brings information
to bear on a participant's estimate of the costs of achieving an
objective. Sometimes, however, X simply tries to make vivid and
concrete Y's perception both of his own preferences and of the
relevant facts. Still again, short of communicating threats and
promises, discussion may deceitfully allege difficulties or incon-

sistencies or, following another strategy, create a mood designed to alter another's judgment. This range of interaction in coordination through negotiation will be called *partisan discussion.*

Where participants enter into an exchange of conditional threats and promises we shall appropriate the term "bargaining" despite the looser way in which we used the term earlier. X makes demands on Y, to which demands are attached credible conditional promises or threats.* "If you do this for me, I will do that for you," or "Do this, or else. . . ." The phenomenon is illustrated when policy makers trade favors, as in Congressional porkbarreling, or threaten each other with destruction as do the United States and the Soviet Union, or achieve a complex mixture of threat and promise as in the threats of insurrection and implicit counter-promises of French Algeria that brought General de Gaulle back to power in 1958. To limit the term "bargaining" to an exchange of conditional threats and promises is to follow one line of customary usage. But because there are also other usages of the term, it is of some importance that the word is hereafter in this study understood to mean neither more nor less than what it is here defined to mean.

Although the distinction between partisan discussion and bargaining is sometimes difficult to make, and although negotiators commonly practice both at the same time, it is useful to hold to the distinction. In partisan discussion, the interchange is limited to reassessing the gains and losses attached to various possible settlements; in an exchange of threats and promises the gains and losses are themselves deliberately altered by participants in order to influence other participants.**

* Although a threat or a promise that lacks credibility is, of course, often delivered in the course of a negotiation, the second type of negotiation needs to be defined in such a way as to exclude the possibility that none of the threats and promises are credible, for in such a case one would find this second category insignificant.

** What if a conditional promise or threat, although believed, turns out to have been false after it had already achieved its manipulative effect? Strictly speaking, X has, by lying, changed Y's perception of gains and losses without himself altering them. Thus he has engaged in partisan discussion, not bargaining. In repetitive bargaining, which is common, lying is curbed and the case is not one on which we shall have anything further to say.

Thus, *bargaining* is defined as: *A form of partisan mutual adjustment in which in a symmetrical relation X and Y each, as a recognized condition of making effective his own decision, induces a response from the other by making conditional threats of deprivation and/or conditional promises of gratification.*

And partisan discussion is defined as: *A form of partisan mutual adjustment in which X, as a recognized condition of making his own decision effective, induces a response from Y by effecting through communication a reappraisal by Y of his partisan interests and the means to satisfy them without X's actually altering the objective consequences for Y of any of his possible responses, where Y may or may not, in a symmetrical relation, do the same with respect to X.*

What is to be said, in light of the definition of partisan discussion, of a situation in which through, say, facial expression alone X communicates to Y a belief that a proposed course of action is less rewarding to Y than he had supposed and at the same time actually does reduce the pleasures of that course of action to Y because Y now associates it with X's expressed skepticism about it. We include gesture, drama, pictures, and other communicating symbols other than words in the concept of partisan discussion; that is why we used the word "communication" in the definition. We shall bypass, however, the question of whether, strictly speaking, it is possible to change Y's appraisal of the gratifications and deprivations attached to various courses of action without actually changing the gratifications and deprivations themselves. For our purposes it is enough to distinguish between changing Y's income and changing his estimate of what his income will be, changing Y's chances for advancement in public office and changing his desire to win the advancement, or adding to the obstacles to Y's policy and changing his estimate of how many and how severe the obstacles will be. Certainly many manipulations of one decision maker by another work almost exclusively on perceptions and evaluations rather than on manipulation of the things perceived and evaluated, and it is the former that we want to capture in the idea of partisan discussion.

One of the reasons for singling out partisan discussion for special attention is, of course, that it is a relatively noncoercive kind of coordination. Another reason, however, is that cooperative discussion of quite another kind is widely alleged to play a fundamental role in democratic politics, and we shall want to raise the question whether partisan discussion in fact plays the role attributed to the other. Illustrative of a common concept of discussion is the following:

Ultimately . . . democracy is simply group action, the decision of group questions by group process. It is practically identical with discussion, the intellectual-coöperative quest of right answers to questions. Right answers are known by the the the fact of agreement that they are such. Hence the very notion of a "right" answer implies some society, and social recognition of truth or norms which have "validity" in contrast with merely individual opinion or preference.[1]

Or consider Barker's view of democratic discussion:

Not only must the issues formulated and presented be similar in the sense of having the same sort of power of exciting *general* or widespread interest. They must be similar in a deeper sense. Thus must all alike suppose, and all alike be addressed to, a *common* or identical interest.[2]

The view of political discussion as a cooperative search for and application of agreed criteria is as old as Aristotle.[3] Is it, however, cooperative discussion with agreed criteria, with a common purpose, or is it instead the rougher discussion of partisans that carries the burden of democratic politics?

Of the decision, referred to earlier, on the location of a county hospital branch in Chicago, Banfield comments on the Welfare Council's attempt to discuss the problem with Ryan, President of the Cook County Board:

In public hearing it was indispensable to preserve the fiction that the public interest was all that would enter into the discussion. But the Council might have recognized, explicitly in private discussion and implicitly in its public statements, that it would be persuasive only if it showed that certain private interests would be served, or at least not harmed, by a South Side branch. Had it, for example, shown Ryan that a South Side branch would be an asset rather than a liability in his next campaign, it might have had more success with him.[4]

In this case, at least, it appears that cooperative discussion was ineffective where partisan discussion might have achieved a desired result.

COMPENSATION

As we noted earlier where bargaining proceeds exclusively through an exchange of conditional promises and benefits, the mutual adaptations of X and Y are not coercively achieved and, moreover, are advantageous to both. In effect X compensates Y for whatever he asks of Y, and Y similarly compensates X for his response. We can refer to this happy state of affairs as coordination through bargained compensation. But the unilateral use of compensation in partisan mutual adjustment is ubiquitous and not to be neglected.

When, for example, President Franklin Roosevelt attempted to pack the Supreme Court he fixed upon a policy, communicated his wishes to the Congress, refused to bargain, and set out to bring Congressmen around to his predetermined policy by a variety of devices, among which compensation was conspicuous. He is thought to have offered Senator Wheeler the privilege of nominating some new justices; he promised leaders of the farm organizations that he would revive AAA legislation; he used patronage heavily; he held out hopes of generous relief and public works projects in the states of Senators whom he wished to sway; he proposed to manipulate labor leaders by offering wage and hour legislation; and he called in Senators to discuss with them "problems of their states."[5]

One might say, of course, that any offer of benefit in return for a desired response results in an exchange of favors, thus in a trade or transaction and thus in the striking of a bargain. It is useful, however, to distinguish between the case in which X and Y both actively bring demands to each other, at least after negotiation begins, where both seek a response from the other, and the case in which X seeks a response from Y and Y simply accepts or perhaps declines after some discussion of terms. Granted that in both cases a trade has been made, a bargain (by some uses of the term) struck, the one meets the conditions of symmetry (each decision maker seeks, as a condition of making his own decision, a response from the other) and the other does not. Thus compensation of the unilateral kind can be distinguished from bargained compensation.

Market transactions are often described as bargaining. But for those many transactions in which a buyer seeks to induce the seller to provide a commodity or service by offering its price and the seller passively sells or fails to sell as the buyer decides, making no effort to induce buyers to buy, the coordinating method is better described as unilateral promise or compensation than as bargained compensation.

Compensation is defined, therefore, as: *A form of partisan mutual adjustment in which X, as a recognized condition of making his decision effective, induces a response from Y by a promise of gratification, where Y either does or does not do the same to X.*

Reciprocity

In the preceding chapter three possible reciprocal manipulations were mentioned and subsequently appeared in the table on page 63. First, in negotiation X will sometimes make a concession, knowing that this places on Y an obligation to reciprocate. In haggling over price, for example, in the first stages of negotiation it is incumbent on Y to make a reciprocal concession if X has just made one. Among governmental decision makers reciprocity as a norm is no less powerful. It is not an absolute norm, nor is it an application so unambiguous as to prescribe a reciprocal concession for every concession. And it leaves room for disagreement about the size of the reciprocating concession. Still, if Northern liberals voluntarily concede a point on racial policy to Southern negotiators in, say, writing the party platform in convention, they can expect something of consequence in return. The original concession must have been made, however, not in extremity but in conditions that suggest that at the option of the Northerners it could have been withheld.

This first type of manipulation through exploiting the norm of reciprocity is, however, not always found in negotiation. Similarly, the second and third types will be found both within and outside of negotiation. The second, it will be remembered, consists of calling in an existing obligation: X can obtain the response he wants from Y because Y acknowledges an already existing obligation. Political discussion is full of reference to this kind of reciprocity. For example, "This time the *Tribune* had the support of the newly elected governor, William G. Stratton. Stratton owed the *Tribune* a great deal. . . ."[6] The third kind is inducing a response by making a request that is accorded to because Y knows that by acceding he puts X under an obligation that he, Y, can call in later. Powerful decision makers induce responses in this way almost without thought; they are in a position to return favors and it is assumed without discussion that they will return favors; hence, their expressed wish is powerful without recourse to threat, promise, persuasion, or any other tactic. A political boss, for example, does not, for most of the responses he induces, need any instrument other than his assumed willingness to reciprocate.

To be sure, this third kind of reciprocity shades off into coordination through compensation where X asks for a response in return for a benefit offered. There is a small difference between the two, though not one we shall have occasion to make anything of. In compensation, the response waits until the offer is made, and presumably the offer must be worth the response requested. In this third kind of reciprocity, by contrast, one responds in the expectation of future benefit, but just what the benefit will be and whether it will actually ever be forthcoming are uncertain. At the time of the response itself X need not trouble himself to decide to what he is willing to offer in order to win the response he wants from Y; hence additional differences are that the exploitation of reciprocity in this way is quicker than compensation and it leaves unfinished business.

Where compensation produces adjustments that are mutually advantageous, reciprocity may not. To concede in negotiation in order to induce a concession is sometimes to be coercive; so also, sometimes, is calling in a past obligation where the sense of obligation rests heavily on Y and he feels he is bound to respond although at greater loss to himself than the original benefit was worth. None of this denies that reciprocity achieves coordination as defined, but it does suggest that in later chapters we will sometimes be able to make some claims for compensation that can be made only in weaker form for coordination through reciprocity.

We define *reciprocity* as: *A form of partisan mutual adjustment in which X and Y, either symmetrically in negotiation or otherwise, as a recognized condition of making effective his own decision, each induces a response from the other because the response discharges an accepted obligation to the manipulator or because it creates an obligation, valuable for the future, of the manipulator to the responder.*

Nonsymmetrical Manipulations: Unconditional Manipulation, Prior Decision, and Authoritative Prescription

AUTHORITATIVE PRESCRIPTION

A critical kind of manipulated adjustment arises, we saw, when one decision maker is conceded, by those other decision makers whom he wishes to manipulate, the authority to control their decisions. In such cases all that is necessary when X wishes to induce a response in Y is for X to prescribe the desired response to Y. This type of manipulation is to be distinguished sharply from that in which authority appears in conditional threats and promises, as when X threatens to fire, demote, or cut the budget of Y or promises to hire him, promote him, or raise his budget. Authoritative prescription denotes manipulation through an actual prescription that is to some degree obeyed.

"Authority" is a key word. In defining it, however, we wish to avoid taking on the troubles of the often related concept of legitimacy. Pushing, therefore, the irrelevant (for present purpose) question of legitimacy to the side, the term "authority" will be used to denote a relation in which a person tends to obey X without first calculating the probable gains and costs of doing so in each case in which X gives an order. One's authority is the other side of the coin of the other's habitual tendency to obey. Thus authority is *conceded,* and clearly the term refers to an interpersonal relationship. Moreover, persons often concede to X the authority to assign or allocate authority to others, whom they in consequence immediately tend to obey without *ad hoc* calculations of the probable gains and losses of obedience.

Authority is thus defined as follows: *The relation of authority exists (a) when a person receives an explicit message from another; (b) when he then adopts it as the basis of decision or action; and (c) when his grounds for doing so are that messages received in this way from the other ought to be obeyed without his subjecting them to independent evaluation in terms of his own criteria of judgment.**

People concede authority to others for various reasons, as is well known. While their concessions may sometimes simply reveal habitual fear, more typically they find quite practical advantages in fastening on certain persons certain responsibilities together with the capacity to discharge them. The concession of authority is often collectively agreed upon if only tacitly.

That authority is an interpersonal relationship, that it is conceded, and that the concession is sometimes quite explicit is illustrated in the oath of the four estates of Aragon to their king: "We, who are as good as you, swear to you who are no better than we, to accept you as our king and sovereign lord, provided you observe all our liberties and laws; but if not, not."[7] Moreover, the stress on equality in the concession of authority contained in the oath suggests (although the authority in this case is presumably central authority) the possibility that since authority can be conceded among equals, it is often conceded by one partisan to another.

Although authority as a concept is familiar mostly in connection with central coordination, our point is that authority is a powerful method of noncentral coordination. The authority to prescribe is widely employed by various noncentral participants in interrelated decision making. Xs employ it in order to achieve the subordination of various Ys where no X plays a central role in coordinating or considers himself to be playing a coordinating role. He may employ his authority to achieve his partisan purposes.

Thus we noted that the Port of New York Authority pre-

---

* The definition of authority is David Easton's and is almost a verbatim quotation from his *A Theoretical Approach to Authority,* Technical Report No. 17 for the office of Naval Research (Stanford: Stanford University, Department of Economics, April 1, 1955), p. 28. The "ought" in the definition is not necessarily a moral "ought."

scribed on some points to the legislature of the State of New Jersey; the legislature prescribed on some points to the New Jersey State Highway Department; the Highway Department prescribed on some points to local police officers, and, finally, local police officers prescribed on some points to the Port of New York Authority. Depending on what points each decision maker prescribes, such a system of linked authoritative prescription, we said, achieves a coordinated set of decisions since there is an established superior and subordinate on each critical point of conflict, without any central coordination or any explicit attention to a coordinating function.

Authoritative prescription is, then, defined as: *A form of partisan mutual adjustment in which X, as a recognized condition of making effective his own decision, prescribes a specific response to Y, who accepts X's authority on the prescription.*

UNCONDITIONAL MANIPULATION

The most immediately understandable form of unconditional manipulation of advantages and costs attaching to a course of action is providing funds so that Y can do what Y is prevented from doing only by lack of funds. In such a case X needs to attach no condition to the grant of funds. The element of promise is absent and there is no reason to negotiate. Similarly, to withdraw funds is to manipulate unconditionally. Some forms of unconditional manipulation are easily confused with authoritative prescription. If X orders Y to do or not to do something, that, we have said, is authoritative prescription. But if X uses his authority to control or enlarge the funds allocated to agency Y, or to assign personnel to that agency or to withdraw it, authority so employed represents unconditional manipulation of the advantages and costs to Y of a course of action that Y might consider. The common tactic of Congress in reducing the budget of an agency to which it is hostile is sometimes an example of authoritative prescription, although not always, for Congress may prescribe no course of action to the agency.

Unconditional manipulation is, then, defined as: *A form of partisan mutual adjustment in which X, as a recognized condition of making his decision effective, induces a response from Y by unconditionally altering advantages and costs to Y of Y's specific response.*

Some methods of unconditional manipulation operate only indirectly through non-decision makers. X, for example, is an administrative agency in conflict with Y, another agency. X cannot move against Y directly, nor can X even directly move against any other agency Z who can order a change in Y's decision. Perhaps X can, however, create among the clientele of Y such opposition to Y's policies as to lead either to Y's changing its policies or Z's instructing Y to do so. Or X may discredit Y in the eyes of important sectors of the public, or obstruct Y's work with its clientele by inducing members of the clientele to become overly demanding or intransigent.

After President Kennedy's blocking of a price increase for steel in 1962, for example, business groups seem to have exploited fears about his decision to undermine Congressional and public confidence in him generally. This is a method by which these groups hoped to increase the difficulties facing the President were he to contemplate intervening again in business pricing policies.

During World War II the Department of Agriculture and the Agricultural Adjustment Administration aroused the farmers' opposition to the farm bureaus and county agents, and the bureaus and the agents in turn undermined popular support for Department of Agriculture policies on price control and subsidies.[8]

The methods by which X influences non-decision makers and they in turn influence Y are not, of course, identical with those by which decision makers directly manipulate each other. Relations between the decision makers and non-decision makers show in some significant ways (to be outlined in the succeeding chapter) special characteristics not well represented in the categories we have been developing. Yet X's manipulation of Y by influence on non-decision makers belongs in the family of partisan mutual adjustment.

One might suppose that in any manipulation of Y, X manipulates non-decision makers and that this is, therefore, not a new category. Let us see. In partisan discussion X needs involve no one other than Y himself. In bargaining he may threaten Y with injuries that can only be inflicted with the cooperation of non-decision makers (he threatens, for example, to undermine voter support for X, a politician); but the threat itself can produce the response without actually calling on non-decision makers to make a response. Prior decision is, of course, also possible without activating non-decision makers. In reciprocity X can clearly call in an obligation without asking for response from any other person than Y. So also can he employ his authority to require Y to respond. It is required only that Y concede the authority, regardless of whether other persons concede it or not, and certainly without X's exercising his authority on other persons.

Non-decision makers may be participants in unilateral manipulated partisan mutual adjustment by giving credence to threats or promises, by assisting in the discharge of obligations under reciprocity, by behaving so as to make X's claims to authority persuasive to Y, and in many other ways. But the distinction we drew seems useful: sometimes non-decision makers are the object of X's indirect attempts to influence Y, and sometimes they are not.

All these forms of unconditional manipulation lie outside the domain of negotiation and are almost always unilaterally employed. They are worth emphasis in order to make obvious the place of unilateral manipulation in partisan mutual adjustment. For, as we have seen, it is easy to lapse into a mistaken identification of mutual adjustment with symmetric adjustment, even with negotiation alone.

PRIOR DECISION

A form of unconditional manipulation that will turn out to be especially important for understanding relations among interest groups is prior decision. To recapitulate what has already been said, it is a form of unconditional, manipulated adjustment close in appearance to, but different from, tacit bargaining. X perceives, as in negotiation, an interdependence between his decision and that of Y. He also believes that Y sees similar interdependence. In X's eyes it is to his own advantage and to Y's that their respective decisions are coordinated. But he does not negotiate. Instead, he makes his decision before Y does, to force Y to adapt to X's decision. He may strengthen the inducement by moving his own decision in the direction preferred by Y. For example, the House, without negotiation with the Senate and shortly before adjournment, may move from its preferred policy position on a bill to one closer to that which it estimates the Senate prefers. It thus hopes to induce the Senate to move from its preferred position to the intermediate one.

Prior decision is defined as: *A form of partisan mutual adjustment in which X, knowing that there are advantages to both X and Y from coordination of their respective decisions, makes a firm, noncontingent decision before Y decides, thus compelling Y to adapt to X in order for Y to reap any advantages of coordination.*

Where the prior decision has not moved in the direction of Y's preferences, this a method of coordination that forces all the adjustment onto Y. Wanting the advantages of coordination with X, Y has no recourse but to take X's decision as governing or to forego the advantages. Where X tries to seduce Y by first altering his own decision to make it more attractive to Y, X and Y share the burden of adaptation unless, as is not impossible, in searching for a position attractive to Y, X finds a new policy that combines the virtues of attractiveness to both X and Y. Just as the search in deferential adaptation will sometimes produce advantages for both parties, so also the search for a policy sufficiently attractive to Y to make the gambit of prior commitment operative may uncover a decision possibility without excessive burden on either X or Y.

In 1957 when Senator Neuberger and others in pursuit of conservationist interests were proposing that the federal government buy up shares of the dissolving Klamath Indian Reservation, to prevent the land's being rapidly cut over by logging companies who stood ready to buy the shares, Secretary of the Interior Fred A. Seaton—responding to logging interests—with the collaboration of the Department of Agriculture, proposed legislation that continued sales to the logging companies but also allowed cutting only under strict government supervision. Seaton's commitment to this policy is an example of prior decision, one in which the manipulated decision maker speaks eloquently of its seductiveness. Senator Neuberger writes:

Now the dilemma was mine. If I insisted on my own bill and it bogged down in a partisan political debacle, the economy of my native state would suffer grievously. I desperately needed the unified backing of all my colleagues on the Indian Affairs Subcommittee if we were to have any chance of success with the Senate as a whole. And if only one or two large blocks of Indian timber were purchased privately under the Interior Department's bill, its total cost would be $90 million as contrasted with $120 million under my original bill. This was decisive with me, for I knew that many of my fellow Western Senators—rebuffed on relatively small reclamation and public-works project in their own states—would wonder why scores of millions of dollars were necessary to buy an Indian reservation in Oregon.

I took the bill which Secretary Seaton had sent to me and dropped it in the Senate hopper "by request." If I had not crossed the Rubicon, I at least had crossed the Upper Klamath Lake. It was my bill now.[9]

The resemblance of prior decision to tacit bargaining, it will be remembered, is this. If such a move as described above were made only tentatively—that is, with an indication that the new decision was not a firm move but a contingent proposal for a decision (as Neuberger's earlier bill was but Seaton's was not)— it would still be a part of a game of bargaining. For it would be an offer of a benefit made contingent on a response from Y. By prior decision, however, we mean a firm, noncontingent decision. Prior decision is a method of coordination that can be operative where, for any one of many possible reasons, bargaining and partisan discussion are impossible or not desired by the decision makers in question.*

Moreover, although tacit bargaining is a symmetric relation, adaptive adjustment is not. In adaptive adjustment X chooses a decision point to which Y simply does or does not respond. Only if Y could choose another decision point to which X could be lured would the relationship between the two become symmetric. This is possible only where, as in tacit bargaining, the moves of X and Y are only proposals: where X has already made a firm prior decision, Y only can take it or leave it.

* Prior decision bears an obvious relation to Schelling's concept of commitment or of binding oneself, except that he has seen commitment as a bargaining tactic, specifically as a preface to striking a bargain, explicitly or implicitly. (Thomas C. Schelling, *The Strategy of Conflict* [Cambridge: Harvard University Press, 1960], pp. 22ff.)

On a small technical point it might appear that prior decision is not a form of manipulated adjustment since X makes his decision without first manipulating Y, as he would do in all other forms of manipulation. To be sure, X makes his own decision without first waiting for Y's decision; nevertheless, winning Y's response is part of the strategy that constrains his own decision. To a degree his own decision fails, by our assumption, if Y does not respond. To put it another way, even if X moves first, as though independent of Y as he would in fact be in adaptive adjustment, the decision X makes is designed to induce Y to alter his decision; X wants a particular response from Y because it makes his own decision more efficacious for himself. Clearly X manipulates Y deliberately; Y's response is not simply a by-product of X's decision, which is all it can be in adaptive adjustment.

Indirect Manipulation

We took note above of, and incorporated into the tabular summary on page 63, the probability that X may seek to induce a response from Y by employing a manipulative method on a decision maker Z, who in turn can induce the required response from Y. A pressing problem, for example, to the incoming administration of President Kennedy was to induce the House Committee on Rules to permit consideration of liberal legislation on the floor. The President's principal direct move was not to the Committee at all but to induce the Speaker of the House to make it his problem. The Speaker then negotiated with the Chairman of the Rules Committee to win him over to an expanded Committee with increased representation of liberals. This failing, he subsequently tried to replace one conservative member of the Committee with a more liberal member, but was dissuaded by protests. He then undertook—indirection again—to induce the membership of the House to enlarge the Committee over the objections of its Chairman.[10]

Indirect manipulation is defined as: *A form of partisan mutual adjustment in which any of the other types of manipulative adjustment are used to manipulate Y indirectly by X's manipulating a third decision maker who then manipulates Y.*

The example cited earlier in the chapter of organized opposition to the New Jersey jet airport illustrated indirection through manipulation of other decision makers than the Port Authority. A conspicuous feature of manipulation by indirection through other decision makers is alliance building, where X requires coordination between himself and a variety of other decision makers in order to effect the response he wishes from Y. The United States Department of Agriculture's Extension Service, the Farm Bureau, and many of the agricultural colleges, for example, have long practiced manipulation on each other in order to manipulate still other decision makers such as the Soil Conservation Service and the Farm Security Administration. Formation of alliances is a complication in partisan mutual adjustment about which a good deal will be said in later chapters.

Summary of All Critical Types of Partisan Mutual Adjustment

In summary, then, all the forms of adaptive adjustment and the critical forms of manipulated adjustment can be summarized as follows, certain other manipulated forms appearing only in the tabular summary on page 63.

Adaptive adjustments: parametric
deferential
calculated

Manipulated adjustments: negotiation
partisan discussion
bargaining (always a form of negotiation)
compensation and bargained compensation
reciprocity
authoritative prescription
unconditional manipulation
prior decision
indirect manipulation

Part
3

The Process
in Government

Chapter
6

THE

GOVERNMENTAL

PROCESS

IT IS NOW TIME TO PLACE THE methods of partisan mutual adjustment in the governmental process more formally than in the examples of the preceding chapters. Accordingly, there will be laid out here a simplified picture or model of a governmental process. Among other purposes served, it clarifies the assumptions about the character of government that underlie the argument to be developed on partisan mutual adjustment. It is a picture not of government in general but of a more or less democratic or polyarchal government, of a presidential rather than parliamentary system, and of a two-party system. As a picture of American government, it is easily recognizable. The restrictions make for concreteness and even more for simplicity, values that justify not attempting to analyze partisan mutual adjustment in all forms of government. The descriptive propositions to which we want to call attention and which constitute the picture or model are stated somewhat formally and are numbered partly for emphasis and partly to facilitate later reference.

Agencies

(1) *One set of policy decision makers are government administrative organizations, to be called agencies.*

The organizations here referred to are governmental in a specific sense. It is not enough to establish that they participate in the governmental process; they must be part of the formal machinery of government and not private associations.

For the sake of simplicity the agency rather than its members is taken to be the decision-making unit. That some agencies are composed of other agencies is not denied by this proposition. But, except for agencies within agencies, we abstract from processes internal to an agency. The abstraction is for convenience; it would be feasible, if any important purpose were served by doing so, to regard an agency head as the decision maker and treat his relations to others in his organization in the same way that decision making among organizations is treated.

In actual fact, at sufficiently "low" administrative levels, agency decisions deal less with policy than with implementation or administration of policies decided upon elsewhere, but this distinction is difficult and dangerous to make, and unnecessary for present purposes. In any case we are concerned only with those agencies that make policy decisions, even if they do not make policy decisions exclusively or at a very high level. Governmental organizations that do not make policy decisions at all are simply ignored.

(2) *Each agency makes policy decisions in only a restricted, specialized area.*

We leave open, however, the basis of specialization among the agencies. It may be by area of public concern (farm problems, for example), by area of the traditional division of policy-making labor (foreign relations), by objective (soil conservation), or by means of technique (monetary management). If one thinks of fairly large social functions or problem areas—control of inflation, for example, or national security, economic development, transportation, regulation of urban land use, structural reform in government, or education—it is not in fact typically the case that any one agency monopolizes or even dominates the whole area; nor does the proposition so imply.

(3) *Each agency possesses and employs governmental authority over some participants in the governmental process (officials, agencies, nonofficial leaders, citizens), restricted and specialized, however, to its policy-making area.*

That each agency has and employs authority appears to be trivial. But we shall make much of the use of the concept of authority; mutual adjustment is not a contest of naked power but a ritualized process in which the principal counter is authority. "Authority" was defined in the preceding chapter; "governmental authority" denotes authority conceded to a decision maker by virtue of his position in government. Agency authority includes prescriptive authority over other agencies; all the other uses of authority mentioned in the preceding chapter, such as budgetary authority; and, of course, authority over citizens.

(4) *While in its area of specialization each agency makes policy decisions, some agencies also confer governmental authority on other agencies; and, of those that do, all make some decisions designed to coordinate the agencies on which they have conferred authority, and all occasionally prescribe a particular decision to such an agency.*

This proposition merely specifies that agencies are often formally related to each other in a way ordinarily called hierarchical.

Legislators and Executives

(5) *Another set of policy decision makers are legislators and executives.*

"Executive" denotes chief officers like a president, governor, or mayor.

(6) *Unlike the agency, which is specialized, each legislator and executive possesses and employs, among other powers, governmental authority conceded by almost all citizens ("citizen" to be defined later) over all or almost all areas of policy making by that government.*

(7) *The exercise of the legislator's authority in any given situation is commonly but not always contingent on some degree of formal agreement with other legislators, the agreement to be reached through and tested by certain formal procedures, such as legislative voting.*

(8) *With their authority legislators and executives allocate authority and assign functions to all government agencies (including those agencies to which other agencies also allocate authority and function).*[1]

(9) *Legislators and executives, individually and collectively (if collectively, through the legislative procedures referred to), sometimes make some decisions explicitly designed to coordinate the decisions of agencies; sometimes prescribe a particular agency decision; and sometimes make directly, without any allocation of authority or function to an agency, a policy decision.*

In these last five propositions, there are introduced what would ordinarily be called in question-begging language the top decision makers in government. They have the power to establish and dissolve government agencies in every field of public policy making, and their particular powers are relatively unrestricted. The set includes chief executive, legislators, and some kinds of judges, but not party- or interest-group leaders who lack the authority referred to in proposition 6.

Proposition 7 takes account of the fact that a legislator's share in a collective authority—his authority, say, to allocate authority over taxation to a revenue bureau—depends on agreement among legislators through some such formal procedure as legislative discussion and voting with some formula for deriving a "decision" from the pattern of votes cast. The procedures required have not been specified in detail because they are numerous, including as they do, for example, special procedures for moving to a decision after an executive veto of a prior legislative decision, or, for another example, special procedures for judicial reversal of legislative and executive decisions. All that needs to be said at this point is that the legislator's exercise of authority is often dependent upon agreements reached through ritualized procedures. One need not even specify, for present purposes, the origin and sources of support for the formal procedures. They may in fact rest on the indoctrinations of the citizenry or indoctrinations shared specifically by legislators. Or they may be respectfully observed because no one legislator dares challenge them, even if there is no prescribed punishment for a challenge. Still again, there may be an effective and tangible enforcement procedure. One way or another, these procedures exist.

Conventions

The importance of conventional, formal procedures; the parallel importance of concessions of authority, which is itself a convention; and the significance to be given to still further conventions in the behavior of participants in the governmental process all lead to the proposal of a tenth proposition:

(10) *The behavior of each participant (including each citizen) in the governmental process is greatly controlled by conventions about ends and means that have the effect of prescribing behavior conditionally or absolutely.*

The conventions are explicit or implicit prescriptions that specify to some degree, though only very roughly, what goal values and side values can and cannot be sacrificed to the achievement of other values. They prohibit, to take an obvious example, the taking of human life as a bargaining tactic. They also roughly specify the circumstances or conditions in which certain kinds of means can be used; they sometimes specify, again very roughly, a matching of obligations, thus creating, for example, a strong obligation on X to make a concession, even if small, for every concession made by Y.

Some conventions are written into law, others come to be traditionally accepted without force of law. Others not written into the law are themselves the product of the kind of interchange we are describing in this book. Thus these conventions are both the foundation of and the product of partisan mutual adjustment, even if it is only the former point that needs to be made at this point. Where these are not law people may accept them out of the conviction that the stability of the system demands their acceptance. Or they simply may strategically calculate the advantages of their accepting them, as has been the case, to choose an obvious example, with acceptance of some of the conventions or rules of war. Presumably the acceptance of some conventions is traceable simply to social indoctrination. In the House of Representatives, for example, a favorable committee assignment goes to a "responsible" member of the House. He is one who has a

... basic and fundamental respect for the legislative process and understands and appreciates its formal and informal rules. He has the respect of his fellow legislators, and particularly the respect of party leaders. He does not attempt to manipulate every situation for his own personal advantage. In the consideration of issues, he is careful to protect the rights of others; he is careful to clear matters that require clearance; and he is especially careful about details. He understands the pressures on the members with whom he cannot always agree and avoids pushing an issue to the point where his opponents may suffer personal embarrassment. On specific issues, no matter how firm his convictions and no matter how great the pressures upon him, he demonstrates a willingness to compromise.[2]

The conventions sometimes fix an obligation that all participants in the governmental process are held to accept; but, at the other extreme, they may prescribe that what X is required to do depends on whether Y does or does not follow a certain convention, itself either conditional or unconditional.

These conventions are sometimes referred to as rules of the game; on the other hand that term is sometimes reserved for the more universal and stable of them. That they exist does not make partisan mutual adjustment superficial, for they do not prescribe what X and Y do; they only lay down some general constraints.

Citizens

(11) *There exists a set of individuals, called citizens, who by convention are eligible to vote.*

With this proposition the citizen is identified as an eligible voter, where voting is taken in its ordinary meaning except that we make no place for voting on any issues other than the choice of members of the legislative and executive set. Voting is therefore defined as follows: *A specialized procedure, following certain conventions, whereby individuals express their preferences among candidates for membership in the legislative and executive set and there is made by rule from these expressions of preference a determination of membership in the set of politicians.*

(12) *The rule by which citizens' expressed preferences, determine membership in the legislative and executive set is such that, in choosing among candidates for any one open position in the set, the weight assigned to the preference of any one individual is the same as that assigned to any other.*

In choosing among candidates for a Senate seat in California, for example, no one vote counts for more than any other, even if only a few votes in Nevada are sufficient to elect its Senator and many times more are needed to elect a Senator in California.

(13) *When some or all citizens engage, as they do, in voting, all participants in the governmental process concede the authority of the legislator or executor only to those so determined to be members of that set.*

Interest-Group Leaders

(14) *There exists a set of policy decision makers, called interest-group leaders, each of whom can at his discretion commit, to some degree, each of a group of citizens to the support of at least some candidates or policies he selects.*

(15) There is no barrier to playing the role of interest-group leader other than that of each prospective leader's capacity to win a following.

With these propositions there is introduced a broadly defined, very large category of participants in the governmental process. The category includes the trade-union leader, for example, who can repeatedly commit, to some degree, his members by committing their funds, and who can speak in the name of an organization. It includes also the minister who from time to time uses his pulpit with some effect to organize public opinion, as well as the self-appointed spokesman for one cause or another who, merely by the currency given his remarks, pulls the opinions of some like-minded citizens in the direction he wishes. At an extreme the concept even embraces a Walter Lippmann simply because he has a following, that is, because what he writes in part commits some group of individuals through the authority they concede his ideas. Clearly the concept as employed here is not limited to the recognized leader of a formally organized group. Moreover, individuals are classified as interest-group leaders whether they claim to speak for private interests or for their conception of the general welfare.

(16) Interest-group leaders, on one hand, and citizens, on the other, control each other in a specialized exchange of benefits having characteristics described in the following sub propositions:

(16.1) Interest group leaders, actual and prospective, freely compete among one another for followings, whether intentional or not.

A following is a group of people who can be committed in some degree at the discretion of the leader. Leaders compete at least in the sense that, for any citizen confronted with any given policy issue, more than one would-be or actual interest group leader offers advice. In other cases group leaders may explicitly compete by criticizing each other's positions and by explicitly asking for support.

(16.2) For his part the citizen picks and chooses among various interest-group leaders, choosing to follow one at least for a time on one category of issues, and choosing to follow another at least for a time on another category.

(*16.3*) *The interest-group leader appeals for support by aiding citizens in adapting realizable, specific policy preferences to their underlying attitudes and evaluations and vice versa.*

(*16.4*) *In choosing to follow any given interest-group leader citizens confer on him some capacity to control their political positions in the future; they also put him in a position, because of the support he commands, to influence governmental decisions more heavily than can an individual citizen who is not an interest-group leader; and they of course also offer him certain gratifications such as prestige and the pleasure of wielding power, at least for those whom it is a pleasure.*

Given the complexities of public policy making, any given citizen is heavily dependent on others for information, diagnosis, and prescription, whether he reserves to himself a final judgment on an issue or prefers to take his position from someone else whom he believes has found a suitable position to take. He cannot take anyone's advice, diagnosis, or position at random; what he wants is proffered diagnosis, advice, or prescription that takes account of his own basic attitudes and evaluations. He wants to shortcut a process of working through the whole policy analysis himself because he may lack competence or time or both; yet he wishes to emerge at roughly the same outcome as if he had competently performed the whole analysis himself.

Moreover, even though he wants advice that respects his underlying attitudes and evaluations, he also wants advice as to what these should be. He does not want his attitudes and evaluations to be treated as wholly satisfactory for all time. Even given a deep general commitment to certain existing attitudes and evaluations, he wants to be able to adapt them, at least gradually and marginally, to the needs of policy making. That is to say, if no feasible policies seem suited to his underlying attitudes and evaluations, he will sometimes want to alter the attitudes and evaluations rather than look further for new policy alternatives.

Thus, both with respect to underlying attitudes and with respect to particular policy issues, he wants the help of opinion leaders who in one sense "think like I do" and at the same time can be sufficiently different from him to change the way he thinks. He wants, therefore, the help of a leader who will both respond to his preferences and at the same time substantially determine for him what they are to be.[3]

He dares surrender a great deal of immediate control over his own political opinions to interest-group leaders because competition among them permits him to sample their opinions and dispositions on many fundamental attitudes as well as on policy choices. If he chooses to follow his trade-union leader on, say, policies with respect to race relations, it is because he has already found that his trade-union leader, or perhaps any trade-union leader of a certain category, is sympathetic to his own attitudes on some other matters on which he believes himself to have some competence to judge.

On the leader's side of the mutual relationship (would-be or actual leader), he is held responsible by the followers' capacity to sample, by criticism from other would-be or actual leaders, and by the freedom with which a citizen can abandon any one leader on any one kind of issue and turn instead to another. Even a trade-union leader whose members cannot leave the union can be disestablished as an interest-group leader by the members' refusal to vote as he wishes. He may find, and politicians may clearly see, that on certain political issues his members do not follow his leadership but instead follow their religious or ethnic leaders, or perhaps the editorialist or columnist of their daily newspaper. Hence every opinion leader has to satisfy his following or be deposed. Therefore, he must not simply announce to them what he wishes them to believe on policy issues, but must satisfy them that he is in fact adapting his positions on particular policy issues to their underlying beliefs, and vice versa.

(17) *Many interest-group leaders are linked to each other in the same way that interest-group leaders and citizens are linked to each other.*

A local Chamber of Commerce secretary, acting as an interest-group leader on certain business issues for a small group of businessmen, will often acknowledge another Chamber official higher up in the hierarchy as his interest-group leader on the same issues. In so far as leaders at one level play the role of followers to leaders at another level, a pyramidal structure of leadership sometimes develops. In a governmental structure of greatly dispersed policy-making responsibility such as is being described, however, the pyramid always lacks an apex. And often the relationships do not constitute a pyramid at all. A national interest-group leader, like the President of the National Farm Bureau, may be a follower of a local leader on issues pertaining to local community affairs. On national nonfarm issues, he may follow a leader, say, on space technology issues who in turn follows him on farm issues.

Party Leaders

(*18*) *There exists a subset of interest group leaders, called party leaders, itself divided into two competing subsets each of which takes proximate responsibility for maintaining and directing a relatively stable association of legislators and executives (potential or actual), interest-group leaders, and other citizens cooperating to win various elections.*

(*19*) *To achieve this purpose, party leaders seek, in addition to their activities as interest group leaders: (a) to discover and mold both reconciliations of disparate citizen preferences and common interests that will appeal to at least a plurality of voting citizens, and (b) by public declarations and by influencing the selection of candidates and the policies followed by legislators and executives in the party, to identify the party's candidates in the citizen's mind with the presumed plurality preferences.*

(*20*) *These competitive party efforts at discovery and molding, reconsidered and redirected as a result of each electoral success and failure, eliminate before each election a wide variety of alternative candidates who might otherwise be considered; and they exercise heavy influence toward keeping policy alternatives within the relatively narrow range within which each party thinks plurality support is most likely.*

These three propositions on political parties identify the last set of participants in the governmental process. They are especially important in indicating the role of the political party in reconciling conflicting citizen preferences and in discovering common interests and thus in moving toward actual policy choices. If both parties competently diagnose citizen preferences and both parties find sets of reconciliations and common interests capable of competing for plurality support on election day, then each party has already rejected a great variety of candidates and policies that could otherwise have been espoused. And where political preferences are single peaked in their distribution, the effect of party competition is to bring the candidates and espoused policies of the two parties into the relation of two slightly different versions of fundamentally the same preferences and perceptions of common interest.

Thus the activity of party leaders, as described above, accomplishes a large part of the selection process in government. Although this activity is disciplined by elections—each party wants to win—citizen choice is in some very large part already completed by election day. In short, to an important degree citizens do not choose on election day; but the fact that they could choose compels choices and commitments responsive to their preferences to be made earlier by party leaders, so that whichever way the election goes they will enjoy fundamentally the same aggregation of their preferences and will have, in effect, influenced the choices made earlier.

To emphasize that any given participant in the governmental process may play several roles, we may finally add that a party leader is often himself a legislator or executive.

Partisan Mutual Adjustment

One can now finally specify just how partisan mutual adjustment fits into the governmental process.

(21) *Actual and potential legislators and executives, agencies, interest-group leaders, and party leaders constantly engage in partisan mutual adjustment with each other, both bilaterally and multilaterally, in all possible combinations.*

This proposition locates all those mechanisms of the preceding chapters in the governmental process: parametric, deferential, and calculated adaptation; negotiation; partisan discussion; bargaining;

compensation; prior decision; reciprocity; authoritative prescription, and unconditional unilateral adjustment.

It should be noted that citizens do not participate directly in partisan mutual adjustment. It will be remembered from Chapter 2 that partisan mutual adjustment occurs among decision makers, defined as a subset of all individuals. Here that subset is defined to include not citizens but legislators and executives, agencies, interest-group leaders, and party leaders. Among them partisan mutual adjustment is ubiquitous.

(22) *Participants in partisan mutual adjustment who manipulate each other employ a wide variety of influences, among which five are especially important: persuasion; authority, not limited to its use in authoritative prescription; appeals to conventions; votes; and wealth.*

Persuasion alone is, of course, the moving force in what we have called partisan discussion, as is authority in authoritative prescription. But authority, we saw, has other uses such as the control of personnel and budget, and in the implementation of official function; through all of this authority comes to be a counter in bargaining and other negotiation, in prior decision, and in unconditional unilateral manipulation. Negotiation of all kinds is full of appeals to conventions,[4] although in negotiation and other methods wealth and votes also count heavily. Wealth is of course a source of influence in compensation and bargained compensation, especially among nongovernmental participants in mutual adjustment. To speak of votes as an influence is to abbreviate drastically. More fully stated, any participant in mutual adjustment who can influence how citizens vote can use this capacity to manipulate agencies, executives and legislators, and party leaders.[5]

(23) *There is no highest prescriptive authority in government: no agency, legislator, executive, or continuing collectivity of legislators can prescribe to all others yet concede no authority to any other, even if indirect prescription is allowed for (the authority controls Z by prescribing that X prescribe to Z).*

This is an important proposition for what follows in later chapters, and it of course describes the state of affairs in American government as well as in most others. The reference to a "continuing collectivity of politicians" in the proposition is designed to rule out the possibility that, though no individual legislator is a supreme prescriber, an association of them—say a legislature or cabinet—becomes so. Both possibilities are ruled out by the proposition. There may be a prime minister, president, or cabinet, but not with the kind of unilateral authority just proscribed.

It is apparent that it is being taken for granted that agencies are not simply independent of each other, each having just such authority and function as to permit it to carry on its work without effect on other agencies, thus escaping any participation in partisan mutual adjustment. Similarly, it is being assumed that interdependence among legislators goes beyond the ritualized procedures through which they reach the agreements often required for a collective exercise of authority. These assumptions can be made explicit.

(24) *No allocation of authority or function can be found that eliminates interdependence among participants in partisan mutual adjustment; and among legislators there is interdependence other than that implicit in their participation in the rituals by which they reach the agreements necessary to the collective exercise of authority (for the definition of interdependence, see page 21f).*

From what has been said so far, it might be thought that the distribution of authority and other powers and functions might be static. Hence three last propositions identify dynamic elements in the governmental process.

(25) *Through the mechanisms referred to in these propositions, including partisan mutual adjustment, those who make policy decisions also make decisions on changes in policy-making procedures.*

Such a proposition calls attention in a useful way to the breadth of the policy-making process that we have been describing. The allocation of authority and other powers to agencies can be changed, thus, by the use of authority and other powers, either within the process of partisan mutual adjustment or not. Even the allocation of authority and other powers and function among politicians can be changed in the same ways, that is, by their use of their own authority and power both within and outside of processes of partisan mutual adjustment. In addition:

(26) *There are specialized conventional processes whereby citizens can alter the authority, function, and power of legislators and executives in addition to those rituals by which citizens determine membership in the legislative and executive set.*

This proposition refers, of course, to specialized rituals for constitutional changes such as, in the United States, the formal process for amendment of the Constitution.

Not only can the allocations of powers and function change, but they do change, ceaselessly, because the exercise of existing powers in many cases is inseparable from the reallocation of power. Thus many authoritative prescriptions of the legislature, for example, establish new agencies and new authority. Or, for another example, the exercise of authority in an impressive way often encourages the concession, informally, of further authority. Therefore, finally:

(27) *At any time the making of decisions by participants in the governmental process itself necessarily alters the allocation of authority, other powers, and function among participants.*

The propositions of this chapter do more than specify the place of partisan mutual adjustment in the governmental process, though that is one of their purposes. Having rounded out the preceding exposition of mutual adjustment, they also constitute the assumptions on which further analysis of the process will be pursued.

Chapter
7

MIXED SYSTEMS:
EMPHASIS
ON CENTRALITY

WE CAN NOW PUT PARTISAN
mutual adjustment and centrally coordinated governmental systems side by side so that they illuminate each other. However, real-
world systems are mixed; hence we will find it even more profitable
to set side by side a number of mixed systems, beginning with one
that suppresses, as far as imaginable, the practice of partisan mutual adjustment in favor of centrality and proceeding step by step
through mixed intermediate systems to one, finally, that represents
an extreme in its heavy employment of mutual adjustment. In so
doing we shall also put some flesh on the bare bones of the preceding chapter by showing just how and where various forms of
mutual adjustment appear in real, more or less democratic systems.

Centrally Coordinated Decision Making in the Extreme

CENTRAL COORDINATION DEFINED

If we are to depict government marked by a maximum of central coordination and a minimum of partisan mutual adjustment we must first define what we shall mean by "central coordinator." The abstract characterization of centrality given in Chapter 2 is inadequate. We cannot mean simply that the adaptation of any one decision to any other in a set of decisions is *exclusively* regulated by some single (hence called central) decision-making individual or cooperative group, since at least some common values and common circumstantial constraints on decisions will achieve in every imaginable case some adjustment of decisions to one another. Might we mean, then, that with respect to explicit and deliberate attempts at coordination, decisions are made exclusively by a single decision maker or group for the whole set? This is not satisfactory either because in partisan mutual adjustment there might be one among the participants who deliberately and explicitly *attempts* to coordinate but whose efforts are overwhelmed by partisan adjusters. We should not want to call this central coordination.

Might we mean, to try again, that central coordination means that with respect to interpersonal control or influence, the controls are unilateral, running from the one (central) decision maker to the others and never the other way round? This is unacceptable since the character of decision makers' responses to any one coordinating decision maker invariably influence or control the character of his attempts to coordinate. Central coordination of investment decisions, for example, through central bank manipulation of interest rates is obviously responsive to, influenced by, and controlled by the strength and direction of desires to invest. For that matter the central controls can best be understood as a set of controls designed to grapple with investment decisions, and clearly one never grapples with anything without being influenced or controlled by it.

Might we then say that central coordination is distinguished not by the absence of controls on the coordinator but by the fact that the one ostensibly central decision maker wins, dominates, or overcomes the controls exercised over him? What might this mean?

That the controls over him finally count for zero, are wholly in-effective? That is impossible; we cannot conceive of a decision maker wholly free from influence from any other decision makers in an interdependent world. Might we mean that the one ostensibly central decision maker has the authority finally to make the deci-sion? This is not satisfactory either. If a central bank has exclusive authority to manipulate interest rates it may nevertheless be unable to coordinate centrally because it fears to use its authority (say because of the possibility of weakening its conceded authority by using it when offensive to investors), or because it chooses not to use it (because there are ways investors can circumvent manipu-lated interest rates), or uses it but unavailingly (because, again, the effect of the rates is circumvented even if the authority is not challenged).

To try again, is coordination central when one decision maker is conceded the exclusive authority to manipulate decision makers in some given set, when that authority actually is employed, and when it is not challenged but obeyed? The shortcoming of this concept is that in any imaginable circumstances the presumptive central coordinator will exercise his authority mindful of the effects his presumptive subordinates have on him; hence, in effect he will find himself in a situation in which, as in partisan mutual adjust-ment, they exercise on him a number of controls other than author-itative prescription while he counters with authoritative prescrip-tion (which they obey). He may have no more influence on the pattern of decisions finally arranged than each of a number of other decision makers. With his power of authority he has overcome, dominated, won out, no more than each of several others with their special powers.

One might suppose that the power of conceded authority would dominate other powers in such a relationship. But this is not so when authority is limited to certain specified permissible prescrip-tions. And it always is, for no decision maker is ever given authority to prescribe to a given set of decision makers anything he pleases. And, on the other hand, their powers to control him enlarge with their inventiveness, for there are multitudinous ways of manipulat-ing people.

It begins to be clear that with or without authority no decision maker can ever approach very closely to unilateral control over other decision makers. Inevitably their beliefs and attitudes constrain him, and they may deliberately seek to manipulate him. There is, however, one kind of control or influence of subordinates over superiors that is quite consistent with central coordination. That is the influence subordinates achieve through information and analysis they provide for their superior. Insofar as presumptive subordinates help a central coordinator to grasp and solve his coordination problem, their control over what he thinks is, by any acceptable concept of central coordination, not inconsistent with central coordination.

Finally, to introduce an additional element often missing from a list of the limits on any one decision maker's capacity to influence others, he can adapt only some past decisions to present decisions. He can, to coordinate highway construction with plans for the expansion of residential area, have a highway torn up and replaced with building lots. But if he can in that sense adapt the historically earlier decision (to build the highway) to contemporary decisions to develop a residential area, he cannot touch the earlier decisions to invest the labor of a thousand men in the construction of the highway. Some past decisions are forever beyond his coordinating reach.*

We shall therefore have to mean by central coordination not the capacity in the hands of some one decision-making individual or organization unilaterally to arrange the adaptations of decisions to one another in a set but instead an approximation to that.

Central coordination is therefore defined as follows: *Among a set of decision makers, coordination is central to the degree that there is in the set one decision maker who (a) is in a symmetric control relation with every other member of the set; (b) in every such symmetric control relation, is much more powerful than the other, except for the other's control through information and analysis; and (c) explicitly recognizes his task to be arranging the adaptations of decisions one to another, and to some significant degree arranges such adaptations.*

* It will be remembered from the discussion of parametric adjustment in Chapter 3 that we include in the concept of coordination the adaptation to each other of all decisions, past, present, and future.

How powerful must a decision maker be to approximate unilateral power closely enough to be called a central coordinator? We can only answer that the more powerful (relative to those coordinated), the more central, bearing in mind that exclusively unilateral power is an impossibility. If central coordination were conceived of as exclusively unilateral power in the relations of one to a group, it would be at best a limiting analytical case never closely approximated in the real world. Although there are many circumstances in which none of a set of decision makers *attempts* to manipulate the central coordinator, there are no cases in which they do not control him; hence there are no cases in which they do not share influence on the coordinating decisions ranging, in the case of any one of them, from merely substantial influence to influence greater than that of the ostensible central coordinator.*

Let "decision maker" in the definition above refer either to an individual decision maker or to a committee or other group, even a large one, who agree immediately on all decisions or resolve their differences through cooperative discussion in the light of agreed objectives. Among them partisan mutual adjustment is absent, and they speak to all other decision makers with a single voice. In that way we can incorporate, for simplicity's sake, coordination through cooperative discussion into the concept of central coordination. Typically, of course, central coordinators are not single individuals but groups.

With these clarifications we shall imagine now a government in which central coordination is dominant.

A HYPOTHETICAL EXTREME: NO PARTISANS

Imagine a government in which, to begin with, the executive and the legislators either share an adequate set of criteria for the actual resolution through cooperative discussion of any problem about the relation of any governmental decision to another, or they all agree on who among them is to control the relations. Assume also—admittedly contrary to fact—that they possess the intellectual

---

* In Chapter 5 manipulative relations were described as either unilateral or symmetric. But control is always symmetric. That is, X can manipulate Y without Y's manipulating X, but X cannot control Y without being controlled (influenced) by Y.

competence to apply the criteria conclusively in every case required. Make a similar assumption for agencies. Either all agencies agree on an adequate set of criteria for decisions, which they are competent to apply conclusively; or the instructions specialized to each agency respectively are sufficient to resolve any doubt as to what the appropriate decision is; or there is a hierarchical superior, possibly at the highest level the chief executive, to whom they delegate the decision when they find their criteria inadequate.

By "inadequate criteria" we mean criteria that suffice to prove one decision correct and another incorrect or, to put it another way, criteria such that all decision makers agree, because they can and do competently test the decision by them, that a given decision is to be desired or not.

By "delegate the decision when they find their criteria inadequate" we mean that they concede that a coordinating decision should be made by one of them, that they accept and obey the coordinating decision, that they do not attempt to influence the coordinating decision by any partisan appeals or manipulations other than offering information and analysis, and that they permit no doubts in the coordinating decision maker's mind as to their intention wholly to follow his decision.

As further assumptions, interest groups do not exist, nor do parties and party leaders.

Under these assumptions there are either no partisan decision makers in the governmental process; or those who are present simply accept, without attempting to alter, the decisions of others to whom decision making is delegated on points of disagreement among them.

To maintain a high degree of centrality in coordination such extreme assumptions are required. But some people will say they have no such extreme assumptions in mind when they speak of central coordination. They may suspect that a straw man is being constructed. Let us see.

These assumptions are indeed necessary in order to suppress as far as possible the role of partisan mutual adjustment in coordination. In the first place, if decision makers do not cooperatively pursue decisions in the light of agreed values or, failing that, do not turn over the controverted decision to someone whose decision is simply accepted, they are by definition introducing the noncentral devices of partisan mutual adjustment with respect to each other. What if they delegate the formal authority to make a coordinating decision to a presumptive central coordinator but do not delegate exclusive control over the decision to him and instead manipulate him through partisan appeals, threats and promises, prior decision, and the like, as, in fact, subordinates typically do to their superiors? This question brings us to a second point which is that if we are looking for a *high* degree of central coordination, as in the present hypothetical case, we must look for a situation in which the presumed coordinator is *extremely* powerful relative to other decision makers. We can make him so only by reducing as far as possible the power of other decision makers, either by eliminating other conflicting decision makers, as we do when we assume they become cooperative discussants, or by assuming that they wholly accept and do not fight or resist the presumed centralist's decisions where cooperative discussion is not attempted or fails.

Thirdly, the common claims for central coordination demonstrate the necessity for these extreme assumptions. If it is claimed, for example, that central coordination is desirable when a decision is urgently needed and there is no time for negotiation, it is implicitly assumed that a coordination decision can be made, and made effectively by some one decision maker or harmonious decision-making team that can save the time otherwise needed to work out relations with other conflicting decision makers. But this is a possibility only if some one decision maker or team is extremely powerful relative to each other decision maker. If it is claimed, as is perhaps more common, that central coordination brings intelligence to bear on coordination (specifically, that it facilitates an overview of the interrelations among decisions as a basis for the adjustment of those interrelations), it is implicitly assumed that the coordinating decisions finally reached are those of an overseeing mind (individual or team) and not merely the results of the hauling and pulling of various participants in a decision, a possibility, again, only if one decision maker is extremely powerful relative to each of the others so that he suppresses the pulling and hauling. If it is claimed that central coordination fixes responsibility definitely, it is again assumed that there exists some one decision maker extremely powerful relative to the others who can as a consequence be charged with responsibility.

But why assume that there are no interest group or party leaders? Because an interest-group leader is a partisan decision maker, one who participates in making governmental decisions but not solely by appeal to agreed criteria. And it is his role not simply to accept decisions of presumptive coordinators but to bring whatever manipulations to bear on such a coordinator as he can. If he were to meet the conditions of our assumptions, we would no longer recognize him as an interest-group leader. For there can be interest-group leaders in our hypothetical centrally coordinated system only if they do not pursue any segmental interests and only if they foreswear trying to influence any other decision maker except through cooperative discussion in the light of agreed criteria. As for party leaders, we could permit their entrance on the scene only if they meet the criterion for those already introduced: that they seek no influence over policy other than through cooperative discussion.

In this hypothetical state coordination is perhaps as central as it conceivably can be. But citizen influence on policy will compromise centrality even in this extreme case unless we assume that they have absolutely no influence on decision making. Assuming more reasonably that although they do not organize into interest groups that influence governmental decisions, they do to some degree still influence decisions, their participation in government limits central coordination. A further remaining limit on centrality, already mentioned, is the coordinator's inability to reach into the past to adapt past decisions to present and future decisions. By some usages an extremely powerful decision maker would, by definition, have that power. Clearly our decision makers do not.

Contrariwise, partisan mutual adjustment is almost wholly suppressed. As a constraint on the coordinator it remains in a greatly weakened form to the extent that the coordinator must adapt to some past decisions and to the extent that although counting on obedience from all other contemporary decision makers, he must inevitably permit his decisions to be influenced by the other decision makers insofar as they have behavior characteristics (other than disobedience, which is ruled out) that are important for the success or failure of the coordinator's decisions. In short, partisan mutual adjustment remains as a constraint on the coordinator because he must practice at least parametric and calculated adjustment to some limited degree.

An Additional Increment of Partisan Mutual Adjustment: Interest Groups

THEIR REDUCTION OF CENTRALITY

By altering the assumptions stated earlier we can introduce a new range of possible mixtures of centrality and partisan mutual adjustment into coordination. In doing so we move from the hypothetical to the real. Keeping executives, legislators, and agencies unchanged, let us simply introduce interest groups and their leaders, the latter as partisan decision makers. Thus we sharply reduce the degree of centrality in coordination and inject a conspicuous element of partisan mutual adjustment previously suppressed, for the cooperating executives, legislators, and agencies must now fight off or submit to the wishes of a number of decision makers who do not share their agreed criteria and who are not willing to accept the decisions of some one decision maker to whom decision making is delegated.

To be precise about the role of interest-group leaders in mutual adjustment, let us state clearly that as they operate in the real world and, in this hypothetical case, do not merely humbly petition legal authorities for the decisions they wish, in no way influencing the decision other than by the expression of preference. They share in decision making by exercising controls over executives, legislators, and agencies, thus practicing manipulative adjustment; and, on the other side of the relation, they are decision makers to whom government officials must sometimes defer and to whom they must commonly practice calculated adjustment. At an extreme one interest group leader alone may wholly overpower, in his effects on the coordination of decisions, the effect of any executive, legislator, or agency; short of that his participation in decision making moves coordination far away from the centrality of the previous hypothetical case.

Of interest groups in the government of New York City, Sayre and Kaufman write:

As a consequence, the inner core of each group develops close relationships with one, or at most, a few agencies. In some particular segment of officialdom, leaders of each group are usually received whenever they request an audience, their advice considered seriously when offered and often incorporated in official decisions, their views canvassed when not volunteered. In a manner of speaking, many group leaders become intimate parts of the city's machinery of governmental decision in certain spheres. They are nongovernmental in the sense that they cannot *promulgate* binding orders and rules the way officeholders clothed with public authority can, but they often have as much to say about what officeholders promulgate as the officeholders themselves, let alone the parties and other contestants for political prizes. Officeholders feel compelled to cooperate with them because they have so much influence, knowledge, and interest. Out of this official acceptance grows an integration of portions of government with relevant nongovernmental groups.[1]

There are often, of course, differences between the position of interest-group leader and of government official in their mutual adjustments to one another, though they are not differences that deny that the participation of the former moves coordination far from centrality. In many circumstances, for example, group leaders will have to manipulate the other participants in mutual adjustment if they are to achieve coordination of decisions on terms satisfactory to themselves, whereas, by contrast, the other participants—executives, legislators, and agencies—need not manipulate the group leaders. The group leaders need the cooperation of the officials as a condition of making their own decisions effective; but the officials do not need the cooperation of the group leaders as a condition of making their own official decisions effective. The officials have authority, as described in the preceding chapter. No decision, it will sometimes turn out, can be made effective without the exercise of their authority; hence interest groups, lacking grants of authority themselves, must manipulate the officials who possess it.

Reaching back into the 1920's, there has been, for example, opposition on the part of certain farm organizations to the close ties between the Extension Service and the farm bureaus because, among other reasons, the Extension Service sometimes acts as a recruiting and organizing agency for the bureaus, which are private organizations. An appropriate remedy often demanded by the Grange, the Farmers Union, and other organizations has been thought to be an order from the Secretary of Agriculture forbidding ties between the Extension Service and farm bureaus.[2] Here clearly is an example in which the interest groups cannot act without the cooperation of a government official, who alone can authoritatively issue the order.

Even in these circumstances, however, the officials cannot ignore the group leaders: they must defer to them or practice calculated adjustment for fear of how the group leaders may react to decisions made. In the case of the separation of the Extension Service and farm bureaus it seems clear that the farm bureaus overpowered successive Secretaries of Agriculture, despite their ostensible positions of strength. Neither Secretaries Wickard or Brannan ordered the separation though both had strong reason to wish to do so. The separation was not ordered until, under Secretary Benson, the farm bureaus assured the Secretary (because circumstances had changed) that they would not resist the order.[3] More than the Secretaries, the farm bureaus made the decision.

Authority is not enough to achieve the power necessary for central coordination. Not enough because, as we said, the official may not wish to use it for fear of reaction. He practices calculated and deferential adjustment instead of authoritative prescription, or some combination of the adaptive and the manipulative. But not enough, again, we can go on to say, because he may wish the cooperation of interest-group leaders in ways that run beyond his authority to prescribe even if it were fully employed. Hence he must practice, just as do the group leaders, other forms of manipulation such as compensation, prior decision, or partisan discussion, or he must enter into negotiation.

Often, of course, it is not enough that an official practice deferential or calculated adjustment with respect to interest groups; he must also manipulate them, being as dependent on group leaders as they are on him. It must be stressed that officials whom the group leaders wish to control are not typically passive, simply resting on their position as government officials to respond or refuse to respond to pressures on them. In their relationship with any one group leader officials often are already on the move, that is, they are in the process of moving toward or implementing a decision toward which they have been disposed already for any of a number of reasons. Wishing to move in directions already determined, they often find the cooperation of one or more interest groups essential, and the official then becomes the petitioner to the group leader. In such a case the agency or legislator has, as has every participant, at least the possibility of partisan discussion. But he can also of course try to strike a bargain with the interest group, or practice prior decision, reciprocity, or compensation, for example.

When, for instance, during the Korean hostilities the War Labor Board undertook wage regulation, clearly the administration could carry on its program of wage control only by inducing the active cooperation of the unions who could at any time successfully ask for the resignations of the union members of the Board (and at one point did so).[4] Or, for another example, just as the Extension Service cannot do its work without the cooperation of private groups, neither can the Securities and Exchange Commission which does part of its work by inducing, through negotiation, private organizations to share the task of securities regulation.[5]

Then, too, the official instead of the group becomes the petitioner when he requires, before he dares make his decision, the consent of one or more interest groups, as when Mayor Richard Lee of New Haven, intent on urban redevelopment, sought the consent of New Haven business and financial groups.[6] Or when in the steel seizure of 1952 the White House telephoned an official of the Steelworkers Union to ascertain what would happen if the Taft-Hartley Act were invoked at the same time the mills were seized. The union official called back in an hour to report that regardless of what the union ordered, there would probably be a rank and file walkout, and so the idea was abandoned.[7] The frequency of this state of affairs—private group consent needed in advance of official decision—is reflected in the multiplicity of standing arrangements, formal or informal, for consultation of government officials with private groups.

An obvious yet nevertheless noteworthy feature of the coordination of interest-group decisions with official decisions, about which we shall want to say more later, is that prior to that coordination there often takes place a wide ranging coordination of the interest groups to each other. This is most familiar in the form of negotiated alliances. Some of our national interest groups can, of course, be thought of as alliances of smaller like-minded groups: the United States Chamber of Commerce, for example, or the Farm Bureau Federation. But alliance building goes on apace in ways not limited to formal affiliation. It is an activity to which an interest turns almost as soon as it is organized. For example The Salt-Wahoo Watershed Association sprang into life in Lincoln, Nebraska in the 1950's to influence public water projects in the area. It sought allies almost immediately by organizing the Kansas-Nebraska Watershed Council, but also allied itself informally with the National Association of Soil Conservation Districts and the National Informal Citizens Committee on Watershed Conservation.[8] Or, for another example, fifteen leading organizations of manufacturers and producers conferred on tax policy and sent an invitation to 143 trade associations for an expression of their views, thereafter making recommendations to Congress reflective of the interchange among them.[9]

SPECIAL ROLE OF THE METHOD OF PRIOR DECISION

Alliances are not always explicitly negotiated and sometimes develop through prior decision as well as through tacit bargaining. The manipulative method we have called prior decision plays an especially important role in the coordination of interest groups with one another, and it deserves emphasis. As many interest groups as the following became participants in the decision finally made in connection with one important change in government policy toward the American Indians in 1934 (and we give the list in some detail to make vivid the point to come): American Indian Defense Association; National Association on Indian Affairs, General Federation of Women's Clubs; American Civil Liberties Union; Indian Council; California Conference of Social Work; National Society of Daughters of the American Revolution; American Federation of Arts; Indian Rights Association Incorporated of Philadelphia; National Indian Association; American Indian Association; Indians of

California; Mission Indian Federation of Southern California; Board of County Commissioners of Rolette County, North Dakota; Crow Indian Baptist Mission in Montana; Presbyterian, Baptist, and Christian Reform Church Missionaries at Fort Defiance, Arizona; Massachusetts Congregational Conference and Missionary Society; Northern California Regional Indian Defense Association; National Council of American Indians; Ojisto Council; All-Pueblo Council; Navajo Council; Colville Indian Association; Women's Club of the Flathead Tribe; and, finally, a large number of tribal organizations, religious organizations, and business organizations not already listed.[10]

Even allowing for the possibility that some organizations on the list might appear twice under different names, this was a larger number of participants in the decision process than can usually negotiate with one another. The stake of some of these organizations in what they could gain by negotiation was not large enough to motivate them to incur the expenses and other demands of participation in negotiation or any other active manipulation of other interest groups or of officials. Yet they did not remain wholly inactive, for all those listed appeared in an account of participants in the decision. In large part their effect on the decision was achieved by adding their voices to the voice of one or another alliance which was itself not negotiated, except perhaps among a few of the most active groups, but was cumulated on the basis of the prior decision of the more active—the prior decision of an official or of one of a group of interest-group leaders—whose proposed decisions were taken as a rallying point by the others. Negotiation is costly in time, energy, and money; adapting to an initiator's prior decision is cheap.

It is not only an accidental process. Certainly some officials and interest-group leaders count on dissuading group leaders from making demands on them through negotiation or other manipulative devices by deliberately making prior decisions. When, for example, President Kennedy produced his medicare proposals in 1962 he no doubt had calculated the advantages to various potential interest-group allies with whom he had not consulted of associating themselves with his proposal rather than with others each might initiate. Or when business groups begin a campaign against the union shop, they calculate how they can state their so-called right-to-work proposals so as to enlist the support of still other business and nonbusiness groups who, looking for any one of a number of ways to attack labor unions, might be induced to converge rather than go their own independent ways.

Prior decision is, as we have said, a tactic that shades off into tacit bargaining. When in 1955 four unions allied themselves in lobbying to increase the legal minimum wage, their decision not to push for a $1.25 minimum, which was their strong desire, represented a coordinating adaptation, it would appear, to a prior decision reached by various Congressmen to advance the minimum wage by some amount less than that. Rather than fight the Congressmen and dispute among themselves over the issue, they coordinated with them and each other by going along. Yet if this decision was based on a survey of commitments already made by Congressmen to themselves and others, there was also apparently some tacit bargaining over just what the minimum would be, with both legislators and union representatives trying out different positions on each other (in addition to explicit negotiation).[11]

MIXED SYSTEMS:

MUTUAL ADJUSTMENT

DOMINANT

Another Increment of Mutual Adjustment:
Political Parties

IF WE NOW ASSUME THAT
there are party leaders in the hypothetical governmental process, in
addition to interest-group leaders, we open up a new range of
variation in the practice of partisan mutual adjustment.

To begin with party leaders will sometimes play a role that we
need not distinguish for present purposes from the role just attributed to interest-group leaders. They are partisan decision makers,
reducing the possibilities of centrality in decision making and forc-
ing upon legislators, executives, and agencies (whom we still
assume are agreed on either a decision or a delegated decision
maker) a partisan response.

In Chapter 6, however, we gave party leaders an entrepre-

neurial role; even though we shall assume they remain partisans
with respect to each other they try to organize combinations of
voters sufficient to win elections. This being the case, they come to
play the role of organizers of alliances and other less formal coalitions among interest groups; hence they bring some degree of
central coordination into the mutual adjustments of these groups.
They do not bring a great deal, however, for in making coordinating arrangements they are not necessarily very powerful relative to
the group leaders whose decisions they seek to influence toward
coordination. At one extreme in their coordinating role among
interest groups party leaders may be distinguished from the interest-
group leaders only in their wish to play a coordinating role and
their view of themselves as attempting to do so; yet no other participant in the mutual adjustment they seek to facilitate may concede them any recognition or in any way grant them any influence
in this respect. They also may be distinguished in some cases by
their playing down the pursuit of any policies or decisions other
than those that will bring about agreement among the groups. But
even this conciliatory interest is a partisan interest, since it is one
that the interest-group leaders, not necessarily interested in party
success at the polls, do not necessarily share. Hence, although this
interest is distinctive, it leaves the party leaders in a position of
practicing partisan mutual adjustment with interest-group leaders
on the same terms as do interest-group leaders themselves.

Suppose, however, that through party discipline party leaders'
decisions commit executives and legislators to decisions from which
they would feel free to depart in the absence of party discipline. In
such a case interest groups may find it to their advantage to turn
more of their attention to influencing party leaders than otherwise.
The party leader now appears in a more prominent role in partisan
mutual adjustment, and he may, in effect, draw partisan interest-
group activity away from executives and legislators. At an extreme
we can imagine the case, sometimes alleged to correspond to a
degree with party practice in Britain, in which the agreed criteria
that unite executives and legislators (and which also give guidance
to any decision makers to whom they will sometimes delegate
decision making) take the form of a party platform which is
worked out in partisan mutual adjustment among interest-group

leaders and party leaders. In providing an agreed set of criteria party leaders, though indulging heavily in partisan mutual adjustment among themselves, have set the stage for subsequent increase in the centrality of coordination of official decision making by carrying out the party line, to which interest group leaders cannot now so effectively oppose themselves.

As for the role of partisan mutual adjustment internally in the party, party discipline does not prove internal centrality. The disciplined support of a line of decisions by party leaders may be the result of a bargain struck internally or a result of any of the other methods of partisan mutual adjustment within the party. Our point is, however, that once achieved, and however achieved, party discipline opens up the possibilities of greater centrality in the coordination of those decisions—participated in by executives, legislators, and agencies—that thereafter implement the line taken by the party.

Suppose further, to clarify the range of possibilities, that party leaders seek an agreed basis for a disciplined party not by partisan mutual adjustment among themselves but by cooperative discussion guided by a single criterion: to maximize the possibility of electoral success. Clearly this is an important criterion to party leaders, and it is not altogether fanciful to imagine party leaders wholly committed to it. In such a case whatever partisan mutual adjustment party leaders participated in would not be among themselves but only between themselves as a unified group, on one hand, and the variety of interest-group leaders, on the other.

In summary party leaders may:

1. simply further complicate partisan mutual adjustment and reduce centrality in coordination by playing the role of interest-group leaders; or
2. practice partisan mutual adjustment among themselves and with interest groups in such as way as to settle on an agreed party policy which thereafter, when the party wins an election, provides agreed criteria for executives, legislators, and agencies, thus providing at least that component of centrality in government decision making; and
3. in so doing, draw partisan activity away from executives, legis-

lators, and agencies, thus further protecting centrality at that level in decision making, even if at the expense of an increase in partisan mutual adjustment between party leaders and interest-group leaders; or

4. in single-minded pursuit of electoral victory, constitute themselves as a cooperative group for the resolution of their common electoral problem, hence eliminate partisan mutual adjustment among themselves though not between them and interest-group leaders.

There are elements of all these party strategies in American politics. Illustrations are complicated by the fact that a party leader is very often also a legislator or executive, but we can try to separate the two roles. Taking the fourth listed possibility first, many people would say that the Republican Party's failure to win a presidential election from 1932 until 1952 is evidence that party leaders did not attach as much importance to winning presidential elections as to the pursuit of other goals, the other goals varying among different party leaders from the maintenance of local control of the party to holding the national party to certain policy commitments. If so, we can clearly say of these leaders that they acted toward each other almost wholly as partisans and in any case were more partisan and less cooperative than some Democratic leaders like Roosevelt and Farley who regarded internal party politics more as a process of cooperatively constructing a winning coalition of voters. It would be dangerous to stress the contrast since there was no weakness of partisan mutual adjustment among some Democratic leaders and, on the other hand, at least some Republican leaders sought to suppress partisan mutual adjustment within the party in the hope of developing a winning coalition.* Yet Rooseveltian politics had a touch at least of the fourth listed possibility, even if a cooperative, nonpartisan internal reconciliation of conflict never went far enough to produce a disciplined party line that sharply reduced the

---

* The point is not that developing a winning coalition in fact requires the suppression of partisan mutual adjustment. Not at all. It is that the difference between the two parties corresponded very loosely and roughly to the difference between the cooperative and the partisan mutually adjustive approach to party politics implicit in point 4 of the summary statement above.

practice of partisan mutual adjustment between officials and interest groups.

Insofar as, under the second and third listed possibilities, party
leaders work out party positions through partisan mutual adjustment, American examples are largely of impermanent and ambiguous adjustments that by no means serve to supply officials with
agreed criteria for decisions. There are, however, some extraordinary examples in American history of party negotiations pushed to
the point of bargains of supposed contractual force even involving
other parties, as for example the Compromise of 1877 that dealt
Tilden out of the presidency, or the Missouri Compromise of 1826.
These compromises do not go far toward providing agreed criteria
that facilitate centrality in the coordination of subsequent decisions
generally, but they do so along certain lines. The Compromise of
1877 might be said to have taken certain policy questions on the
South and on Negroes out of further partisan mutual adjustment
for decades.[1] One might interpret the Compromise to have therefore strengthened central controls over government decisions along
certain agreed lines, even if simultaneously the Compromise threw
back into partisan mutual adjustment within the states certain decisions that had been more centralized at least temporarily in
Washington and in the military.

If we are looking for illustrations of the possible role of party
leaders in partisan mutual adjustment, American history displays
many examples of the first possibility listed above. That is, party
leaders in the United States appear in much the same role as
interest-group leaders in partisan mutual adjustment. Like group
leaders, party leaders in the United States appeal to and manipulate
government officials with the same techniques that are used by
group leaders. Their interests are not even necessarily broader or
more integrative than those of interest-group leaders. The Committee To Defend America by Aiding the Allies or, say, the League
of Women Voters are examples of interest groups extremely broad
in view. Party leaders are, of course, sharply distinguishable in that
other interest-group leaders do not seek to win proximate formal
control of the governmental machinery as do party leaders, who
organize to win elections for themselves and their party associates.

It is this, of course, that accounts for the presence of a mixture of the second, third and fourth listed possibilities with the first.

Mutual Adjustment Among Agencies and Between Agencies and Legislators and Executives

We began the exploration of mixed systems with the assumption that agencies worked out their relationships with each other through cooperative discussion in the light of some agreed criteria adequate to provide any guidance needed; or that they were issued specific criteria from "higher up" that were adequate to resolve any problem of coordination and that they had the intellectual competence to apply them; or that, where criteria failed, they delegated the decision to some agency, executive, or legislator in such a way as to leave that decision maker wholly free and uninfluenced. If we now remove these constraining assumptions, the role of centrality in government falls sharply; and, conversely, the practice of partisan mutual adjustment is greatly extended.

Agencies, which up to this point we have considered as engaging in partisan mutual adjustment only with interest groups and party leaders, can be considered as now engaging in it with respect to each other. To be sure, adequate criteria and delegation are coordinating devices that are in the real world neither wholly present nor wholly absent. Hence the removal of the assumptions opens up a spectrum of partisan mutual adjustment. The form it takes will depend upon whether criteria and delegation remain in a large coordinating role or shrink to a small one. Common background and training, as well as professional traditions, among public administrators will support some common standards to guide agency decisions; and we have also introduced in the preceding section the possibility that party discipline provides a basis for laying down a policy line that serves as a centrally coordinating influence.

The range of variation opened up by the removal of our previous assumptions about agencies embraces the possibility of an extremely heavy dependence on partisan mutual adjustment by agencies in order to coordinate themselves; examples from American politics appear to support the idea of heavy dependence. Earlier illustrations, for example, have already shown how the coordination of the Soil Conservation Service, the agricultural work of the agricultural colleges, the TVA, the Extension Service, and the Agricultural Adjustment Administration has been worked out largely through partisan mutual adjustment among them. This is also borne out by, in large part, the coordination, year after year, of the Treasury and the Federal Reserve System, though not to the exclusion of legislative and executive participation from time to time. Or, as we have seen in the case of schools at military posts, there is coordination of the Department of Health, Education and Welfare, local school boards, and the military largely through parametric adjustment.

Sometimes the coordination of agencies through partisan mutual adjustment is formalized, as among the Joint Chiefs of Staff where these procedures brings the military services together for negotiation. But more typically the adjustments are worked out in formal organization arrangements that look hierarchical and central.

From his own experience as an agency head, Marshall Dimock vividly describes the working out of coordination between the Recruitment and Manning Organization (RMO) of the War Shipping Administration and other agencies. His is an account of coordination achieved largely through partisan mutual adjustment rather than central coordination. Commenting first on the jurisdictional difficulties he found the RMO to be facing, Dimock goes on to say:

In our case, the first priority was to stabilize our own internal situation in the WSA. Accordingly, Captain Macauley and I approached Admiral Land and emphasized the necessity of a clarification of jurisdiction within the WSA. . . .

Our next step was to define the relationships that were to exist between the RMO and the maritime unions . . .

. . . .

. . . We were prepared at this point for our second jurisdictional struggle. This had to do with the government seaman-training program, then located in the Coast Guard which, accordingly, controlled our most reliable source of manpower. On this question our natural allies were the maritime unions, the state maritime academies themselves, and the ship operators, all of whom might be expected to favor a civilian administration of seaman training as against the military type of supervision exercised by the Coast Guard.

In our attempt to regain control of the training program we had to work through the Bureau of the Budget. . . .

There was a further aspect of our relationship with the Coast Guard which also seemed important to us. This had to do with the control of entry into the merchant marine. Under law, the Coast Guard was responsible for the issuing of certificates to men in the entry ratings and licenses to those in the skilled ratings. . . .

Estimating the strength of our opponent, however, it did not seem that we could be successful in this [transferring the licensing and inspection functions of the Coast Guard to the WSA] and so, rather than fail on two fronts for lack of concentration, we worked on the transfer of the training program alone, hoping that a more favorable opportunity would later present itself so far as the licensing and inspection functions were concerned. The Bureau of the Budget proved co-operative and saw the point of our arguments, with the result that in three months . . . the training program was retransferred to the WSA.

Dimock then explains the development of conflict between the RMO and the new Training Organization, both now within the WSA, indicating that his RMO produced a proposed solution. He then goes on to say:

We were finally successful in getting this recommendation accepted, but the achievement was slow and painful. . . . The sense of institutional survival and of power, although natural and universally shared, was a force in the Training Organization with which we had to reckon in a serious way.

Nor were we free of other potential competition. The Army Transport Service, for example, . . . made it clear that they intended to take care of their own placements. . . . Eventually, after nearly a year, we were able to enter into an understanding with them. . . .

And finally . . . was the threat that the navy might take over the merchant marine . . . we felt confident that if we did a good job we could avoid the rocks of navy expropriation. In this, of course, we were supported by the operators and by the maritime unions.[2]

The point that agencies indulge heavily in partisan mutual adjustment in their relations with one another hardly needs elaboration. Let us therefore simply sort out some points that should not be confused. First, the removal of the assumptions about agencies with which the preceding chapter began opens up the possibility of widespread practice of partisan mutual adjustment; and we cannot doubt that in any real-world situation agencies do in fact engage in negotiation, compensation, reciprocity, authoritative prescription, and prior decision, as well as in parametric, deferential and calculated adjustment with one another. Proof would be pedantic. Secondly, this is to say something more than merely that agencies feud with one another, which is sometimes the way in which interagency relations are dismissed. Thirdly, we do not claim that the interagency coordination achieved through partisan mutual adjustment is satisfactory. Without doubt it is coordination as defined in these chapters; but it may or may not—we have not said yet—fall far short of achieving the pattern of relations that might be desired. Later we shall want to inquire into the merits of interagency coordination through partisan mutual adjustment; here, however, we simply want to identify interagency relations as a specific locus for partisan mutual adjustment.

If agencies have become partisan with respect to each other because they do not share criteria or simply accept a superior's decision, then they also have become partisan with respect to executives and legislators. Hence we locate a further extension of the practice of partisan mutual adjustment in their relations. If, as by our assumption, the executive and legislator are unified by agreed criteria or by their delegation of decision making to the chief executive, then the element of centrality in coordination is great, for on their side of the mutual adjustment processes the legislators and executives speak with a single voice and presumably act with the power of a cooperating team in their manipulations of agencies. If, on the other hand, the executive–legislative group is not unified, then centrality is pretty much lost in the overwhelming influence of partisan mutual adjustment. To look into this possibility let us next remove the assumptions that have constrained our treatment of executives and legislators.

Partisan Mutual Adjustment Dominant

If we remove the assumption that executives and legislators share adequate criteria or submissively delegate authority to a chief executive, we see at once a possibility for partisan mutual adjustment in the adaptations one to another of Parliament and cabinet, Parliament and Prime Minister, legislature and President, legislature and governor, and so forth. In these pairs relations are in part governed by certain agreed rules such as the Prime Minister's right of dissolution, the presidential veto, and legislative overriding of the veto, all laid on top of the requirement that decisions reached by either in the pair must be sanctioned by the other. The effect of these rules is not, of course, to dispense with partisan mutual adjustment but instead to influence the practice of partisan mutual adjustment by the way in which authority is allocated and restricted.

That, say, the President and Congressional leaders threaten or promise each other, negotiate, seize the advantage of prior decision where possible, build elaborate networks of reciprocity or, where their autonomy permits, simply play a parametric, deferential, or calculated game with the other is not to be doubted as an illustration of the range of practice of partisan mutual adjustment opened up by relaxing the earlier assumptions. It is a commonplace to say that the British cabinet, or the Prime Minister himself, has much greater power on specific issues relative to Parliament than does the President relative to Congress. Without debating the point we simply observe that even in British practice partisan mutual adjustment is ubiquitous between executive and legislator. For example, here is a description of negotiation, tacit bargaining, and prior decision:

By now the Minister's position was threatened: some of his own side put up an amendment to delay the proposed superannuation increases until the teachers' salaries had been reviewed. The Minister countered by promising to sanction interim increases in teachers' salaries *immediately,* should the Burnham Committee propose them. As the crucial clause was approached in the committee stage, it was apparent that the Labour members would join with dissident Conservatives. The Minister would almost certainly have been beaten, so, just before this amendment was reached, he introduced an amendment of his own post-poning the operation of his Bill for six months (by which time the review of salaries would have taken place).[3]

Again, one can imagine a range of possibilities. At one extreme legislator and executive engage in partisan mutual adjustment on each policy issue as it arises. At the opposite extreme they engage in it for the determination of certain broad lines of policy, in sub-sequent subordination to which the legislature accepts some degree of dominance, hence in effect accepts central direction from the executive. American practice exemplifies the former; British prac-tice moves (though in what degree is much debated) toward the latter. As noted earlier in the discussion of party-leader participa-tion, the difference may depend on the role that party leaders play in effecting party discipline.

Finally, then, we come to the coordination of legislators with each other. Let us assume that they not only lack criteria or willing-ness to delegate decisions in their relations with the executive but lack it as well in their relations with each other. Here is still another area for partisan mutual adjustment.

Because the legislator is sometimes a participant in a ritualized decision-making procedure in which he does not act alone but only participates in a collective, voted decision, we need to spell out the legislative practice of partisan mutual adjustment with care. The individual legislator operates in ways other than through his vot-ing. His membership in the legislature opens up for him significant possibilities for manipulating other decision makers: through hearings or the threat of hearings, through the promise or threat that he will undertake to get legislation voted, or merely through the expression of his wishes to an agency. It is clear that in these ways he exercises control over other decision makers quite apart from the formal collective decisions of the legislature as a whole. But does he in any similar way adapt to or manipulate his fellow legislators through the methods of partisan mutual adjustment?

The answer is that the voted collective decisions of the legisla-ture are often the result of coordination through partisan mutual adjustment among legislators, not a substitute means of coordina-tion. Clearly, legislators do not simply engage in cooperative discussion in the light of agreed criteria, then cast their votes to formalize the agreed decision. Nor do they, for lack of agreed criteria, simply coordinate their decisions by a vote, from which emerges a single legislative decision which integrates their various divergent preferences. Instead they try to influence other legislators' votes, or adapt their own to the others, by all the coordinating devices of partisan mutual adjustment.

A citizen can, and often does, come out of a kind of political retirement to cast his vote and then lapse back into retirement again; the vote is therefore a choice mechanism that can serve him independently of any other participation in the political system. But for the legislator casting a vote is clearly part of a continuing political activity and is significant in relation to that activity. He may vote in a particular way to live up to his part of a bargain; or he may vote as he does simply to ratify a decision reached through negotiation beforehand; or he may vote as he does to weaken the prestige of position of a political adversary in the legislature; or because he wishes to defer to the wishes of a legislative committee in whose affairs he does not wish to assert his own competence. Quite aside from the role his vote plays in his relations with other legislators, the legislative decision as a whole, reached through a vote, is itself understandable only in the light of legislative relations with politicians outside the legislature and with agencies. A legislative vote is often only a move in a conflict with the President or with an agency.

That the vote is no substitute for partisan mutual adjustment in coordinating the decision of legislators is indicated, at an extreme perhaps, in the frequency of unanimous decisions in legislative bodies. They are unanimous because the coordination of legislators has already somehow been accomplished—by partisan mutual adjustment, among other influences; and the unanimous vote gives emphatic testimony to the fact that it has indeed been accomplished.[4] In a study of a local community we find the following:

Within the formally constituted governing agency of the village, the village board, politics is conducted on the principle of unanimity of decision. In two years of observation of village board meetings in Springdale, all decisions brought to a vote were passed unanimously.

The dissent, disagreement and factionalism which exist in the community are not expressed at board meetings. Through a process of consultation prior to an official meeting and by extended discussion involving the entire group during the meeting itself, a point is reached when it seems reasonable to assume that everyone will go along with the proposed action.[5]

In a study of politics in Connecticut, we find another example:

> In more recent years, however, the Democrats in the Senate have been an extraordinarily cohesive group. . . . Indeed in 1951, not a single Democrat deserted his party colleagues on any roll call of the session. The caucus of Senators, which takes place daily, is the scene of some protracted disputes and debates on bills. . . .[6]

We do not argue that the vote is unimportant. It is because the final ratification of a collective decision must take the form of a vote that anyone who can cast a vote has power to manipulate others in the partisan mutual adjustment that precedes the vote. To be sure, he may have other sources of power—perhaps an important committee chairmanship or even his own reputation and prestige, but his vote is a counter with which he bargains and practices other forms of adjustment.

It might be argued that even though the legislative vote is the product of partisan mutual adjustment, by finally reaching a vote the legislature speaks with a single voice to the executive and to agencies. If so, this result, in the relatively greater power it gave to the legislature, would be evidence of more centrality than if speaking with a single voice were not the case. Or one could argue directly that a single voice represented more centrality than partisan mutual adjustment with executive and agencies in which various legislators or legislative groups each followed a somewhat independent line of decisions.

But partisan mutual adjustment among legislators opens up the possibility—and, again, it is verified by American experience—that the legislature, even though it registers a single, collective decision on many issues, does not speak with one voice. Individual legislators and groups of legislators directly manipulate, for example, agencies that have to be, say, especially respectful of certain committees or their individual members. Certainly, for example, the Armed Services Committee of the House and the Appropriations Subcommittee on Defense act to a degree independently of the Congress as a whole and of each other in manipulating or adapting to the armed services. Moreover, because the Congressional vote often ratifies, with little investigation, the recommendations of various powerful committees of Congress, the Congressional vote cannot itself be described as a single voice. It speaks sometimes for one committee and another time for another, and the two voices are not necessarily consistent. Legislators may go to great lengths to permit subgroups to make decisions for the legislature as a whole. Here is a description of the autonomy granted to subcommittees of the House Appropriations Committee.

The point at which a subcommittee makes its recommendations is a potential point of internal friction. Subcommittees could clash with one another and engage in tests of strength to control the full Committee. Conflict among subcommittees (or between one subcommittee and the rest of the Committee) is minimized by the deference which is traditionally accorded to the recommendation of the subcommittee which has specialized in the area, has worked hard, and has "the facts." "You don't go barging into another man's field unless something is patently wrong." "It's a matter of 'You respect my work and I'll respect yours.'" "It's frowned upon if you offer an amendment in the full Committee if you aren't on the subcommittee. It's considered presumptuous to pose as an expert if you aren't on the subcommittee." Though records of full Committee decisions are not available, members agree that subcommittee recommendations are "very rarely changed," "almost always approved," "changed one time in fifty," "very seldom changed," etc. The optimum condition for changing a subcommittee recommendation occurs when the fight is led by a dissident member of that subcommittee—by a man, that is, who can draw on the norm of specialization and its concomitants of information and hard work.[7]

Similarly, the House as a whole accepts the decisions of the Appropriations Committee to an impressive degree. One study showed that of 443 separate case histories of bureau appropriations examined, the House accepted the Committee's recommendations in 87 percent of them.[8]

This is not evidence that the legislative vote is merely a rubber stamp, for there are devices through which legislative subgroups are held in line, to a degree, by the legislature as a collectivity. We make the point of subgroup autonomy in the legislature only to indicate that, as a decision maker, the legislature is not monolithic; that its voted decisions are to some degree ratifications of decisions of subgroups within the larger body; that its participation in partisan mutual adjustment with agencies and executives is not that of a highly unified decision maker. V. O. Key, Jr. has written:

> Congress, House of Representatives, and Senate are terms evoking in the mind the notion of an assembly that debates, deliberates, and decides. Such notions must be supplemented by more adequate conceptions if we are to comprehend the interplay between legislature and administration. Congress as a whole can really master and decide only a few main issues. So great is the volume of legislative business and such are our parliamentary practices that we have in reality not one legislative body but scores of small legislative bodies. When we seek to understand the relations of Congress with the executive branch, we must speak, not of either, but of this Senator, or that Representative, or this committee, or that bloc and the administrative establishment. The actions of Congress are in the great majority of instances those of a single member, or two, or a handful—actions which their colleagues ratify or to which they raise no objection.[9]

A conspicuous type of sub-Congressional participation in partisan mutual adjustment is through the association between the administrative bureau, the interest-group constituency, and the relevant Congressional committee. The interest group, the public agency serving that group as a clientele, the legislative committee, and the Appropriations Committee all together constitute a more or less permanent alliance.[10]

Common Values as a Limit on Partisan Mutual Adjustment

Through a gradual relaxation of the assumptions with which the preceding chapter opened and a successive introduction of new participants in decision making, we now have made partisan mutual adjustment a dominant element in the governments we have been considering. We need finally to take note of common values as a limit on partisan mutual adjustment.

Like conventions, as we saw in Chapter 6, common values lay down some general lines of policy; they are, therefore, not to be deprecated. But, abstractly stated, common values do not at all make mutual adjustment unnecessary, for to use these values in practical application to concrete decisions is often impossible, or possible only with such disagreement about proper application as to make cooperative discussion fruitless. Partisan mutual adjustment comes into play to the extent that common values cannot be formulated in such a way as to be adequate for testing policies and the correctness of their adjustment to each other.

Typically some values are widely shared and at the same time are specified in sufficiently concrete and unambiguous forms as to permit cooperative discussion. Cooperative discussion then narrows the range of alternative policies over which the mechanisms of partisan mutual adjustment may thereafter achieve a selection and coordination. We need not and shall not try at this point to go much further in specifying how far such common values go, that is, how much their existence constrains the practice of partisan mutual adjustment. We shall only add that their significance for, decision making and its coordination can and does vary greatly from one political system to another and, within a given system, from one time or circumstance to another.

Franklin Roosevelt's urgent appeals to Congress in his "Hundred Days" both took advantage of and stimulated a value consensus that heightened the role of centrality in governmental decision making for the time. So also did Lincoln's assertion of the values of the Union and the American egalitarian tradition in order to mobilize common values to support, in the North, some diminution of partisan mutual adjustment on some policy questions. One might argue that Lincoln's rhetoric and governing acts alike left a heritage of heightened, widespread commitment to these values. In less critical times a political leader may appeal widely for, say, relief funds for a disaster area, unified opposition to Roosevelt's plan to pack the Supreme Court, desegregation, or massive resistance to desegregation. For a large number of decision makers such an appeal will reduce the practice of partisan mutual adjustment on some issues and, contrariwise, raise the prospects of cooperation and centrality (with respect to the responding group) in decision making.

Although many circumstances will govern the rise and fall of applicable common values, in the examples above we have stressed the role of a conspicuous political leader. Clearly, conspicuous leadership can make a difference, an important point that can easily be lost sight of in a preoccupation with the mechanics of partisan mutual adjustment. It is important to make a place for that kind of leadership in a picture of partisan mutual adjustment, especially since a highly influential national leader appealing for broad agreement at least begins his appeal as a partisan. Even the leader who, like Lincoln, makes an appeal to the nation to commit itself, not to a mere reconciliation of sectional or other segmental interests but to an overriding national, collective purpose, has to make his influence on policy felt in large part through partisan mutual adjustment, although once he has done so he may thereafter reduce its role. He is forced into it if only because he must overcome adversaries who themselves practice it.

In a later chapter it will be argued that *it is in partisan mutual adjustment itself that, in some large part, common values originate.* Hence, even if once they arise they, to some degree, reduce the role of mutual adjustment, they require mutual adjustment.

The Allocation of Power

Finally, the range of possible employments of mutual adjustment embraces a range of allocations of authority and other powers among participants in the process. Hence it is essential to distinguish the process of mutual adjustment from an allocation of powers within such a system of adjustment. This is a simple point, but it will be critical when we subsequently try to distinguish between the defects of mutual adjustment and the defects of particular allocations of power that make the results of mutual adjustment less satisfactory than would an alternative allocation. For example, is legally protected featherbedding on the railroads a feature of partisan adjustment? Or a feature of a particular allocation of authority in a system of partisan adjustment?

Part
4

Problem-Solving Strategy
and Mutual Adjustment

STRATEGY IN

PROBLEM SOLVING

Synoptic Problem Solving

FOR AN ANALYSIS AND AP-
praisal of mutual adjustment and centrality as policy-making systems we now need some clarification of decision making as a
problem-solving process. How is decision making thought to solve
problems? What features of decision making promise success or
failure in problem solving?

A common answer that will run through almost everyone's
mind can be put down as a kind of paradigm of problem solving.
To solve a problem, a decision maker:

1. identifies, scrutinizes, and puts into consistent order those objectives and other values that he believes should govern the choice
   of a solution to the problem;
2. comprehensively surveys all possible means of achieving those
   values;

3. exhaustively examines the probable consequences of employing each of the possible means;

4. chooses a means—that is, a particular policy or combination of policies—that will probably achieve a maximum of the values or reach some acceptable level of achievement.

We shall call such a method "synoptic" because of the high degree of synopsis or comprehensiveness of view the decision maker seeks to achieve in such a method.[1] To adopt the term is to assume that a problem is solved by understanding it. Understanding requires a comprehensiveness of information and analysis. It is also to assume that one cannot be rational without first knowing what one wants and proceeding only thereafter to a comprehensive examination of alternative means to the attainment of what one wants. This method of decision making is, of course, consistent with scientific canons, including the prescription that purely scientific analysis is to be kept free from contamination by ethical components of the problem-solving process.[2]

Nevertheless, for complex public policy problems no one can approximate the synoptic ideal. Policy makers invariably have to make policy in the face of an incomplete formulation of governing values, typically in the face of some significant disagreement on values. Moreover, we all know that no one can complete or even reach a high degree of comprehensiveness in the analysis of a complex policy issue, where consequences run on forever and where they also run off in a wide variety of directions. Not all of the important possible consequences of recent American policy decisions on Cuba, the NATO, on Angola, on taxation, on social security, on farm policy, or on antitrust can be incorporated into the analyses of these policies before decisions are taken.

Precisely what are the difficulties of synopsis for complex public policy problems? We can identify some principal respects in which synopsis is not adapted, even as an ideal, to the difficulties of complex problem solving.

(1) The synoptic ideal is not adapted to man's limited intellectual capacities.

If, as is the case, puzzles and mathematical problems can easily be constructed that outrun human intelligence, we cannot doubt but that many policy problems will run beyond man's intellectual capacity, even when he extends these capacities, as he does, with analytical aids of various kinds ranging from new words or concepts to electronic computation. A specific failure of the adaptation of the synoptic ideal is that in the face of man's limited capacities, it offers simply a prescription: "Be comprehensive!" Such a prescription is one that advises problem solvers simply to disregard a fundamentally important characteristic of man and its consequences for his problem-solving activity.

(2) *The synoptic ideal is not adapted to inadequacy of information.*

(3) *Nor is it adapted to the costliness of analysis.*

If, as is typically the case, some important information is not available and either cannot be made available or can be had only at great expense, the admonition to be comprehensive fails badly. Some kind of adaptation to the situation is necessary: some pieces of information, presumably, are sufficiently critical to be worth the cost of their acquisition, others not; and some account has to be taken of the absence of those pieces not available in the way conclusions are drawn. We do not deny that men make these adaptations—indeed it will be a major point that they do somehow make them—but we point out that inadequate information is inescapable and that the synoptic ideal is simply not adapted to this fact. Moreover, wholly complete information, if one can conceive of it, is indigestible. To the extent that information becomes complete, it imposes increasingly severe strains on man's cognitive faculties. Hence, the demands of the synoptic method on man's intellectual capacities and its demands for information are related: insofar as the second can be met, the first is less well met.

(4) *The synoptic ideal is not adapted to failures, which must be anticipated in many circumstances, to construct a satisfactory set of criteria, as, for example, in the form of a welfare function.*

In synoptic analysis the common requirement that values be clarified and systematized in advance of analysis is impossible to meet in many circumstances in which, on the one hand, the relevant values are unknown until the analysis is far advanced or in which, on the other hand, disagreement on values guarantees that no stated principles or welfare function can command the agreement of those whose values are presumed to be governing. Moreover, no one has been able to construct a set of criteria adequate to specify formally the "correct" solution for a complex policy alternative; hence what an analyst or policy maker requires, in the absence of such criteria, is some looser criteria or guidelines. But he cannot turn to the synoptic ideal for them.

Disagreement on values calls for some special attention because of its importance to later chapters. Those who espouse the synoptic ideal assume that those whose values are to count agree. Otherwise, the prescription to clarify the values that are to govern choice is not only often impossible to follow but would also in many cases be an obstruction. In the United States, for example, at least two groups of citizens with quite different values agree on the gradual extension of Social Security benefits. One group, of generally conservative opinions, favors extension in order to avoid union demands for employer-financed pension schemes; the other group, of generally less conservative opinions, favors extension out of equalitarian sympathies. Policy making in this field would be paralyzed by an attempt to clarify values in the way called for in the synoptic ideal, for there is no formulatable set of values that policy makers can take as governing from which the desirability of extending Social Security can be inferred. An often better and nonsynoptic prescription asks that policy analysts and policy makers work directly toward agreement on policy without regard to a prior establishment of a set of governing values.

Because the synoptic ideal is not applicable in the absence of a formulatable set of governing values, it is tempting to think that, after all, every decision maker has a set of his own. Despite conflicting preferences among citizens, might a decision maker nevertheless find an adequate criterion for resolving the disagreement? Can he not simply follow the principle of equality in the weighting of individual preferences?

This is a defective criterion. Who believes in equality between the immediate preferences of a policeman and a law violator when it is a question of whether the violator shall be taken to court or not? Who advocates equality between the President and a citizen, between the President and a Congressman, between a judge and a litigant, between an officer and an enlisted man? Obviously, differences in social function call for inequalities in the weighting of preferences relevant to the performance of those functions, and for other reasons other inequalities are called for. The case for equality in weights has never been pushed seriously except for the special case of equality in a kind of "last say" decision, as in elections in which all citizens are equally weighted in the expression of their preferences. But even in "last say" expressions of opinion we are not agreed on equal weights; many persons wish to depart from them to take account of intensity.

Moreover, even if one does in fact endorse equal weighting of preferences there seems to be no feasible way ascertaining preferences on all the policy decisions that must be taken in government, or even on any substantial minority of them. In part this additional difficulty simply reflects the extraordinary number of policy decisions taken each day by any government. In addition, however, the silence of citizens as to their preferences is attributable to their inability to inform themselves sufficiently on the vast range of questions that come up for decision. Citizens thus seek advice as to what their opinions should be; until political leadership has spoken they have no opinions on many issues. But since they have no opinion until leaders have advised them, one can hardly prescribe to a political leader that he resolve interpersonal value conflicts by weighting conflicting preference equally.

Nor can decision makers use the most recent election returns as a guide to the preferences of the majority on even the limited number of issues raised during the campaign. For a party can easily win a majority of electors to it by appealing to each subsection of the electorate on an issue on which it is an intense minority, thereby winning the election with a majority of the electorate opposed to the party's policy on each point.*

(5) The synoptic method is not adapted to the closeness of observed relationship between fact and value in policy making.

* In considering how conflicting values are weighted in partisan adjustment we shall later return to the egalitarian–majoritarian principle for more extended discussion. See Chapters 16 and 17.

In the actual process of policy making fact and value elements are in fact closely intertwined in ways proscribed by the synoptic ideal. As already noted a decision maker often will not know what values are relevant to his problem until he has undertaken an empirical analysis of the possible consequences of the alternative policies under consideration. To prescribe that he clarify his values before undertaking his analysis implies that he is capable of organizing in his mind all the values that might possibly turn out to be relevant—in short, all values. And, indeed, such an assumption is implicit in prescriptions that values be organized into a set of principles or in the form of a welfare function. Because no one has ever been able to achieve such a feat, a reasonable question might be how to move more modestly back and forth from the empirical element in analysis to the value element as each throws light on the other.

(6) *The synoptic ideal is not adapted to the openness of systems of variables with which it must contend.*

If we ask what the important possible consequences of a choice among several alternative policies for dealing with racial discrimination in the public schools are, we should have to concede that they might easily include consequences, first, for the quality of education for Negroes and whites, a consequence that spills into further private consequences for the students immediately concerned, and into consequences for, say, their economic productivity, which in turn spills into consequences for our economic rivalry with the Soviet Union, and its consequences for a variety of intangible values we think linked to the survival of a free society in the United States. They might, secondly, include consequences for social relations in areas in which Negroes and whites are mixed, which are consequences that spill over in a variety of directions, including consequences for the structure of political parties, the performance of local governments, the power of trade unions, and the indoctrination of Americans in the aspects of their social and moral codes that bear on such issues as equality, fair play, and opportunity. They might, thirdly, include consequences for altering the distribution of citizens between urban and rural areas, which in turn will have consequences for the severity of business fluctuations, for a variety of political institutions, and even for such a specific phenomena as tax revenues to local, state, and national governments.

Now it cannot be hoped that an analysis can follow through such an open system of variables. An important question then is: How does the analyst close his own analysis? How can he satisfy himself that he can work his way to useful answers to policy questions without following through each of a multitude of variables? All that the synoptic ideal has to offer is, again, the impossible prescription to be comprehensive, which is blind to the problem here posed.

(7) *The synoptic ideal, lastly, is not adapted to the diverse forms in which policy problems actually arise.*

Public policy problems like inflation, unemployment, social security, reform of the judiciary, relief of urban congestion, and segregation each encompass a host of disparate but interlocked problems of individuals and groups. If what is to be achieved, then, is not simply (as in the usual concept of a problem) removal or substantial reduction of the frustrations in a goal-seeking activity, but also, and sometimes instead, reconciliation of interests, then problem solving is a more continuous process than it is ordinarily conceived to be. For whether a possible reconciliation is satisfactory today will depend not solely on the characteristics of today's problem, but also on what yesterday's pattern of reconciliation was and what tomorrow's might be made to be.

Disjointed and Incremental Problem Solving

Given these difficulties in the practice of synopsis for complex public policy problems, decision makers fashion adaptations or tactics in order to make headway against their problems. Among these are some that will turn out to be consequential for centrality and mutual adjustment. We describe them only briefly here because they are in rough outline familiar.[3]

COMPARISON AND EVALUATION OF INCREMENTS ONLY

Decision makers do not attempt a comprehensive survey and evaluation. In the examination of the consequences of possible alternative policies they do not investigate all of them, but only, at most, those with respect to which the policies are thought to differ. In these senses, therefore, attention is focused on increments by which social states and policies differ. For example, a farm-policy decision maker does not ask about all the implications of present and possible alternative farm policies, but only about those aspects by which each differs from the other. Moreover, policy making in many political systems is typically, though not always, a part of a political process in which the only feasible political change is that which changes social states only by relatively small steps. Hence, decision makers typically consider, among all the alternative policies that they might be imagined to consider, only those relatively few alternatives that represent small or incremental changes from existing policies. In this sense, too, decision making is incremental.[4] In short, policy makers and analysts take as their starting point not the whole range of hypothetical possibilities, but only the here and now in which we live, and then move on to consider how alterations might be made at the margin.

Proceeding incrementally, the decision maker need not ask himself whether security is more to be prized than liberty, or full employment more than price stability, or a high standard of living for this group more than for that. Such questions as these are converted into relatively concrete choices among values at margins where the values are in effect traded against each other. Thus, the full-employment-versus-price-stability choice is converted into a choice between some specific estimated amount of inflation that can be avoided by a certain policy choice and some specific amount of unemployment that the same policy choice risks.

Incremental problem solving enormously reduces the range of investigations that the decision maker must undertake, and enormously reduces the strains on his cognitive capacity that attend the attempt to comprehensively evaluate social states. Thus it adapts to his limited intellect, reduces his demands for information, and makes concessions to the costliness of analysis. Moreover, incremental analysis turns his attention to materials which are most familiar to him, least speculative, and relatively concrete.

A focus on evaluation at margins where small amounts of values are exchanged renders unnecessary either the construction of a social welfare function or a set of principles that cover all possible situations. One need not try to organize all possible values into a coherent scheme, but, instead, can evaluate only what is relevant in actual policy choices; one need not determine priorities even among these limited number of values, but, instead, can choose more or less of one as against more or less of another in a concrete case; and one need not try to conceive of values and take a position on them abstractly, but, instead, can choose directly among those embedded in actual policy choices.

CONSIDERATION OF A RESTRICTED NUMBER OF POLICY ALTERNATIVES

As decision making is actually practiced the total number of alternative policies considered at any time by an analyst is greatly restricted. If he limits his attention to the incremental he has already limited the number of policies he will consider. But he further limits his attention by disregarding a host of conceivable incremental alternatives simply because they appear to him to lie outside a familiar path of policy making. Then, too, he restricts the alternatives out of concern for political feasibility.

That restriction on the number of alternatives considered adapts to the difficulties of problem solving is obvious; the adaptations are much the same as those just discussed for incrementalism. The restriction is an adaptation to the limits on man's intellect, the inadequacy of information, and the costliness of analysis. And, again, the restriction pulls the attention of the analyst toward those policy alternatives on which there is some reasonable possibility of his proceeding with tolerable competence.

CONSIDERATION OF A RESTRICTED NUMBER OF IMPORTANT CONSEQUENCES FOR ANY GIVEN POSSIBLE POLICY ALTERNATIVE

Even in synoptic analysis unimportant consequences are presumably neglected; but here we make the point that as decision making is in fact practiced, important consequences of policies under analysis are simply disregarded, often deliberately. Forthright neglect of important consequences is a noteworthy problem-solving tactic.

What kind of important consequences are neglected? The answer is, any kind. For illustration we can imagine a decision maker with special responsibilities for or attachments to certain groups or classes of citizens; he therefore typically neglects values highly prized by other classes or groups. Or we can imagine a decision maker who has worked out his conception of the public welfare; hence he thinks of himself as responding to the values of all citizens, but, in fact, he does not take account of certain values in his concept of the public interest. Or we can think again of the decision maker who neglects some important consequences or values simply because he believes he cannot master his decision-making problem without simplifying it.

Neglect of consequences is defensible because, like incremental focus and the limitation of the number of policies considered, it drastically reduces demands on the intellect and demands for information. Where the prescription to be comprehensive may be impossible to follow, the practice of outright neglect at least makes what remains within the analysis manageable. Thus, a decision maker will find himself impossibly over his head if he seriously tries to work through all the consequences of, say, United States policy in Berlin; but he can make a more or less defensible decision if he makes that decision on the basis of a limited number of explored consequences. Between incompleteness because of neglect of consequences and incompleteness because of an aspiration toward comprehensiveness that cannot in fact be satisfied, the former is not necessarily more alarming. Decision makers must choose between errors of omission and errors of confusion. In many circumstances a decision maker comes to terms with his own abilities and with available information when he turns from an analysis so complex that he will bungle it to a simpler analysis that, even if incomplete, can be done well within its limits.

RECONSTRUCTIVE ANALYSIS

Decision makers do not fix on a nicely defined problem. Ends are adjusted to means as well as the other way around. To be sure, a decision maker may hold firmly to a stable abstract value like liberty, but specific evaluations brought to bear on policy choices are always part of a process of exploration of ends and means together. Hence, "the problem" is continually redefined.

While this fluidity might appear to complicate problem solving, it is a method of simplification. What we here call reconstructive analysis is a tactic of altering a problem to make it manageable rather than fruitlessly attacking an impossible one. It is not always a successful tactic, to be sure; but it will often permit a decision maker to slough off part of an earlier problem, either because it is solved or unsolvable, and attack a new one. It also permits him to incorporate into his concept of his problem whatever new insights his work on it has so far given him.

SERIAL ANALYSIS AND EVALUATION

Characteristically, public decision makers pursue, for any policy problem, a never-ending series of attacks on it. Thus labor legislation, for example, is not simply enacted but reenacted endlessly. Decision makers know, therefore, that they need not understand all aspects of a problem and find its "right" solution. Given a problem's complexity and the inevitable opportunities to return to it, they would be foolish to try to accomplish more than a serial step in the attack on it. *Moreover, if they return again and again to the same problem area their neglect of certain consequences and values at any one step is less alarming.*

REMEDIAL ORIENTATION

Given the incremental, reconstructive, and serial character of policy making as actually practiced, it is not surprising that public problem solving is also dominated less by aspiration toward a well defined future state than by identified social ills that seem to call for remedy. Thus problem solving will be directed toward the suppression of vice even if virtue is not defined, will be concerned with mental illness even if we are not clear as to just what is healthy, will be bent on curbing the expansion of the Soviet Union even if we do not know what positive objectives in foreign policy to set against the Soviet's objectives. The decision maker does not wholly turn his back on such general aspirations as liberty, economic growth, or justice; but he makes these abstractions less dominant in his analysis than particular imperfections which he wishes to remove. The simplification of immediate problems achieved by focus on the remedial ill is obvious.

Strategy in Problem Solving

The synoptic idea of problem solving is fairly straightforward. To solve a problem one must first understand it—one masters it. In contrast, behind the incremental and disjointed tactics we have just summarized is a concept of problem solving as a strategy. In this view public policy problems are too complex to be well understood, too complex to be mastered. One develops a strategy to cope with problems, not to solve them.

Consider a society in which values or preferences and means at hand do not change. In such a society the difference between the intellectual organization of the problem-solving process under the synoptic ideal and under a view of problem solving as strategy would roughly parallel the difference between solving a mathematical problem by exact computation, on the one hand, and by sucessive approximation, on the other. The advantages of strategy would be just those of successive approximation: the latter is superior when exact computation is relatively too difficult, and it is necessary when exact computation is impossible.

In such a society the strategic concept of problem solving would be this: The decision maker makes an incremental move in the desired direction and does not take upon himself the difficulties of finding a solution. He disregards many other possible moves because they are too costly (in time, energy, or money) to examine; and, for the move he makes, he does not trouble to find out (again, because it is too costly to do so) what all its consequences are. He assumes that to the extent that his move was a failure or was marked by unanticipated adverse consequences, someone's (perhaps even his) next move will attend to the resulting problem. If policy making is remedial and serial, his assumptions will be correct.

To be sure, his assumptions will not always be correct, and

sometimes a great deal of damage will be done permanently or before a corrective next step can be taken. Neither his strategy nor synoptic problem solving is infallible. He does find, however, that his strategy is often desirable and unavoidable in view of the failures of the synoptic method. His view of problem solving as successive approximation is a practical and sophisticated adaptation to the impossibility of actually attaining the synoptic ideal, and to the consequent need for moving to an alternative concept of problem solving whenever he judges, on the basis of the multiple adaptive features present in successive approximation, that the degree to which he can approximate the synoptic ideal leaves him with a poorer solution than can be had with successive approximation.

In the real world, where preferences and means constantly change, the strategic concept of policy making through successive approximation needs some amendment. It needs to be emphasized that in a real-world society, in which tastes and means change and in which information about them is growing or at least changing, the decision maker is no longer approximating a solution in the sense in which "solution" is conventionally conceived—as in pursuit of the synoptic ideal. (And, as we have already pointed out, it is in their conception of social ills as well defined problems with solutions that aspirants to the synoptic ideal go wrong.) In a nonstatic society objectives and other values continue to shift, as do the actual possibilities of change; hence such a process as we have been describing for the strategy does not successively approximate to any solution but continues to move apace with changing values and policy possibilities. But what we have said about the static society remains relevant. In a nonstatic society, even more than in a static society, the obstacles to the successful practice of anything approaching exact computation, as in the synoptic ideal, loom increasingly large; and the possibilities of moving in a series of remedial steps come to look increasingly appropriate.

Following the strategy the decision maker's possible errors of commission or omission are of two kinds: (1) adverse consequences and failures in policy unanticipated because of limited analysis, and (2) adverse consequences and failures at least roughly anticipated but nevertheless not permitted to influence the decision maker's choice among policies.

If the decision maker's approach to his policy area is both remedial and serial, he can catch either kind of neglected adverse consequence or failure in policy as it begins to reveal itself and he can at that time devise policies to cope with it.

For the second kind of consequence or failure—those at least in part anticipated—the policy maker can also actually anticipate ways of meeting consequent problems. But, if he can be expected to anticipate the emerging problems and deal with them, why, it will be asked, did he neglect them in the first place? The answer is that, on top of his other burdens, he could not incorporate an analysis of the neglected consequence and ways of coping with it in his original policy analysis, but he can make it the focus of a subsequent policy analysis. He can cope with two quite separate successive policy problems where he cannot cope with an integrated problem.

A city traffic engineer, for example, might propose the allocation of certain streets to one-way traffic. In so doing, he might be quite unable to predict how many serious bottlenecks in traffic, if any, would develop and where they would arise. Nevertheless, he might confidently make his recommendations, assuming that if any bottlenecks arose, appropriate steps to solve the new problems could be taken at that time—new traffic lights, assignment of a traffic patrolman, or further revision of the one-way plan itself. He might also have quite correctly anticipated certain other consequences, such as business losses from rerouting customer traffic. Some of these he nevertheless ignores as a consideration in his traffic plan. Instead, he proposes subsequently to alter parking regulations, ease pedestrian traffic in certain areas, or turn to still some other policy to reduce the business losses ruled irrelevant to his first policy problem. The remedial and serial character of his strategy in effect achieves remedies for emerging problems.

In short, if decision making is remedial and serial, anticipated adverse consequences of any given policy can often be better dealt with if regarded as new and separate problems than if regarded as aspects of an existing problem. And unanticipated adverse consequences can often be better guarded against by waiting for their emergence than by often futile attempts to anticipate every contingency as required in synoptic problem solving.

The Need for a Multiplicity of Decision Makers

Looking at complex problem solving as a strategy, one can wonder whether serial and remedial methods are enough to provide reasonable assurance that adverse consequences and policy failures will be straightened out. One can easily imagine a decision maker who can return in later policy steps to no more than a few of a variety of neglected adverse consequences resulting from an earlier policy step. This possibility points directly to the need for a multiplicity of decision makers and, more than that, to a multiplicity marked by great variety of attitudes and interests, so that no line of adverse consequence fails to come to the attention of some decision maker.

The great multiplicity of decision makers in, say, American public policy making can be seen, therefore, as a great strength where problem solving cannot be synoptically accomplished but must be strategically pursued. Multiplicity copes with the inevitability of omission and other errors in complex problem solving. Were there no decision makers with a stake in international trade, we might wonder whether farm policy might not put strains on international trade to which the farm-policy decision makers might themselves be inadequately sensitive; but we know that, if the strains appear, those decision makers who have a stake in international trade will attack them as their own problem. Were it not for decision makers with an interest in parks and recreation, we might wonder whether an urban redevelopment board could be trusted to make decisions on the relocation of commercial houses within a city.

If, through multiplicity, decision makers mop up the adverse consequences of each other's inevitably imperfect decisions, multiple decision makers will, in addition, compellingly call to others' attention aspects of the problem they cannot themselves analyze. Moreover, just as the single decision maker will sometimes anticipate adverse consequences that he must nevertheless treat as separate problems for fear of making his existing problem unmanageable, so also other decision makers can anticipate what they either cannot anticipate or cannot attend to. They can then treat the anticipated adverse consequences as their problems, even attacking them simultaneously with their attack on the initial problem.

The relation of strategic problem solving to partisan mutual adjustment now begins to be clear.

COORDINATION

THROUGH A

MULTIPLICITY

OF STRATEGIC

PROBLEM SOLVERS

Coordination through Multiplicity

A PROCESS BY WHICH DECISIONS deal with adverse consequences of other decisions, either as they come to be felt or in anticipation of them, is, we now need to recognize, a process of coordination, although possibly a weak one. Thus the strategic approach to problem solving is also at least a weak method of coordination.

Decisions are coordinated, we said, if they are adapted to one another so that at least one decision maker prefers the adjustment to no adjustment at all. Why would a decision maker prefer an adaptation to no adaptation at all? Because the adaptation reduces adverse consequences for his decision of one or more decisions in the coordinated set.

We now can restate the definition as follows: *A set of decisions is coordinated if adjustments have been made in it such that the adverse consequences of any one decision for other decisions in the set are to a degree and in some frequency avoided, reduced, counterbalanced, or outweighed.*

This concept of coordination does not strain ordinary usage. If we say of a group of policies that they are badly coordinated, do we not indeed often mean specifically that some of the policies hinder others, perhaps even stultify others, or that some of the policies do not make the contribution to the success of other policies that could be arranged? In short, do we not mean that, on one hand, policies may be positively adverse in their consequences for others and that, on the other hand, they may be adverse in failing to support others, that is, adverse in their sins of omission. Sometimes, of course, we say that a set of policies somehow does not add up to an integrated attack on a problem. But this is merely a way of speaking, again, of the relations among policies and of their adverse consequences for each other, with emphasis on errors of omission.

Thus, it is useful to consider decision making as coordinated—in a fundamental but not necessarily satisfactory way—if adverse consequences are acted upon as though they were regrettable. This is, of course, still a loose concept of coordination, as was our earlier one. We cannot use it to specify just when, where, which, and whose adverse consequences ought to be taken care of as a condition of calling a set of decisions coordinated in a more ambitious sense. It is, however, open ended; that is, rather than specify a certain pattern of adjustments to adverse consequences as necessary to coordination and make irrelevant the exploration of any other adjustments, it will ultimately direct our attention to a range of adjustment possibilities that we do indeed want to explore.

We have shown that a single decision maker acting remedially and serially to some degree attends to adverse consequences of any one decision with other decisions. Thus, we now say, he at least weakly coordinates his decisions. When there are many decision makers pursuing problem solving as a strategy they greatly strengthen, we have said, the process of attending to neglected adverse consequences. Hence, fragmentation of policy making to a multiplicity of strategic problem solvers achieves, we now say, coordination, though perhaps only in a weak form. Now that we recognize that coordination is achieved through a multiplicity of strategic problem solvers, the process through which it is achieved, described only briefly at the end of the preceding chapter, calls for further clarification.

As an illustration of the process, the attack on problems, or on any single problem, of income distribution in the United States is fragmented among various taxing authorities: Social Security agencies at the local, state, and national levels; trade unions; business groups; agencies performing public services on such terms as affect the distribution of income; and the market, which is itself a highly fragmented decision-making process. To take an example of what might appear to be a more specific problem, educational inadequacies are attacked through a variety of public and private organizations.

For a more extended example, the President and some of his advisers agree on a greatly expanded program of highway expenditures. Their objectives are national defense, reduction of highway congestion for civilians, and economic development. Consequences of the program for the parity of the fifty states as recipients of federal funds are ignored, as are possible consequences for auto fatalities, design of automobiles, profits of existing toll roads, destruction of homes and recreational areas, sale of automobiles, sale of home furnishings, character of home life, participation in organized religion, and so on. When the program is presented to Congress, if not before, some of the neglected values will be spoken for, say, by representatives of the states or of toll-road authorities. These interests may come to terms immediately with the original proponents of the program, not necessarily by each representative's taking into account each other's values, but by direct agreement on modification of the program. Other interests will wait until Congressional consideration of the program is under way, and still other interests will be brought to bear on the administrative officials eventually responsible for implementing the program. Years later, when it becomes apparent to churchmen that too many people are out driving on Sunday rather than attending religious services, churchmen will stir themselves to find ways of combating the tendency. When they do they will not necessarily attribute the tendency to the earlier highway program, and it is not at all necessary that they do so in order to deal with their then current problem.

We stress the distinction, very briefly referred to at the end of the preceding chapter, between dealing with a neglected consequence only as it shows itself, on the one hand, and anticipating it, on the other. Where there are many decision makers both possibilities are open, just as they were shown to be open for any one policy maker. Groups become watchdogs for values they fear will be neglected by other groups; each group consequently develops sensitivity to certain lines of consequences and becomes more competent to explore them than do other groups to whom these consequences are incidental because subordinate to other objectives and values. It is possible for each decision maker to specialize in this way since, as we have said, none are required to anticipate all the possible failures and adverse consequences of a decision. Nor are they required, as they would be by the synoptic ideal, to bring their anticipation of failures to bear as an objection on the very policy that stimulates the anticipation. Instead, they more simply employ the anticipation by designing a next step to deal with the anticipated failure or adverse consequence of the last step.

The relationships among the multiplicity of decision makers which account for their coordination are—to make explicit what is now obvious—characterized by mutual adjustment. In explaining the coordination process for strategic problem solvers we have made no reference to centrally controlled adjustment of decision makers to each other. They adjust because they are pursuing a partisan purpose. Thus we conclude that partisan mutual adjustment is a method for coordinating decisions of strategic problem solvers, although to what degree and with what success we cannot yet say.

There is a paradoxical quality to this argument. One ordinarily assumes that the more numerous the decision makers, the more difficult the process of coordination. We are instead suggesting that given that decision making is incremental and disjointed, more rather than fewer decision makers can facilitate coordination. Because of the necessity for a division of labor and for other reasons, where decision making is dispersed over a large group of decision makers—and in complex problem solving it always is—their very numbers afford them the possibility of coordination. And if they represent different interests and look at problems differently, then the possibilities are even greater. If numbers sometimes create a problem of coordination, it is only traditional bias that causes us to overlook the contribution numbers can make to its solution. A multiplicity of energies, interests, and intelligences can itself be exploited to achieve coordination.

Alternative Forms of Mutual Adjustment in Strategic Problem Solving

We can now very quickly identify the role, in fragmented decision making, of various types of partisan mutual adjustment in processes by which adverse consequences of strategic decisions are to some degree and with some frequency attended to. To begin with, the place of deferential adjustment (defined as decision making intended to avoid adverse consequences for another decision maker) is clear by definition. As for calculated adjustment (in which X considers repercussions for Y before making his decision, even though he is able to make his decision without Y's cooperation) it is a kind of decision making in which X's decision is typically tailored to reduce or avoid injury to Y, or to offset injury with benefit so that Y's reaction will not be disadvantageous to X. To be sure, X sometimes makes a decision calculated simply to leave Y in no position to redress his injuries from X, in which case adverse consequences for Y are neither avoided nor offset, even if adverse consequences for X of Y's potential decision are avoided. Still, this is not always an open possibility for X; therefore, frequently and to a considerable degree, he will alter his decision to avoid diverse consequences or to levy offsetting benefits on Y. When, for example, a state highway department fears unfavorable public reaction it may plan new highway routes to reduce injuries to municipalities in the highway area; or when it wishes to compensate for land surrendered reluctantly by a town it may offer a bonus to the town in the form of state maintenance of some local roads.

In parametric adjustment the decision maker simply takes another's decisions as he finds them and adapts to them without deferring to or calculating repercussions on others. The adverse consequences of others for him are not forestalled, as they might be if he engaged in manipulated adjustment; but they are reduced in effect—at an extreme wiped out—by his autonomous decision to make the best of the situation for himself. It may seem to be laboring the obvious to say that X reduces adverse consequences on himself by making a decision designed to cope with adversity to his own advantage. Yet it is a significant point. For while such a move is open to him in partisan mutual adjustment, it will often not be open to a decision maker assigned a specific role in a centrally coordinated system. In their ideal forms noncentral and central systems are different on this point, the latter carefully constraining each decision maker. Dimock's adroit maneuvering in the War Shipping Administration described at some length in Chapter 8, for example, represented a course of adaptations that a genuinely centralized coordinating system could not tolerate.

Of the three adaptive forms of adjustment the simple parametric form, of course, carries an enormous burden of attending to adverse consequences. A parametric adjuster makes no other move to reduce adverse consequences than to protect himself—unlike the deferential and calculating adjuster. But, as we pointed out earlier, a sequence of round-robin of parametric responses involving a large number of decision makers opens up to each in turn a possibility of reducing adverse consequences. The heavy burden carried by purely parametric adjustment arises from the fact that neither a central decision maker nor a willing negotiator or manipulator of any other kind can attend to more than a very small minority of the adverse consequences, potential or actual, of other decisions on him. In an interdependent world we are all injured, as well as benefited, by actions so far removed from us that we do not know the origin of our injuries. We cannot go to the source; we can only react in a self-protecting way to the injury as we see it bearing on us. In reacting to our injuries we do not, then, either defer or calculate with respect to most other decision makers. There are too many others—more than we can take account of. This is a universal experience for decision makers, no less than for all of us.

The Federal Reserve Board, for example, cannot stop to take account of those decision makers who deliberately or unwittingly obstruct the Board's management of the monetary system. Or, if it does take account of all of them, it cannot find the capacity to manipulate all; it must instead manipulate only a few. And, on the point of acting, it can take only limited account of its repercussions on others not deliberately manipulated, hence it can defer or calculate with respect to a handful of decision makers and must act parametrically toward a thousand others.

As for manipulated adjustments, they are obviously not merely devices by which decision makers try to enlist the cooperation of other decision makers, which is the emphasis we gave them in Chapters 4 and 5; they are also devices by which decision makers try to head off decisions adverse to them in commission or omission. These are the devices which, by definition, permit X to share in the control of Y's decision, and thus permit X to protect himself before Y's decision is made or permit him to avoid adversity in the first place rather than try to overcome it once it bears on him. The symmetric forms of manipulative adjustment, of course, permit a give-and-take on a given decision such that X's and Y's potential adverse consequences for each other are taken into account by each before the decision is made.

That negotiation coordinates is everywhere accepted as obvious, but its capacity for coordination is often wrongly attributed to the equality or near equality of power among the participants. Conversely, striking inequality of power in unilateral manipulation is incorrectly taken as evidence that it cannot coordinate. In fact, however, coordination is achieved because the decisions of X and Y are brought by manipulation into a relationship to each other so as to reduce their adverse consequences for each other. It is, therefore, achieved quite as easily by unilateral as by symmetric manipulation, even though the terms on which the conflict is settled will differ accordingly.

Often we will say that symmetric manipulation is preferable to unilateral on ethical grounds, and on this score one is tempted to attribute a superior coordinating potential to symmetric manipulation. But the ethical superiority of symmetry evaporates on close examination; clearly, we often find it necessary, on ethical grounds, to make power run in one direction almost exclusively, as in the relation between a judge and a convicted criminal, between a parent and a child in some circumstances, and between many pairs of civil servants. In any case, however, the alleged ethical superiority of symmetry is not to be confused with the question before us, which is the comparative strength of unilateral and symmetric manipulation as coordinating processes, in the defined sense of "coordination."

It may be helpful to note how alike the two forms sometimes are. In multilateral bargaining, for example, which is typical in politics, the differences in power from bargainer to bargainer can be very great, e.g., the difference of influence in negotiation of the Senate Majority Leader, on the one hand, and a freshman Senator or representative of the Railway Brotherhoods, on the other. Now if unilateral manipulation does not give X more control over Y than he would have in negotiation with him, if X is aware of Y's interests (as he sometimes must be in order effectively to manipulate him), and if X knows that although today he manipulates Y, at some later date and on some other problem their positions may be reversed, then there is no obvious difference in the way in which unilateral and symmetric manipulation will handle adverse consequences. Moreover, if X unilaterally manipulates Y through compensation there is no adversity at all; therefore, again, there is no reason to look more skeptically on unilateral than on symmetric manipulation.

The comparison of the two forms is quite inconclusive; it has been pursued only far enough to call to attention to at least some respects in which the apparent coordinating merits of negotiation are shared by unilateral manipulation. It is, therefore, a very small point that we make; we do not even go so far as to claim that the apparent merits of negotiation are real.

Although no central synoptic mind can possibly anticipate all the possible repercussions of a decision, or even, if able to list them, grasp them well enough to accommodate them in its decision, each neglected value that has a protecting decision maker who is a manipulator can be incorporated, without intellectual incorporation into the mind of any one decision maker, into the pattern of decisions reached. For any other neglected value, as we have seen, adaptive adjustments must serve to incorporate it into the pattern. We shall have to investigate in later chapters the terms in which, either way, the incorporation takes place.

Finally, it is worth noting that the devices by which partisan mutual adjustment attends to adverse consequences, hence coordinates, will be seen only in part by anyone who conceives of coordination solely in connection with overt, recognized conflicts among decisions. Clearly, most adverse consequences are visited on decision makers indirectly, as a result of decisions unnoticed by them. The consequent burden of indirect, long-distance, enormously complex coordination carried by partisan mutual adjustment (especially, we noted above, by parametric adjustment) should not be missed. By our definition federal policy on Western reclamation projects and policy on school lunches in California are coordinated with public housing policy in New York City (if only because they cannot both use the same funds, but, in fact, for other reasons as well), although, by intellectual habit, their interrelations would never raise a question of coordination in many people's minds.

Unanswered Questions

If multiplicity of strategic problem solvers accomplishes coordination, is there not also some residue of truth in the common notion that multiplicity itself creates a problem of coordination? It is, of course, true that if decision making is carried on by a large number of persons and organizations, it needs coordination; but our point is that the decision makers themselves provide a great deal of coordination by their attentions to each other. Moreover, it is not logically necessary that many decision makers require more coordination than a few. For, as we have seen, even a single decision maker's decisions need coordinating. If when faced with complex problems he abandons synopsis and pursues the tactics of problem solving described in the preceding chapter, the coordination of his decisions, which he can accomplish only serially and remedially, constitutes the same problem as the coordination of the decisions of many. But he is without the help of many. Our point, again, is that a multiplicity of decision makers brings new energies and skills to the task of coordination; and multiplicity does not necessarily create any new problems of coordination.

One can imagine, however, that the coordination of decisions through a multiplicity of decision makers might, for certain special reasons, create new problems of coordination for which an overlay of central coordination might be required. A multiplicity of decision makers, for example, might, one could fear, produce a kind of irrational mixture of values. That is to say, the interplay among decision makers pursuing different partisan values might result in the accidental dominance of this or that value, or this value at one time and that value at another—in any case without rhyme or reason. We shall appraise this criticism and others like it in a sequence of analytical steps in succeeding chapters.

Since it has been shown that coordination is achieved when X defers to Y, when X ignores Y, and when X dominates Y, it would seem to follow that any pattern of yielding or dominance is as consistent with coordination as any other. This being the case, it would then seem to follow that any kind of relation among decision makers must be pronounced coordinated. Obviously, for further analysis we need a fuller concept of coordination than has yet been introduced. All we have shown so far is that in partisan mutual adjustment there are a variety of ways in which, through mixtures of yielding and dominance, adverse consequences can be attended to. Only later can we ask when one pattern of yielding and dominance would seem appropriate to coordination and when another.

Part
5

Comparative Analysis of Central Coordination and Mutual Adjustment

Chapter
11

COORDINATION
BY OVERVIEW

Claims Made for Central Coordination

UP TO THIS POINT WE HAVE
laid out the mechanisms of partisan mutual adjustment, examined
their special adaptibility to strategic problem solving, and seen
that these mechanisms coordinate in at least a weak sense. Now it is
time to ask whether they coordinate in any fuller sense.

The difficulty in answering this question is that whether a set
of decisions are fully coordinated or not, other things being equal,
depends, finally, on the values by which one judges the set. A set of
policies nicely adjusted to achieve a maximum of price stability is
not necessarily nicely adjusted to achieve a high level of employment. An administrative organization whose decisions are
all coordinated to achieve a specified combination of agency "out-
put" and institutional security against attack does not look well
coordinated to, say, an official of the agency or an observer who
favors more (or less) action and less (or more) caution.

We cannot say, however, what values should be employed in

judgment. Complex problem solving, as we have seen in Chapter 9, proceeds in the absence of criteria sufficient to indicate when a decision is correct or incorrect. If criteria are inadequate for decision makers, they are also inadequate for an evaluator of partisan mutual adjustment, for that evaluation itself constitutes a complex problem. We cannot in this very study be synoptic and must, instead, approach our problem of evaluation in a strategic way.

Rather, therefore, than try to formulate even limited criteria to help distinguish systematically between better and poorer co-ordination, we are going to pursue the question of how well partisan mutual adjustment coordinates by making some specific empirical comparisons between it and central coordination. These comparisons are suggested by the principal claims typically made for central coordination. Meeting these claims head on with further descriptive material will permit us to sharpen the analysis of partisan mutual adjustment.

As coordination has so far been defined there is no question at all that partisan mutual adjustment accomplishes coordination. But the claims commonly made for central coordination attribute to centrality some characteristics that are not ordinarily attributed to noncentral systems. Central coordination is described as intelligent. This is not to say that coordinators are never unintelligent; it is claimed, however, that central coordination represents an application of human intelligence to a problem. Central coordination is a method that approaches the question of the relations among decisions as an intellectual problem. It is a reasoned approach, and it represents a method of attacking a problem by trying to understand it. It is therefore not arbitrary. One also says of central coordination that it represents a method of adjustment that proceeds to a determination only after an overview of all the interrelations among decisions or policies. For all these reasons, there is also an element of correctness or rightness to the coordinating decisions reached.

By contrast, the kind of pulling and hauling that we have formalized as partisan mutual adjustment is typically seen to be just that: pulling and hauling rather than the exercise of human intelligence. Problems of coordination are not approached as intellectual problems but as games, contests, even bitterly fought struggles. If coordination results it is not because of human understanding and not, certainly, because relations among the decisions were adjusted in the light of anyone's overview of their repercussions on each other. These rough processes are unreasoned and arbitrary.

To do justice to these claims and the consequent ostensible points of distinction between centrality and mutual adjustment we shall sort them out into the following points. Each point claims a feature for central coordination that is thought to be absent from partisan mutual adjustment.

1. In central coordination the adjustment of relations among decisions or policies is made in the light of a survey and consideration of all important possible interrelationships among them.
2. The coordinating decisions are reasoned, in the sense that there are criteria or guidelines of some sort for what the interrelationship should be, and these the coordinator employs.
3. Decisions or policies to be coordinated are at least made more or less consistent with one another.
4. Centrality imparts a consistent bias or pattern to the decisions of the coordinator so that coordination in one situation or at one time does not produce results quite at odds with those in other situations and at other times.

The first claim will be investigated in this chapter, the second in the immediately following chapter, and the others thereafter.

It needs to be remembered that we are not comparing organizations and sets of decisions in fact centrally coordinated with those that are not, for a high degree of centrality is rare in any circumstances and, on the other hand, partisan mutual adjustment is ever present. We are analyzing centrality as a conceived rather than achieved form of coordination. To put the comparison in another useful form we are appraising the claims made on behalf of movements toward centrality and are therefore comparing more central with less central coordination.

Competence and Complexity

To begin with the first claim, if one says of central coordination that decisions are adjusted to one another in the light of an investigation of all their significant repercussions for one another, one conceives of central coordination as a form of synoptic decision making. If so, the grounds for suspecting that synoptic decision making is impossible for complex problems become relevant to the claim. With complex problems it is not to be taken for granted that men, individually or in a team, have the necessary information or can get it, can process it if they have it, can afford to get and process the information even when it is in principle available. It is an assumption made on behalf of central coordination that these barriers to problem solving simply do not exist, and it is an empirical question whether for any given problem the capacities for an overview exist. That is, it is a question of fact not faith or assumption whether information, intellectual competence, time, energy, and other resources permit an overview.

No man or team, no individual or organization in any government undertakes, we know, a systematic overview of all the important repercussions of policies on others. Most people would look upon anyone who tried to do so as foolish. In the United States, for example, the interrelations of policies on agricultural price supports, aid to Latin America, desegregation, education, space technology, urban redevelopment, monetary policy, reclamation and conservation, and legislative reapportionment are not given a systematic overview by anyone; their interrelationships pass far beyond what most of us consider to be a manageable intellectual problem.

We tend to justify breaking these policy problems into relatively independent subgroups by arguing that they are not intimately connected with one another, that, specifically, policy can safely be made in one or a group of these areas without regard for consequences to another one or group. Yet every single one of these policy areas has important consequences for our rivalry with the Soviet Union, every one also is consequential for the level of public expenditures, and every one is consequential for the role of government in the economy. For at least these three reasons they are not independent of each other but are instead closely interlocked. Moreover, there are some decisions in each of these fields that can obstruct the success of policies in any other. There are also possibilities in each field for contributing to the success of policies in the other fields. Policies on legislative reapportionment within the states, if they were to be centrally overviewed, would have to be examined for their consequences for a shift of public funds toward urban development as the political strength of urban voters increases (if that were the direction of reapportionment), then that in turn would have to be examined for consequences for Negro housing and education, then that in turn would have to be examined for consequences for effective desegregation, and so on.

Any reasonable view of the relations among the vast array of interconnecting public decisions leads to the conclusion that if they are to be coordinated, it must be largely without an overview of their consequences for each other. Hence a more reasonable claim for central coordination is that it achieves an overview not of the whole but of each of various subsections of public policy. Thus it would be claimed that central coordination achieves an overview of interrelations among various policies bearing on such subjects as, taken separately, monetary management, the position of the Negro in the United States, farm incomes, national security, or administrative organization of the federal government. These claims are somewhat more reasonable, but shifting to them does represent a surrender. If this is all that is to be claimed for the overview of central coordination, the conclusion is inescapable that for the larger pattern of relations among decisions either coordination does not exist or it is somehow achieved without an overview, which means, perhaps, not centrally at all.

Even the more restricted claims are questionable. Does anyone in fact systematically overview all decisions bearing on desegregation in the United States? or on national security? or any other large policy area? Public decisions that bear on desegregation, for example, are those of all public housing, zoning, and planning authorities in local governments, the armed services, commissions on employment practices, the National Labor Relations Board, numerous federal agencies responsible for housing and home finance policies, educational authorities at all governmental levels, and still others. All these decisions are not given a systematic comprehensive overview; and, again, few people seriously propose that one be attempted. The attempt would appear to carry us beyond man's capacities to gather and digest information.

But, it may be replied, granted the quite limited capacity of man to deal synoptically with his problems generally, at least he can come to grips successfully with the relatively limited task of overview *for coordination.*

By subdividing the problem and assigning responsibility to hierarchical subordinates, for example, he turns his problem-solving task into the more restricted task of overseeing the subordinate parts.* But how limited is the task of overview for coordination? It is a task that requires the unraveling of chains of interlocked consequences; there is no more difficult part of decision making.

Paradoxically, preoccupation with central coordination may encourage one to underestimate the magnitude of the task of coordination, even to form a misconception of the nature of the process. The task of coordination is often identified with that part of it which is in fact attacked through central coordination; what comes clear on second thought is forgotten—that an enormous amount of coordination is inevitably achieved through various mutual adjustments. But the most visible part of the coordination iceberg, explicit central coordination, may be only a small part of all those processes through which coordination to a degree is achieved. One would beg many questions about the nature and difficulty of coordination if he were to argue that coordination must be within man's synoptic capacities because it appears to him that synoptic central coordinators are doing the job.

The heart of the matter is that to look upon an overview of mutual repercussions among decisions as a merit of central coordination is to conceive of central coordination as an exercise in synoptic problem solving. But synopsis, we have shown, is an impossible method of problem solving for complex problems. We do not prove by this argument that central coordination is impossible or that, by default of it, partisan mutual adjustment is a desirable

* "Factoring out" parts of problems through hierarchical arrangements among decision makers is, of course, a recognized adaptation of centrality to the complexities of problem solving. It pushes back the limits of man's capacities, not, however, without introducing new problems of communication and organization. While achieving great gains in man's coordinating and problem-solving capacity, its possibilities do not invalidate the arguments we have been developing about the difficulties of synopsis, although they greatly raise the level of complexity that can be synoptically handled. We have been careful to state the difficulties of synopsis in such a way as to make the presence or absence of "factoring out" not critical to them.

alternative. We make the point only that one traditional claim for the superiority of central coordination over other forms of adjustment is invalidated for sufficiently complex problems.

This limited move in the argument somewhat changes the perspective with which one regards partisan mutual adjustment. Partisan mutual adjustment imposes on no one the heroic demands for information, intellectual competence, time, energy, and money that are required for an overview of interrelationships among decisions. It has been shown how incremental and disjointed decision making constitute a set of adaptions to these difficulties in problem solving; and partisan mutual adjustment has, of course, been shown to be adapted to the coordination of that kind of decision making.

With respect to the overview the actual choice between centrality and partisan mutual adjustment in a real-world situation will appear sometimes in the form of two such alternatives as the following: On one hand, one might impose a responsibility upon a central coordinator to carry the overview as far as possible, to strain for comprehensiveness even if not to achieve it; on the other hand, one instead might ask a set of decision makers to take account, as in calculated adjustment for example, of just those very few consequences of possible decisions that might backfire through their effects on a few other decision makers.

The overview will of course be incompetent to some unspecified degree for all the reasons given; it will not, in fact, be an overview but only the beginnings of one. Insofar as the central coordinator has the responsibility and authority to make controlling decisions in the situation, his responsibilites to some degree will run beyond his competence to overview; and his coordinating decisions to some degree will fail to achieve what was hoped for or intended by them. For any complex problem there will certainly be some degree of failure; whether it is large or small will depend on the interplay between competence and complexity, as well as, of course, on luck.

Attacking much more precisely defined and simple intellectual tasks, partisan adjusters will neither attempt nor succeed in an overview; but they will sometimes solve their limited intellectual problems more successfully than will the central coordinator. If they are interlocked with other decision makers in appropriate forms of partisan mutual adjustment, the consideration finally given in policy making to the various consequences of the policies to be coordinated will sometimes be more precisely thought through than they would be if the decision makers had been centrally coordinated; and the final pattern of coordination, although not at all wholly a product of intellectually guided rearrangement, will sometimes be superior by any reasonable standard to the error-ridden attempt at central coordination.

A case in point is one already referred to earlier: the change-over in the California Department of Employment to electronic data processing. The chief of the tabulating section, who made the decision to install electronic processing, had made an intensive study of the desirability of the changeover which guided the central decision to install the new system. But, although he conceded the importance of protecting employee morale and job security, his analysis somehow failed to take these factors into account. One reason was that the decision presented a very complex intellectual problem; and the chief of the section was hard pressed even to carry his analysis of the desirability of the changeover as far as he did.

A comprehensive overview of the factors in the decision problem having failed to attend to employee morale and job security, how might they be attended to? They were in fact attended to, as we saw, by the parametric adjustment of the Department's personnel director who, shocked to hear of the decision to change over, promptly set himself the task of reconciling the decision, which he took as given, with the Department's interests in morale and job security. Acting parametrically at first and subsequently bringing the tabulating section into negotiation, he achieved a final solution that reconciled the new processing with morale and with no loss of a suitable job for any of the employees whose jobs were abolished.[1]

None of this proves the superiority of partisan mutual adjustment to central coordination generally or in any fixed category of circumstances. The discussion and illustration show, however, that given the impossibility of an overview for sufficiently complex problems, the attempt to achieve one can easily result, through mistakes of the intellect, in such failures to achieve the coordination desired as to undermine the claim that centrality is superior to partisan mutual adjustment by reason of its attempt at an overview.

Motivation toward an Overview

Moreover, if it is claimed that a centrally coordinated set of decisions are the product of the coordinator's overview of their mutual interrelationships, it needs to be shown not only that the coordinator can take an overview but that he, in fact, does so when he can. Because the overview, even when in principle possible, is demanding of time, energy and other resources, a central coordinator will sometimes be strongly motivated to avoid it. Can he? Because his authority to make a coordinating decision does not typically depend on his showing how he reached his decision, he can sometimes bypass the overview and make the decision without it. As a result it is not inevitable or even demonstrably probable that a great deal of information and analysis will be brought to bear on the interrelationships among decisions in centrally coordinated systems. For sufficiently complex problems the fear of making a serious mistake troublesome for the future is not a sufficient motivation for an overview, because the probability of serious error remains high for any practicable amount of analysis. Risks may consequently be reduced not by an exhaustive overview but by choosing a decision that for one reason or another—perhaps its popularity among those most likely to criticize—leaves the coordinator less vulnerable.

Congressional decisions, for example, on the allocation of federal expenditures are coordinating decisions on which the motivation to push an overview as far as intellectually feasible is apparently weak. Decision makers have too many other demands on their time and energy. And insofar as failure to attend to an overview exposes Congressmen to criticism because, say, it turns out in retrospect that allocations to distant early-warning systems were not well coordinated with allocations to other parts of the national defense system, that criticism is nothing compared to the criticisms and other pressures more immediately visited on Congressmen by advocates of this or that line of expenditure.

Responding to Congressional interest in undertaking an overview of federal expenditures, Representative Clarence Cannon, then
Chairman of the House of Appropriations Committee, announced
in 1949 that the committee would submit to the House the annual
appropriations in one consolidated bill, permitting Congress to see
the budget picture as a whole. Having tried an omnibus bill in
1950, Congress rejected it in all subsequent years. Having had an
opportunity to push an overview further than before, why did
Congress not pursue it after its 1950 experience? There are several
reasons of striking significance. One is that the overview imposed
intolerable burdens on members of Congress; they simply could
not digest the information and proposals simultaneously submitted
to them for decision. Another reason was that for all the efforts to
take an overview, inevitably the overview remained defective because a large amount of expenditure had to be allocated in separate
bills in the months following the omnibus to meet contingencies
that could not be anticipated in the omnibus. Another reason was
that many individual Congressmen were more interested in particular expenditures of concern to them than the overall coordination
of expenditure.

Now although these reasons bear on the decision maker's capacity to undertake an overview, they throw even more light on his
motivation to do so. They suggest that the decision maker can and
does plead with himself: the overview is too difficult; even if I
attempt it I cannot actually carry it off; and if I attempt it I dis-
tract myself from particular concerns on which I can act with
interest and competence; therefore, I shall not try to do it.[2]

In partisan mutual adjustment, on the other hand, there are
powerful motives to mobilize information and analysis on the relations among possible decisions. To be sure, no one decision maker
is motivated to undertake the comprehensive investigations en-
visaged by the advocates of an overview, but, taken together, a
group of partisan adjusters may generate a great deal more information and analysis than will a central coordinator. Again, they will
not necessarily do so, but they may. There is no valid presumption
that only through centrality is information and analysis brought to
bear on the repercussions of decisions on one another.

Motives for the mobilization of information and analysis in

some forms of partisan mutual adjustment are not hard to find; and they are not weakened, as in central overview, by the discouraging difficulty of collecting and analyzing the required information. A decision maker employing partisan discussion is, of course, highly motivated to find those connections between his decisions and those of another decision maker that he can then cite as reasons for Y's finding it desirable to make the response X wants. If, for example, the advocates of an increase in the minimum wage have no leverage on certain important decision makers other than partisan discussion, they will be pushed toward uncovering every possible relation between a higher minimum wage and the interests of the other decision makers. To be sure, X will sometimes wish to suppress certain information unfavorable to the success of partisan discussion, but then Y is motivated to uncover it for the protection of his own interests.

Deferential and calculated adjustment likewise call for precise information about the consequences of possible decisions for those other decisions to which one wishes to defer or adapt to a degree. And the manipulated techniques, bargaining and the others, succeed only to the degree that the manipulator well understands the connections between his wishes and the interests and positions of those he wishes to manipulate. (Authoritative prescription is an exception, where X can simply order Y to respond, as does a central coordinator.) And they in turn have to appraise, as a condition of deciding whether to yield or resist, the consequences of his proposed decision for them.

In short, to succeed in partisan mutual adjustment—to succeed, say, in avoiding backfiring in adaptive adjustment and to succeed in manipulated adjustment—each decision maker has to meet certain relatively specific, modest, manageable demands for information and analysis. Where a central coordinator can succeed in making his coordinating decisions effective (because, by definition, his decisions control) whether he is informed or not, a participant in partisan mutual adjustment, dependent on finding a satisfying adaptation to others' decisions or dependent on inducing others to make appropriate responses to his wishes, finds information and analysis indispensable to making his decisions effective. In this sense partisan mutual adjustment mobilizes information and analysis that central coordinators can dispense with.

One could take this difference in motivation to be significant in either of two ways. One might claim—although somewhat questionably—for central coordination that it can coordinate without much information and analysis where partisan mutual adjustment cannot do so. But that claim is irrelevent to the one under discussion in this section. The claim being evaluated is that central coordination takes advantage of an overview of all relations among decisions to be coordinated. But the difference between the two systems reveals the invalidity of the claim, for the central system, we are saying, does not necessarily mobilize the information and analysis necessary to an overview when the coordinator lacks motives for mobilizing them.

President Roosevelt's attempt in 1936 and 1937 to pack the Supreme Court is a good example of lack of motivation to gather and analyze information. Roosevelt was confident, especially after his reelection, in his ability to put through Congress a program of Court reform that would reduce the conflict between the Court and Congress. Confident as he was, he did not intend to negotiate a Court reform but took upon himself and some of his advisers the entire task of canvassing alternative possibilities and working up a bill for submission to Congress. He appears to have looked upon himself as a central decision maker with sufficient competence and power to do the job, subject only to Congressional approval, which he expected would come routinely.

Indicative of the way in which a central decision maker might ideally go about the task, Roosevelt asked the Attorney General, together with some of the staff of the Department of Justice, to study the problem of Court reform. He consulted Edward S. Corwin, a noted expert on jurisprudence, and William Draper Lewis of the American Law Institute. Subsequently he enlarged the work of the Department of Justice; the Department produced for him surveys of each of alternative approaches thought worth considering.

But indicative also of the ease with which a centralist may stop short of critical considerations, Roosevelt did not consult any of his political advisers who presumably would have given him not legal advice but advice on the various values that had to be taken account of in any reform bill. This aspect of his problem he confidently disposed of out of his own store of political information; he did not doubt that he knew what was and was not consistent with the various values held by citizens and Congressmen.

Although the Court subsequently changed its line, Roosevelt did not get his bill through Congress, nor did any bill pass that approximated it. What is important for us, however, is to see how little he really knew about the values held by citizen and Congressman. It was only in the partisan mutual adjustment that developed within the Congress that the relevant values came to be identified; and, if their exposition was then overlaid with excesses of rhetoric and tactical misrepresentation, at least it can be said that they were brought to bear on policy making as they had not been brought to bear in Roosevelt's thinking.

One might object to the example by claiming that Roosevelt's refusal to call on his usual family of advisers on this decision makes the case atypical. Granted, he did usually consult his political advisers. He did not do so in this case, we suggest, because he saw himself in a central decision-making role; in more typical circumstances he would have recognized that what he wanted of Congress he would have to win through partisan adjustment. In short, thinking of his decision making as central, he committed just that sin of decision making—not bothering to get the essential information—that he could hardly commit when frankly acknowledging his role in mutual adjustment. By contrast Senator Wheeler and the other principal leaders of the opposition to packing the Court were never under any illusion—they could not be—that they could succeed except through mutual adjustment; and for success at that, gathering information is no luxury that one can choose to forego. They were indefatigable.[3]

A Modified Claim for Overview

Suppose we substantially modify the claim for an overview through central coordination, asserting only that central coordination affords not a comprehensive and systematic overview but only a kind of responsible investigation of the probable principal consequences of each decision for the other most important decisions in a set. Are there any grounds for doubting this claim for central coordination?

We should want to know immediately what account is taken in the decision making process of factors consequently neglected in the coordinating decision. What of the consequences thought improbable that nevertheless occur? What of consequences which though secondary rather than principal are still not negligible? What of consequences for decisions other than the other most important decisions in a set? If they are neglected by the central coordinator in making a coordinating decision, they can only be taken into account in subsequent decisions that, in sequence, remedy the defects in the earlier decision.

In imagining a decision maker taking a limited view of his problem and returning to it in a remedial series, we are in effect asking whether it might be possible for a central coordinator to turn away from synoptic ambitions and become an incremental and disjointed decision maker, a strategic problem solver. If he can do this, then the information he must process, the complexities of the problems that he must grasp, the resources he must be able to command for problem solving are all sharply reduced.

Abandoning synopsis, a hypothetical central decision maker would not try for comprehensiveness in his view of the relations among policies but would instead take up in series each of an unending stream of particular problems, dealing with each with a narrow view of the implications of any policy solution, dealing with neglected implications as quite separate problems, therefore patching up without cease and often anticipating adverse consequences of neglected implications, but in any case dealing with them as separate problems rather than "coordinating." In turning from one problem to another he would presumably turn from one set of relevant values to another slightly different set.

If, however, this is what he does, then it is not at all necessary that each successive problem be dealt with by the same decision maker. Because problem, area of concern, and values all shift from decision to decision, a number of independent decision makers can make the decisions as well as a single, central decision maker.

Moreover, if he is to be a disjointed decision maker, neglecting to consider all possible decisions and ignoring some consequences of those decisions he does consider, the defects of his decisions, although remedied to a degree by serial and remedial decision making, are all the more quickly and consistently caught and remedied if there are many decision makers representing different interests and able to act on neglected consequences or other defects of any given decision. Thus, by the argument of the preceding chapter, there is no point in giving a coordinator who practices incremental and disjointed strategy a central place in policy making.

In his refusing to budget to TVA the funds to build an electric power plant to serve the growing needs of the Memphis area, President Eisenhower in 1953 made a strategic decision that could only be successful, as he himself appears to have recognized, if subsequently some further decision were made to provide Memphis with new power capacity by means other than TVA. He explored the possibility of Memphis's building a municipal power plant, also explored the possibilities for a private power plant in the area, and finally decided on the ill-fated Dixon-Yates contract, by which a private firm would contract with the Atomic Energy Commission to supply TVA with electric power to replace that taken by the AEC from TVA so that TVA's existing capacity would then be able to serve the needs of the Memphis area.

But it was a decision that took too few factors into account and met the preferences of too few groups; the contract was cancelled as a consequence of a group of partisan decisions that, together reflecting a more comprehensive regard for the values at stake, achieved a coordination of a variety of related policies. The adjustment so achieved induced Memphis to satisfy its power needs by building its own plant, kept the AEC out of what some of its commissioners believed to be a questionable political maneuver, left TVA free to expand its capacity in later years by issuing bonds, and satisfied the President himself on the immediate desire to block a new TVA plant. In his detailed study of the affair, Wildavsky writes:

The history of Dixon-Yates suggests . . . that by trying to determine what would be good for other people, leaders are liable to neglect important interests. . . . The President's attempt to serve the interests of all as he saw them . . . led him to arrive at the replacement power decision which . . . did not meet the preferences of a sufficiently wide range of interests to be successful. . . . When the interests concerned fought out their disagreements . . . the end result was a decision which met the most widespread preferences of all concerned.[4]

Most of us have strong habits of thought that lead us to suggest at this point that consistency requires one coordinator, even if he is a strategic decision maker, rather than many. But the suggestion flies in the face of the argument of the preceding chapter that given that decision making is strategic rather than synoptic, neglected consequences are sometimes best dealt with by a multiplicity of decision makers pursuing different, and conflicting, hence not consistent, values. To be sure, we are going to look into the consistency argument as a defense of central coordination in some detail and are not cavalierly dismissing its possible merits. Leaving it aside for the moment, however, there would often seem to be little reason for centrality in strategic rather than synoptic decision making. If a coordinator is a strategic decision maker, he will not accomplish the systematic overview by which his decisions might be defended; and, having reduced his attempt at overview sharply in becoming strategic rather than synoptic, his coordination has, with respect to the character of his overview, no claim to superiority over the views taken of decisions by partisan mutual adjusters.

A central system does not consist, however, of a single coordinator but of a hierarchy of coordinators, each coordinating centrally with respect to decisions under him. If all of them are strategic problem solvers and not synopsists, there is new ground for doubting the merit of giving any one decision maker central coordinating powers at any level of the hierarchy. Given that each central coordinator is neglecting some factors in his decision that his subordinates and coequal coordinators think important to *their* decisions, to permit them to enter into relations with one another on the basis of partisan mutual adjustment would appear to offer no fewer or less efficacious possibilities for dealing with the limitations of view of each decision maker than would subordinating him to another or giving him the exclusive authority of central coordination over another.

Once the task of coordination is large enough to call for a division of coordinating labor—once, that is to say, that coordination requires many coordinators linked together in hierarchical levels—the coordination of the coordinators becomes a task requiring, if it is to be done centrally at all, a high degree of synopsis. The assignment of responsibilities to subordinates, the working out of an organizational plan so that appropriate coordination is provided at each level in the hierarchy, requires that the organization and its functions be seen as a whole. Thus coordination of subcoordinators calls for synopsis or cannot be accomplished well by centrality at all. For coordination of this kind—and it is a typical kind of coordination in government agencies or in any organizations involving a few thousand people or more—nonsynoptic, genuinely central coordination is hardly conceivable. Again, this does not assert the superiority of partisan mutual adjustment; it merely places its possibilities against those that can be claimed, in a considered appraisal, for centrality.

To return, however, to the central issue in the appraisal of the claim that central coordination accomplishes an adjustment of decisions in the light of an overview, let us finally take note that appearances are deceiving in this matter. The ordinary image of the central coordinator is that of a thoughtful, information gathering and processing decision maker. Therefore, one is inclined to impute to central coordination the putative merits of informed and thoughtful decisions. But it is an empirical question, we repeat, how far a thoughtful mind can actually grasp relationships in a competent way and how much information it can digest. It is therefore a question for empirical inquiry whether a coordinating decision made centrally is in fact tailored to take account of the mutual repercussions of decisions any more so than they would be if taken accounts of through what superficially appear to be the arbitrary maneuverings of partisan mutual adjustment. That the coordinating decision is a product of a mind rather than of an interaction among decision makers is no evidence at all.

Chapter
12

REASONED

COORDINATION

The Claim for Reason

THE SECOND CLAIM FOR CEN-
tral coordination is that coordinating decisions are reasoned. The
claim needs to be stated with care and distinguished from the first
claim, discussed in the preceding chapter, with which it is easily
confused. The claim is that the central coordinator works his way
to a desirable set of relations among decisions to be coordinated
by problem-solving intellectual activity. He does not simply flip
a coin to make his decisions, nor are coordinating decisions merely
an outcome of the mutual exercise of power among decision
makers, hence the product not so much of a coordinator's intellect
as of a distribution of power or fortuitous circumstances. Hence
decisions are in some sense rightly or correctly adapted to each
other rather than adapted, say, by the accidents of power.

The claim is still somewhat fuzzy, however. If the determination of any question is approached as an intellectual problem, there
must be acceptable criteria for determining whether, at any point,

the problem is or is not solved. Here we are brought, in trying to specify the claim, to its relation to and difference from the first claim. Let us suppose that a central coordinator has systematically surveyed all possible mutual repercussions among possible decisions. Such a survey is not enough to bring him to the solution of his problem of coordination. What he needs in addition, of course, are some acceptable criteria according to which the best of all possible achievable relations can be preferred or chosen. Leave him without such criteria and he cannot reason his way, no matter how complete his overview, to a satisfactory coordinating decision. Give him such criteria and he can do so unless they are impossibly abstract and cannot therefore be applied to concrete decisions. Hence, the heart of the claim that coordination produces reasoned coordinating decisions is that it tests by acceptable workable criteria the various possible relations surveyed in the overview.

To be sure, the criteria do not need to be explicitly formulated as principles, nor need they be formulated at all in advance of attacking the problem to whose solution they must be applied. They may instead be developed *ad hoc* to meet the needs of the particular problem at hand. But as a minimum there must, by the time the coordinating decision is reached, be acceptable criteria by which the decision can be justified. Otherwise the claim to a reasoned decision is invalid.

In a purely formal sense any decision can, of course, be justified by reference to such criteria as "I like it," or "I thought of this possibility first," or "I say it's good, so it's good." Clearly, the claim that coordination is reasoned asserts something more than that justifications of this quality can be established. This is why we say that a reasoned decision requires not just criteria but acceptable criteria.

But even a partisan in mutual adjustment can justify his decisions by reference to criteria that will refer to important values widely accepted in society. Many will phrase their criteria in terms of the public interest itself, and those who do not will frame them in terms of fairness—as when business groups advocate tax reform favorable to them—or in terms of more specific but still widely accepted values —as when reclamation agencies defend their policies by reference to conservation or development of water resources. It would appear, then, that since partisans can defend their decisions by important criteria, all decisions are reasoned.

It appears that we have not yet stated the claim precisely enough. Those who make the claim will grant that a partisan mutual adjuster reasons his way to his decision and can defend it by reference to important criteria. But, they will add, it is only *his* criteria, and the state of affairs reached by interplay among the participants in partisan mutual adjustment cannot be justified in the light of the criteria that are employed by other participants or in the light of "correct" criteria. There is, therefore, an arbitrary quality to the state of affairs reached. By contrast, conflict of interests in central coordination is examined in the light of some principle or formula that serves to determine how the conflict should be resolved. By applying the principle the coordinator reasons his way to a resolution of the conflict, which otherwise would have to be "fought out," as it is in partisan mutual adjustment.

If, however, the formula centrally applied is one that is not acceptable to some of the interested parties who are being coordinated, or not acceptable to some observers, then to those parties the solution is arbitrary in the same sense as in partisan mutual adjustment. These persons see the solution as justified in terms of the criteria of some but not all persons, which is the situation objected to in the case of partisan mutual adjustment. Thus the only situation in which the arbitrary element we speak of can be removed, the only case, then, in which the solution represents a reasoned resolution of conflict in some sense fuller than in partisan mutual adjustment, is when the criteria are agreed to by all, or when anyone evaluating decisions is willing to specify his own criteria, despite social disagreement on them.

In short, the claim to reasoned coordination implies a claim that central coordination can resolve conflicts in the light of agreed criteria or in the light of criteria satisfactory to whoever makes the claim.

Inadequacy of Necessary Criteria

Now the striking fact to be placed against the claim that central coordination is reasoned is that for many governmental problems the relevant decision makers and citizens cannot agree on criteria. Their inability to agree is not because they have not tried. For the most informed, thoughtful, and searching citizens, for decision makers, and for scholars there is no adequate set of agreed criteria. We return thus to an important defect of synoptic decision making outlined in Chapter 9. If, as we saw in that chapter, criteria are lacking for synoptic problem solving, so also are they lacking for the guidance of central coordination.

We have shown in the earlier chapter that universal or general criteria such as majority preference are inadequate for the solution of complex problems. We may also take note of criteria deficiencies in fairly specific areas in which they might be expected to be satisfactory. Meyerson and Banfield, in their study of the location of public housing projects in Chicago, comment on the Housing Authority's difficulties in finding criteria acceptable both to the Authority itself and to the Aldermen.

It was surprising, one might think, that after so many years of experience in major cities throughout the United States there did not exist a body of tested principles for the selection of public housing sites under various circumstances and on various assumptions. . . .

At any rate, the criteria produced in Chicago (in most cities no explicit criteria at all were formulated) were not concrete and rested on certain assumptions which were perhaps not defensible.[1]

They go on to illustrate the complexity of the criteria problem, and their illustrations go far to indicate the impossibility of finding criteria satisfactory to all relevant parties, for they raise the kinds of questions that have to be faced when any complex policy problem is attacked. (Their exposition runs largely in terms of benefits and costs, and these are terms to which the weighing of alternative decisions can be reduced for any coordinating decision—or any decision, for that matter.)

Why, for example, should so much importance be attached to "economy" as a criterion governing the size of projects? (The Federal agency, probably on the defensive against the attacks of the real estate groups, required that projects be built at the lowest possible costs, and this was a practical reason for the criterion; however, there is no doubt that most of the commissioners approved of it in principle also.) If perchance, most people, not only project residents but neighboring property-owners and residents as well, preferred small projects, would there indeed be any "economy" in building large ones, even if the large ones cost less? Did not "economy" have to be measured as a ratio between costs and satisfactions rather than in terms of costs alone? Similarly, perhaps CHA (admittedly under the mandate of the Washington agency) was wrong in concluding that it was "poor business to build public housing projects on expensive land"; it might be that, measured in relation to the satisfaction (or absence of dissatisfaction) accruing to the community from the use of one site rather than another, expensive land (i.e., high-priced land) would, in some instances, be much "cheaper" than other land. Costs were meaningless and therefore deceptive except in relation to benefits, but what benefits ought to be taken into account and how could they be measured? Some classes of ends may be regarded as immoral or otherwise unworthy of satisfaction, thus the end of not having Negroes in one's neighborhood should not, if satisfied, be counted as a benefit. But if, for reasons which were not immoral (and it was part of the problem to decide which were and which were not immoral), a neighborhood would be better satisfied to have a certain project located on a relatively high-priced site (one which would necessitate the building of a school, perhaps), how many extra dollars ought to be spent to satisfy the people of the neighborhood? The usual practice, which the staff and the commissioners, in accord with Public Housing Administration policy on economy, were accustomed to regard as "good business," did not ordinarily take account of either social benefits or social costs (i.e., benefits or costs the incidence of which was indiscriminate, so that those who benefited or lost could not be charged or compensated accordingly). But it might be that the usual business practice was not appropriate for a public agency, which presumably was under an obligation to attach some weight to everyone's wishes, or even that the usual business practice was wrong and ought to be changed so that it would take account of social costs and benefits.[2]

If we do not have agreed criteria for the location of public housing, neither do we have them for the coordination of policies on national security, where opinions on how to deal with the U.S.S.R. are bitterly opposed; nor do we have agreed criteria on policy toward metropolitan areas, where some people see large and growing cities as growing blights and others see them as indispensable cultural centers; nor on policies toward income security and income shares, where a traditional cleavage between elitists and equalitarians persists. To be sure, in these and other fields some decisions with respect to the relations among policies are resolvable by the application of widely accepted criteria; we point out only that large questions remain that cannot be so resolved.

Since, in some eyes, politics is a process for resolving, through the interplay of power, those questions that do not lend themselves to intellectual resolution, it is surprising that the claim that central coordination is reasoned coordination is so widely made. Perhaps the claim is after all intended as a more modest one. It might be claimed that granted the absence of generally acceptable criteria, at least the central coordinator can find criteria satisfactory to himself and of a kind that he is willing to defend in public discussion. But then, we have seen, the claim that coordination is reasoned turns into a claim that it is subject to criteria unacceptable to many decision makers and citizens. That kind of a reasoned coordination takes on, we have seen, an arbitrary quality. Or it might be claimed that given social disagreement on criteria, the central coordinator takes as criteria the respective power in the society of the persons, groups, and agencies who differ on criteria. That is, he coordinates by asking himself what is politically feasible. If so, again an arbitrary element has been introduced into central coordination since power, not reason, actually dictates the coordination decision.

There are of course those who, in appraising coordination, are willing to make the appraisal by their own criteria. They may draw their standards from mere postulation, from Divine inspiration, or from nature; but whatever the origins, they are willing to use them in confidence despite disagreement within the society on criteria. For these people the problem is then to estimate the likelihood that a central coordinator will employ the criteria they advocate and, similarly, to estimate the likelihood that partisan adjustment will achieve such a pattern of policies as will accord with their criteria. In this study we make no such estimates for them; our method is instead only to throw light on mutual adjustment and centrality in order to facilitate their estimates.

In the light of the questions we have raised about the validity of the claim that central coordination is reasoned rather than arbitrary, let us look again at partisan mutual adjustment. That it achieves arbitrary rather than reasoned coordination is no longer a strong ground for doubting its efficacy. For we now see that, to take the above possibilities in reverse order, the central coordinator who asks what is politically feasible is permitting the same forces to work on coordination that would work themselves out in partisan mutual adjustment. We also see that the central coordinator who guides his decision by his own private criteria is arbitrary in the same sense that any partisan with his own partisan criteria is. And we see, fundamentally, that all coordination must be arbitrary and unreasoned in that area of adjustment of decisions to one another for which acceptable criteria are lacking. *There exists some irreducible area for decision making for which reason runs out, exhausts itself, for lack of criteria; and in that area central coordination has to be arbitrary in the same sense that partisan mutual adjustment is.*

Degrees and Kinds of Arbitrariness

To all this it may be objected that we have missed a more modest claim with respect to the reasoned quality of central coordination. It might be claimed that even if an arbitrary element is introduced whenever agreed criteria are lacking, the element is less arbitrary than in partisan mutual adjustment. For, it will be argued, the criteria to which the coordinator turns will be more generally defensible, more widely endorsed, than the relatively narrowly conceived criteria employed by each participant in partisan mutual adjustment. Moreover, the criteria employed in central coordination will be more or less consistently employed, while in partisan mutual adjustment decisions reached will not be defensible consistently in the light of any given criteria.

Two principal issues are raised here. One is whether the central coordinator will employ more widely endorsed, more generally acceptable criteria, than will mutual adjusters. This we propose to investigate in later chapters. The other issue is whether central coordination is consistent in its arbitrariness where partisan mutual adjustment is not. This we will explore in the next chapter, to determine whether the allegation is true and whether, if true, it is a merit of centrality.

Leaving aside these two issues, are there any other reasons for preferring the arbitrariness of centrality to that of partisan mutual adjustment? In some forms of partisan mutual adjustment the questions of whether the criteria of the participants are narrow or broad and are foolishly or wisely chosen and applied are of little concern to our evaluation of the process; this is so even if, in contrast, a central coordinator's choice and application of his criteria matters a great deal. In some forms of mutual adjustment the kind of arbitrariness we have been discussing is no objection at all to partisan mutual adjustment, although it remains an objection to central coordination. Specifically in partisan discussion and in compensation, whether unilateral or symmetric, we can say of the state of affairs that results that regardless of the participants' criteria, the participants are all satisfied by the results. They have voluntarily chosen their respective decisions because of the benefits of doing so. If Y responds to X, it is because he has, through partisan discussion, now perceived the advantages of doing so or because, through compensation, he receives a new benefit adequate to induce him to do so. One cannot object to these processes on the ground that the resolution of the conflict is dictated by an arbitrarily chosen criterion.

Where coordination cannot wholly satisfy all parties, where all or some must be deprived to some extent, the interaction of negotiation is not demonstrably a more arbitrary settlement process than the imposition of a solution by a central coordinator who has arbitrarily chosen to employ this criterion instead of that one. The subtlety of negotiation, the tentativeness of each move, the sequence of offer, withdrawal, amended offer, the necessity for winning consent—all these features of negotiation, familiar to everyone, leave no *a priori* ground for holding negotiation more arbitrary than central coordination. To be sure, there are all kinds of negotiation, and negotiation with Fidel Castro for the release of Cuban prisoners of war appears to have promised a quite arbitrary solution in that the stakes were too high to permit a prolonged and subtle adjustment of interests through move and countermove. Even here, however, a centrally coordinated adjustment of United States–Cuban conflicts would, if conceivable, be no less arbitrary, depending on who the central authority turned out to be and who the appraiser was. In any case negotiation, like other instruments of social control, can itself be controlled to a degree. Participants can be restricted, for example, to relatively soft instead of murderous threats; and, in fact, in most political negotiation the counters that can be employed are rigorously constrained both by moral agreement and by law.

On other forms of partisan mutual adjustment, the question of whether their arbitrariness is or is not in some sense preferable to that of central coordination will turn on the issue of how, in the various methods, weights are assigned to various conflicting values; this is an investigation, we have said, which will be undertaken later. It is not at all clear that the openness of a system of partisan mutual adjustment, in which all interested parties have opportunities to affect the pattern of decisions, is not a considerable merit of the system, when it is contrasted to coordination by criteria selected by a central coordinator and not agreed to by all. His chosen criteria may give play to fewer interests than would partisan mutual adjustment.

A Paradox

Finally, as a last point on the claim that central coordination is reasoned, we come to a paradox. In cases in which central coordination can in fact be reasoned (where there are agreed and workable criteria), then it need not after all be central. Consider the case in which criteria are available, are workable in that they do not ask for intellectual competence or information beyond that available, and if applied are capable of determining the correct coordinating decision. Under these circumstances central coordination is at its best. At the same time, under these circumstances, any competent mind will be brought by application of the criteria to the same decision as would be reached by any other competent mind employing the same criteria. Hence, in principle, ten independent coordinators are as satisfactory as one, or as nine subject to coordination by one. Thus when the situation is most conducive to successful centrality, centrality is dispensable.

No one would pretend that these hypothetical circumstances can be closely approximated; but the case makes the point that these elements—agreed goals, manageable amounts of information, and intellectual competence—in themselves achieve coordination without centrality. Insofar as they do not—that is, insofar as they leave room for disagreement among coordinators as to the correct decisions to be made—so also do they call into question the competence of any coordinator to exercise the power of central coordination.

One can imagine decision situations on a continuum. At one end are those situations in which intellectual competence is high relative to the difficulty of the problem; at the other end are those in which it is low. As we move to the competence pole correct decisions are possible but do not require a central coordinator. Toward the other end central coordination would appear to be required for fear that incompetent decision makers do not each reach the correct decisions. But incompetence guarantees that no central coordinator will reach them either.

Again, therefore, there are serious grounds for doubting the validity of the claim that a merit of central coordination is that it is necessary to produce reasoned coordination. Having argued that a central coordinator does not necessarily produce it, we have now added that if he *were* capable of doing so, noncentral coordinators could do so as well. This last point is, again, not a positive argument for partisan mutual adjustment; it only, again, seriously undermines a common claim for central coordination. Reason, it turns out, is a possible substitute for central coordination, not always an implement of it.

CONSISTENCY

THE SECOND PAIR OF CLAIMS
made for central coordination follow closely on those claims discussed in the two preceding chapters. They were, as stated in
Chapter 11, that in central coordination:

3. Decisions or policies to be coordinated are at least made more
   or less consistent with one another.
4. Centrality imparts a consistent bias or pattern to the decisions of
   the coordinator so that coordination in one situation or at one
   time does not produce results quite at odds with those in other
   situations and at other times.

In these respects partisan mutual adjustment might be expected
to differ from centrality.

Consistency among Decisions To Be Coordinated

The claim to consistency on behalf of central coordination can
be put in more than one way. Let us begin with the claim in a
strong form, that is, a form in which consistency is defined ambi-

tiously. Not too ambitiously, however, for "consistent" is sometimes defined to be equivalent to "coordinate" so that to ask
whether decisions are consistent is to ask whether they are coordinated. Clearly, this will not do; we do not intend to finish the book
in this one chapter.

One naive view of inconsistency—hence, by inference, of consistency—is to be immediately rejected as troublesome. One hears,
for example, that a government is inconsistent (and hence foolish)
if, on one hand, it encourages crop restriction and, on the other
hand, undertakes expensive projects for reclaiming productive soil
from wasteland; or if it opens up new auto routes from the suburbs
at the same time that it prohibits street parking downtown; or if it
proposes central governmental financial aid to local schools
whether they are integrated or not, while using troops to enforce
integration. These are inconsistent policies only in the trivial sense
that in each of these cases one can think of a value toward which
one of any two paired policies advances while the other of the
pair is indifferent or opposed. By such a test, however, any two
policies can always be shown to be inconsistent, for such a value can
always be found.

In the light of a number of relevant values, rather than only
one, and even in the light of most single values, such pairs of
policies turn out to be quite consistent. It is easy to find a combination of short- and long-range objectives, and of objectives with
respect to growth as well as to distribution of income, that make
crop restriction and acreage increases consistent by any ordinary
meaning of the term. It is even easier to reconcile new auto routes
with parking restrictions; it can even be done by appealing to a
single value—movement of traffic. And, for the third example, a
consistent (by any reasonable standard) attack on integration does
not require that every governmental policy be explicit and direct in
serving that end.

Rejecting the naive concept, we shall choose to mean by consistency among decisions the following: *In a set decisions are
consistent with one another if there is no way to alter any deci-
sion(s) in such a way as to benefit at least one person and harm
no one.*

Such a definition asks of a set of decisions whether it constitutes a Pareto optimum,* and we can explain why it is useful to define consistency in this way.¹ There is an obvious and identifiable flaw in the relations of decisions to each other if the decisions impose adversely on some values without benefit to any other values. Where they impose adversely but at benefit to other values we cannot always say whether the imposition is wise or foolish, regrettable or desirable; but where the imposition is for no one's benefit almost everyone will deplore it. We think that here, at least, is a clear cut case in which decisions get in each other's way. Hence, even if we cannot specify what relations should hold among policies where advancing one value is to retard another, we can at least specify that we want all possible gains that are costless to be reaped, hence all adjustments in coordination to be made that benefit some persons without harming others.

This is, of course, only one useful concept of consistency. But it is worth investigating as a claim on behalf of central coordination. If it is claimed that centrality achieves consistency as just defined, what is being alleged is that even if central coordination cannot always provide reasoned coordination, at least in those cases in which it is possible to advance some interests without retarding others, it will do so with some significant frequency. We can put the claim in another way that shows its relation to the previously discussed claim: Where criteria are lacking for identifying the best set of relations to be arranged among decisions, central coordination will at least arrange decisions so as to avoid unnecessary losses of values, losses that can be avoided without raising any question of conflicting criteria.

It is, again, an empirical question how far a central coordinator can go in discovering and remedying inconsistencies so defined. Again, the argument of Chapter 9 is relevant; to remedy these inconsistencies requires synoptic capacities that can easily run beyond those that men possess. And what we have said about the first claim on behalf of centrality—that coordinators can take an overview of all repercussions among policies—applies here. Remedying inconsistencies requires just that kind of overview we questioned above, even if it does not require solving the criteria

---

* A state of affairs A represents a Pareto optimum for a set of people if it is impossible to identify another state of affairs B such that change from A to B would benefit at least one person in the set and injure no one.

problem. To the extent that the first claim is weak, so also is this one.

By contrast, in partisan mutual adjustment some strong tendencies toward Pareto optima are present in pairs of decisions or other sets of decisions. In his relations with some Y's every X is motivated by his own interests to ask whether there is a possibility of mutual gain, or at least gain to X without loss to Y. And compensation as a form of partisan mutual adjustment opens up the possibility that many situations not immediately promising can be made so. Where X wishes to make a decision that requires Y's assistance and that decision is not of advantage to Y, compensation opens up the possibility that he can make Y's cooperation advantageous to Y. The freedom of participants in partisan mutual adjustment to undertake partisan discussion, compensation, and negotiation sets in motion a never-ending and detailed, even if highly fragmented, search for possibilities of benefiting a multiplicity of Xs without disadvantage to a multiplicity of Ys. For what is negligible detail to a central coordinator is motivating self-interest to X.

Again, the analysis does not prove the superiority of mutual adjustment; it simply calls into question another specific claim to the superiority of centrality.

The question of how successfully partisan mutual adjustment exploits possibilities of making decision consistent with one another turns out, given the definition of consistency, to relate closely to the question of how the process promotes agreement. For a decision that helps at least one party and hurts no other is often the kind of decision that can command agreement. To raise the question as one of encouraging agreement rather than consistency is to see at once that partisan mutual adjustment encourages agreement in a number of specific ways that go beyond what central coordination can do. These will be explored in the next chapter.

Consistency in the Pattern of a Coordinator's Decisions

If the consistency claim, as so far put forth, is no stronger than the overview claim on behalf of central coordination, what of a more modest claim to consistency? Might it not be claimed as a merit of centrality that where it cannot achieve an overview, or where criteria are lacking, or where it cannot achieve a Pareto optimum, it at least applies a consistent pattern to coordination over time? In other words, will not the arbitrary elements introduced by the coordinator be relatively stable? Will not the coordinator be consistent with himself? Consider, for example, the coordination of public expenditures. Granted that an overview is impossible and that the allocation is not sufficiently determined by any agreed criteria, will it not be a merit of central coordination that a more or less consistent bias will govern coordinating decisions and that over time the bias will be relatively stable? A Budget Bureau preference for military over welfare expenditures will show itself in all Budget Bureau decisions; it will not randomly or whimsically appear in one decision or at one time and not in another decision or at another time.

Whether a central coordinator's value biases can, in this sense, stabilize decisions is an empirical question. Even in this limited sense consistency requires synoptic capacities that one can doubt that men possess. Even in this limited sense to show a consistent, effective preference in actual decisions for one value over another, one has to know when the value is at stake, which is more than we claimed for any strategic problem solver. One can be strongly committed to a given value yet quite fail to understand how various possible decisions can best protect or advance it. A pro-farmer bias among Congressmen does not produce policies necessarily in accordance with the bias. It has been repeatedly shown, for example, that farm security programs fail to assist many of the farm groups that the programs are intended to assist;[2] the complexities of crop control and price supports raise issues on which a steady pattern is no satisfactory guide at all. Relatively steady patterns in American foreign relations have been argued to have permitted, if not contributed to, "inconsistent" movements in policy.[3] A bias toward economy, or a steady hostility to the Soviet Union, does not necessarily stabilize policy or reconcile various aspects of it in ways that bear out the claim that consistent bias in values achieves a kind of consistent pressure on policies or decisions. We can say that the bias affects decision making profoundly, but the degree of its effect is problematic.

But all this is merely to express again the same kind of doubt about man's capacity that has already been shown to be generally significant for evaluating centrality. A more crucial point is that it is not at all clear that consistency through steady bias is desirable in decision making. That centrality brings the pressure of a steady bias to decisions might be admitted as an allegation about, but is not necessarily a valid claim on behalf of, centrality. For we have shown how even a single strategic decision maker takes account of values neglected in one decision by returning to the neglected aspects in subsequent remedial decisions in which he gives attention to the values earlier neglected. To attend to neglected consequences of earlier decisions it is essential that the decision maker be able to shift from preoccupation with one value to another. Consistency in evaluation is ideal in synopsis; but for strategic problem solvers consistency in evaluation, for all the reasons given in Chapter 9, would stultify the remedial character of decision making.

In showing how partisan mutual adjustment supports strategic decision making we have, in fact, pointed to the variety of values represented by the many participants in it as one of its chief merits. If, through partisan mutual adjustment, some values are given emphasis in some decisions, neglected values can only be taken account of by giving them—inconsistently, one might say—emphasis in other decisions simultaneously or subsequently taken.

Whether the shift in values from one decision to another or from one time to another, essential as shifts are in strategic decision making, takes a desirable form depends, of course, on how various values turn out to be weighted against certain others. Again we have come to a point that is to be deferred to later chapters. If, however, in those chapters it can be shown that partisan mutual adjustment achieves a satisfactory weighting of values, then the fact that those values are, from one decision to another, inconsistently regarded is no necessary objection to partisan mutual adjustment. If it is true that a consistent central bias applies a steady pressure along the lines of the bias, it will sometimes be an important point of criticism of central coordination.

We have put the argument in favor of an inconsistent bias in terms of the need for a strategic decision maker to shift his values from decision to decision and of the need for a multiplicity of decision makers to favor respectively a multiplicity of values. But we can put the argument just as well in terms of the central co-ordinator who cannot find agreed criteria. Where he cannot and must therefore be arbitrary in that he chooses criteria not agreed to by all, we should not want him always to make the same arbitrary choice; our reasons are, again, these developed in the exposition of the advantage of remedial, serial, and fragmented decision making.

To put the point very roughly, for complex problems both the strategic decision maker and the would-be synoptic decision maker without an agreed criteria will be deficient to a degree, will make decisions that are in some respect unsatisfactory. For any one such decision maker to be consistent he must be consistently wrong. He will have to be inconsistent to be self-corrective. For a group of such decision makers, taken together, to be consistent is, again, to be consistently wrong; they will have to be inconsistent to remedy each other's inadequacies. In 1714 Bernard Mandeville wrote in *The Fable of the Bees:*

> Yet while they alter'd thus their Laws,
> Still finding and correcting Flaws,
> They mended by Inconstancy
> Faults, which no Prudence could foresee.

The pursuit of consistency from one coordinating decision to another in central coordination often degenerates into the pursuit of some kind of superficial uniformity. Given limits on man's capacity and his consequent inability to know whether each in a series of complex decisions does in fact reinforce rather than conflict with the others in the series, the degeneration is not surprising. Among rationing staff units in the OPA during World War II coordination that might have resulted in bringing inferior practices up to the level of the best in OPA instead "became adulterated into a mere insistence on uniform procedures *per se.*" The causes of the adulteration were limits on competence as well as failures of motivation; limited competence and weak motivation both tempt co-ordinators to substitute a routine yea- and nay-saying for a more creative approach to consistency and coordination.[4]

Certainly, however, it will be countered, there must be some situations in which, for the sake of consistency in successive co-ordinating decisions, the need for a single central coordinator is apparent. To be sure, there are "apparent" cases, but they turn out to be only apparent. Consider, for example, a series of expenditure decisions out of a finite budget. It would appear that simply to avoid exhausting the budget each successive decision has to be consistent with each preceding and with each following decision in the specific sense that taken together they must not go beyond what is in the budget—a clear case, it would seem, for centrality. In fact, some would argue, in such a case all the expenditure decisions should be taken simultaneously as part of a planned allocation of the budget. Otherwise they will either underutilize or overcommit the budget. Actually the allocations can in many circumstances be quite satisfactorily made through partisan mutual adjustment in the absence of central coordination. Various combinations of some of the following factors would make it possible: the partisan decision makers, although without any satisfactory agreed criteria, are nevertheless not *extremely* different in their preferred allocations; there is from time to time an additional inflow into the available funds; the inflows are themselves subject to decision either through the same decision makers who allocate or through others who take some account of what the allocators are doing; or all partisan decision makers directly or indirectly control or respond to each other, even if only through partisan discussion.

These conditions, it can be noted, hold for governmental budgetary decisions. They account for the fact that despite fragmentation of decision making and partisan mutual adjustment in the federal budgetary process, expenditures match—that is, are consistent with—revenues no less than would be expected through central coordination. Where they do not correspond the discrepancy is not an accident of miscalculation, except to the degree that neither revenues or expenditures can be exactly predicted and controlled for the budgetary period no matter what the method of decision making, but is symptomatic of reluctance to tax, of reluctance to curb expenditures, or of deliberate imbalance for controlling employment and the price level.

An Example

Some of the points made about both kinds of consistency can be illustrated in their relations to each other. In OPA during World War II a national gasoline eligibility committee was established to develop rules for eligibility for extra gasoline rations, on which rules further eligibility rules for automobiles and tires were to follow.[5] The committee therefore served to coordinate a number of "lower" decisions on gasoline as well as high level decisions on autos, tires, and gasoline. It was composed of one representative each from the tire, automobile, and gasoline rationing branches and one attorney from each of these branches. It appears to have been a committee of high quality with respect to training, intellectual competence, and devotion to the public interest; and it was extremely reluctant to make concessions to special interests. Its central authority with respect to eligibility rules was great; the upper level hierarchy of OPA almost never overruled it.

It achieved some kind of consistency, for in Thompson's study of it he was able to specify the value principles that appeared to guide its decisions, among which are these:

1. Where government is performing some function, private groups and individuals should not be encouraged to duplicate it. (The committee might have held that private activity is a useful supplement to governmental, or even that government should withdraw to the extent that private activity permits.)
2. Much voluntary activity regularly performed for religious organizations does not contribute to the public welfare sufficiently to justify special gasoline rations. (It might have held religious work in much higher regard.)
3. Activities whose purpose is maintenance of an organization do not sufficiently serve the public interest to justify special gasoline rations. (It might have held that maintenance work in an organization did or did not serve the public interest depending on the purpose of the organization.)
4. The most important activity in the public interest is actual physical production. (It might have held that because production

without distribution is impossible, distribution also is extremely important.)

5. Distribution, supervisory, and central management activities do not deserve special rations.
6. Electoral activities of candidates and voters deserve special rations. (It might have regarded them no higher than distributive, supervisory, and central activities.)
7. State and local governments are entitled to special rations.

The pattern of the committee's decisions is inevitably somewhat distorted in so brief a summary, but the summary is accurate in disclosing a distinct and "consistent" committee frame of mind. The parenthetical comments following some of the items simply point up, by contrast, the group's commitments.

For any group that achieves any impressive degree of consistency some such set of principles would arise. Another committee might have opted for an alternative position in each of the points specified, but for any consistent committee it presumably would be possible to derive a set of principles committing the group on such points as listed. The particular principles followed by this committee were by no means eccentric or obviously foolish. Considering the responsibility of the committee—to protect and apportion limited supplies of gasoline—some principles that would otherwise appear quite whimsical, such as those on religious activity, fall within the bounds of considered reasoning.

Yet these principles could easily become intolerable. We can illustrate specific dangerous deficiencies in the committee's thinking. Its distinction, for example, between productive and nonproductive activities, with actual physical production on one side, and distribution, supervision, and central functions on the other, is a distinction long rendered obsolete by economists, who can easily show, on one hand, that physical production often cannot in concept be usefully separated from these other activities (Is a worker who runs a machine by supervising it engaging in physical production or supervision?) and, on the other hand, that where it can be separated, physical production is not necessarily more essential to getting products into users' hands than are the other activities with which it is contrasted. The committee's distinction, serviceable roughly for its work, is a naive distinction and easily could have been extremely damaging to the war effort.

The biases that governed the work of this particular agency were rendered relatively harmless, but not because they were of extremely limited application, for they were in fact of wide application. The committee on eligibility enjoyed an assignment of function that made its decisions consequential for the encouragement and discouragement of almost every kind of activity in the society. The committee's values were made tolerable because they were violated elsewhere and sometimes even within the committee's jurisdiction. For all its apparent authority as central coordinator, the committee was inevitably caught up in a process of partisan mutual adjustment through which values contrary to its own influenced its decisions. It was not often formally overruled, but private groups and other public agencies often were successful in influencing the formulation of eligibility rules. Moreover, the values neglected by the committee, as the committee itself sometimes observed, were allowed to influence decisions of other agencies so that, say, the distribution of seed, to which the committee made no concession, became the object of a special program in the Department of Agriculture. In short, the committee's "consistency" was tolerable only because decisions of the committee and of other agencies were not bound by the committee's values.

Insofar as the eligibility rules, which were influenced by values held by private groups and other agencies, did not follow the committee's own independent wishes were not, of course, consistent in the committee's eyes. (This illustrates the allegation that in the eyes of a putative central coordinator, decisions cannot achieve consistency unless the coordinator's power excludes the power of all others.) An observer, however, might believe that the influences brought to bear on the eligibility rules, because of the committee's inevitable participation in partisan mutual adjustment, made for more rather than less consistency in a larger sense. It also might be argued that decisions as a whole gained in consistency because the values neglected by the committee's rules were looked after by the Department of Agriculture and by many other agencies and decision makers.

Clearly, if we consider that consistency calls for such a set of policies as constitute a Pareto optimum, it is not at all obvious that decisions governed by the committee's principles alone would be more consistent than the decisions that actually emerged. That is to say, given the character of the committee's thinking there is no ground at all for arguing a loss of consistency, because the committee is forced in mutual adjustment to compromise its principles or because what the committee denies is granted elsewhere in the governmental system. One would assume an enormous burden of proof, with the evidence of the listed values against one, to argue that the superficial consistency of the committee's principles constituted a guide to policies that achieved a Pareto optimum.

One cannot even feel confident that if the listed principles were unbrokenly applied, if that were possible, that this consistency would in fact serve the principles themselves. For example, it is quite possible—and an economist would say highly probable—that downgrading distribution to the degree desired by the committee would in fact hamper physical production, if only because physical production depends on efficient distribution of inputs to the producer. Thus an unbroken application would not necessarily represent, from one committee decision to another, a consistent pursuit of the listed values.

Is there any virtue at all in the superficial kind of consistency that the listed values represent? In the allocation of gasoline rations it might be argued that equity requires a kind of decision making that looks uniform to those who apply for rations, similar applicants receiving similar rations. No doubt "equal treatment" is a powerful constraint on rule making, but a variety of principles were available by which applications for allocations could have been "equally" treated,[6] from which fact it seems clear that consistency as represented in the principles is not necessary for "equal treatment."

The point is not an obvious one, however. Suppose the committee receives, as it did, a request for special rations for social workers instructing the blind. It could, in its pursuit of an applicable rule, classify the application as one for social workers, or for teachers, or for the blind. If it has three degrees of leniency, one for each of these groups, it can easily justify any one of three different decisions under an "equal treatment" constraint. Equal treatment, it therefore appears, is not a constraint that imposes a simple unambiguous obligation on decision makers; instead it merely imposes on them the requirement that the decision be justified in relation to some acceptable classification and rule. To so justify a decision does not require the kind of consistency represented in the listed values and can be accomplished in the face of inconsistency in the application of such values.

What the example suggests then, is that the claim that central coordination achieves consistency is dubious on all the points developed earlier. There is evidence of at least superficial consistency in the list of governing values of the committee. But that it constitutes either consistency in the form of a Pareto optimum or consistency from one coordinating decision to another in pursuit of the committee's values is not at all evident. The superficial consistency the committee may have achieved is not to be desired, and the more valuable kind of consistency is not shown to follow from the pursuit of the superficial. The principal merit of the example is that it makes clear what an enormous burden of proof must be assumed if significant consistency claims are to be made for central coordination. It also, however, illustrates the advantage of a decision system in which other decision makers can attend to values neglected by any one decision maker.

Again, then, we see that, just as in our discussion of the claim for overview and for reasoned coordination, the consistency claim is invalid in many circumstances and that partisan mutual adjustment possess merits that are illuminated by the very considerations that question the claims for centrality.

Chapter
14

SOCIAL AGREEMENT

THE IMMEDIATELY PRECEDING chapters force us into an investigation of how conflicting values are weighed against, or otherwise reconciled with, each other in partisan mutual adjustment, for at various points the weighing of conflicting values was critical to the comparison of central co-ordination with partisan mutual adjustment. One would like to establish criteria for the appropriate, proper, wise, reasonable, or correct weighing of conflicting values, then proceed efficiently to establish the respects in which partisan mutual adjustment meets or fails to meet the criteria. But we do not have adequate applicable criteria.

This chapter and several of those following will take up a necessarily more roundabout investigation of the terms on which values are reconciled in mutual adjustment. As a first step we take account in this chapter of the ways in which partisan mutual adjustment encourages social agreement on values. Rather than weigh values, rather then sacrifice one value to another, partisan mutual adjustment sometimes stimulates a reconsideration of values that moves decision makers toward agreement. It is not only a process for resolving conflict among given values, but it also forms values.

There is, of course, one special sense in which, at least in a more or less democratic government, partisan mutual adjustment achieves coordination through agreement in much the same way as does centrality. In both the participants ordinarily shrink from highly coercive control devices; hence, in a sense, almost every decision is an agreed one. Even if a latent threat of force lies behind the use of governmental authority—even if, as some conceive of it, the state has a monopoly of violence—the ordinary course of coordination achieves its effects with little coercion. A legislator, an executive, or an agency ordinarily achieves effects, in large part, through authority which is conceded and in that sense agreed upon. Moreover nongovernmental participants in partisan mutual adjustment—interest-group leaders and party leaders—are ordinarily prohibited from highly coercive measures. To be sure they will maneuver to have governmental adversaries removed from their positions or weakened in their capacity to act, and they will misrepresent themselves and their rivals in appealing to citizens—in these and other ways giving evidence that politics is "rough." Still, their partisan mutual adjustment is not obviously any more coercive than is central coordination; and because they ordinarily play by rules that prohibit highly coercive practices like assassination and blackmail, they, like central coordinators, depend in at least this restricted sense on social agreement rather than coercion.*

* "Coercion" is, to be sure, difficult to define in ways useful for the purposes for which it is ordinarily introduced into discussion. We shall not pursue either a definition or further reference to the term. If our interest in partisan mutual adjustment were the traditional interest in fragmented adjustment processes as a possible guarantee against tyranny, we could not escape an exhaustive investigation of the role of coercion in central and noncentral systems. But, as the introductory chapter tried to make clear, we depart in this book from a long established inquiry that asks

All that is, however, not much more than a digression. The main discussion is of the role of partisan mutual adjustment in inducing social agreement other than on noncoercive rules of the game. A number of propositions will specify just how the role is played. They all explain how partisan mutual adjustment achieves an aggregation or reconciliation of interests, preferences, or values, not by sacrificing, to some degree, one or more of the conflicting values to others, but by modifying values, interests, or preferences, and by dropping troublesome values and formulating new ones, so that agreement replaces conflict to an important degree. Certain common allegations about how noncentral processes encourage disagreement, hence exacerbate lasting conflict, will be considered in a later chapter.

(1) *Many value conflicts that in central systems would constitute barriers to reaching agreed decisions do not constitute barriers in partisan mutual adjustment.*

In purely central coordination the coordinator, having exclusive power over the decision to be made, can achieve whatever decision he wishes by fiat. But if we ask under what conditions he can find his way to a decision that all interested parties will agree to rather than simply accept by fiat, then by one common conception of central coordination he can do so only if he can find agreed criteria in the light of which he can then choose an acceptable decision. In such a view, which makes a synoptic decision maker of the coordinator, decisions are always tested against criteria; and only if there are agreed criteria will there be agreement on the decision.

In partisan mutual adjustment, on the other hand, participants

---

whether fragmented power is an effective way to guard the guardians, protect liberty or democracy, obstruct tyranny, make power responsible—these are a few terms that give the flavor of the older inquiry to which the concept of coercion is central. We ask questions that respond to another kind of concern: Is fragmentation a good way to make decisions? to calculate and weigh alternative courses of action? to achieve rationality in some sense? to avoid foolish decisions? For our questions we can largely dispense with the concept of coercion, although we occasionally refer concretely to aspects of decision making of one kind or another that would bear on a judgment of its coerciveness if such a judgment were to be attempted.

are free to look for agreement on whatever terms they can find it. For example, a decision maker engaged in partisan discussion will cast his appeals to adversaries in terms of the adversaries' own criteria rather than in terms of criteria he himself holds. Bargainers, too, look for any method of striking a bargain, and they do not cripple themselves by asking for prior agreement on criteria. For another example, a calculating adapter looks for a decision suitable to himself that does not promise to stir up retaliation from another decision maker whose adverse responses he wishes to minimize; he does not bother to ask himself whether his own criteria for a decision are shared or not, and in fact he assumes they are not. One might suppose that unilateral manipulation achieves coordination without agreement, that is, coordination forced on Y by X. But this is not necessarily so; X may win the agreement of Y by compensation, by prior decision, or by other means that will result in what by any ordinary standard would be called an agreed outcome. Thus where conflicts over criteria are a barrier to social agreement on decisions in central coordination, they are not so in partisan mutual adjustment.

Suppose, however, the central decision maker is not synoptic to the degree just assumed. Suppose, on the contrary, that he simply sets for himself the task of discovering a decision that will command agreement among the interested parties, even if they do not agree on criteria. (It has to be said in that case that he does not provide the kind of central coordination that can claim the merits alleged in the preceding chapters. If he simply asks of a decision that it be agreed to, he cannot claim to have made a principled decision, nor a carefully researched decision, nor one that has taken account of all implications.) If so, the significant difference between partisan mutual adjustment and centrality with respect to finding agreement on decisions or outcomes in the face of conflict over criteria values will turn on the likelihood that the central coordinator can or cannot in fact find an agreed decision. To that question, the following propositions are addressed.

(2) *Participants in partisan mutual adjustment have stronger motives than do central coordinators to find an agreed decision or outcome.*

In Chapter 7 it was explained that the defining characteristics of a central coordinator were his participation in all the decisions in a given set and his large power relative to any other decision maker participating in that set of decisions. It is the power of a central coordinator that enables him to dispense with agreement (and sometimes he is given his powers for the very purpose of enabling him to dispense with it, where agreement is thought to be impossible or too costly to achieve). By contrast, it is the relative lack of dominating power that turns participants in partisan mutual adjustment to seeking agreement on decisions or outcomes. They do not always seek it, for often a participant will be able to impose his wishes on another participant despite the latter's disagreement. But where a purely central coordinator never need depend on agreement to make his wishes effective, and where, in actual fact, a central coordinator must rely on agreement only to the extent that his decision can be influenced by others, no partisan can well afford to fail to explore the possibilities of winning by agreement; and some partisans can achieve what they want only by agreement.

The ubiquity of mutual adjustment indicates that the motivation to find agreement is not undermined by evidence of conflict, evidence that partisans might be expected to take as proof that agreement is impossible. It appears that, in the first place, a partisan comes to understand that much of the conflict he observes is over criteria values and is not, for reasons already given, a barrier to his reaching agreement with other participants on decisions and outcomes. Thus, as we saw, high level value conflict between conservatives and liberals has not precluded their agreeing in Congressional negotiation to extend Social Security benefits. Secondly, the flexibility of proposal, and of offer and counteroffer in, say, bargaining, suggests that participants in mutual adjustment realize that there are no bedrock social preferences or social values; every value held is a product of and is continually reconsidered in the light of existing circumstances, especially those that bear on the probability of our satisfying our preferences. In any case a participant knows that both he and other participants will change their views in the course of mutual adjustment. Thirdly, he realizes that insofar as men have stable inescapable needs, they can sometimes satisfy them through any one of a variety of instrumental values. On this count he is exploratory; and he counts on other participants to be so, even where conflict is sharp and acute on some existing instrumentality. Fourth, a participant in any decision process as fast moving as partisan mutual adjustment is quick to recognize his own fallibility and is reasonably confident that others will confess theirs.[1]

A further point on motivation of mutual adjusters to find agreement is frankly a hypothesis. It is that central coordinators see coordination as calling for compromise where mutual adjusters see it as calling for what Mary Parket Follett called "integration."[2] A central coordinator may be tempted, by his similarity to a judge or arbitrator, to see his role as achieving a fair allocation of values in dispute. He may easily fall into the habit of believing that what one party gains another must lose, a fallacy that plagued economic thinking until Adam Smith made it abundantly clear that for many transactions all parties can gain. The partisan adjuster, on the other hand, is often powerfully motivated by self-interest to find an outcome in which he gains, and he is often quick to recognize that other participants are driven by the same hope. Hence he is disposed, by a habit of mind, to investigate the possibility of a solution to everyone's advantage, which is Follett's "integrated" solution. At least he tries, as we have already seen, a solution which is to the advantage of some and a loss to none, that is, a Pareto optimum.

To see possibilities for gain without loss the problem at hand often needs to be fundamentally restructured. As long as one conceives of the decision problem in an unchanging way, he is not stimulated to discover new reconciliations of interests. It is, of course, a characteristic of partisan mutual adjustment that what to a synoptic central coordinator would appear to be one problem of coordination takes a variety of forms in the eyes of partisans, none of whom play a central coordinating role. The variety of views taken on a problem sometimes sets the stage for a surprising alteration of the problem that opens the way to a solution, as we noted in discussing the reconstructive character of strategic problem solving in Chapter 9.

(3) The need for allies is an especially powerful motivation toward agreement in partisan mutual adjustment.

Until, in the theory of games, the *n*-person game stimulated an interest in coalitions the study and theory of bargaining, as though excessively influenced by the observation of labor–management bargaining, were preoccupied with two-party bargaining and negotiation. Where bargaining or negotiation is multilateral, especially where the number participating rises into the dozens or hundreds, the process departs far from the traditionally investigated forms. Where, in two-party negotiation, a decision maker X is occupied with resolving his conflict with Y, the possibilities of multiparty negotiation will turn X to a search for other like-minded or potentially like-minded decision makers. In multiparty bargaining one may then spend very little time in actual bargaining. One's major effort goes into the search for allies; and, once won, their presence as allies may quickly bring an end to bargaining or greatly constrain its scope. Similarly, X's desire to manipulate Y when he has no direct means to do so will turn X's attention to the pursuit of allies through whose direct controls over Y he can indirectly manipulate Y.

In governmental decision making it is always possible to find a third party interested in any given issue, and a fourth, a fifth, and so on. As the illustrations scattered through previous chapters have shown, on any given issue partisan mutual adjustment is typically participated in by many decision makers. Thus the search for allies is a fundamental part of partisan mutual adjustment.

In at least two ways the search is consequential for the agreement it achieves. First, decision makers are alerted to the possibility of finding other decision makers with whom they have some interests in common; they develop habits of seeking them out, so much so that decision makers look for permanent allies as a general strategy and even before they face a particular decision. They of course also look for allies that will join them on particular issues if not generally.

Secondly, however, the value of allies is such as to drive decision makers to reconsider their own interests or demands, to see whether there is some possibility of altering them in ways that lose less than will be gained by the ally attracted. It might be thought that in this respect they do no more than has already been attributed to them when we spoke of their motivation generally to find points of agreement with those with whom they appear to be in conflict; but we are in fact adding something. Not only do they look for points of agreement with those with whom they appear to be in conflict, but also they look for points of agreement (and reconsider their own demands to facilitate that agreement) with those with whom they have heretofore not been in touch. That is to say, their search for allies motivates them to explore very widely for points of agreement rather than limit themselves to finding agreement with those with whom they are in conflict.

Now it might be argued that no coordination is accomplished by establishing agreement between an X and a Y that were formerly neither in conflict nor agreement. Their former relationship posed no problem of malcoordination; their new agreement solves no such problem. The objection misses the role of the search for allies in (a) maintaining a conciliatory disposition on the part of decision makers; (b) establishing points of agreement among those not in conflict so that when and if they do come into conflict it is easily resolved or aborted; and (c) directing the energies of decision makers to exploring, as a generally useful strategy, interests they share with other decision makers. In these three respects the search for points of agreement, even when pursued with respect to decision makers with whom one has no conflict, reduces the possibility that conflict emerges and sets the stage for resolving the conflict by agreement if and when it arises.

Quite aside from the resolution by agreement of any conflict at hand, forming alliances achieves, in short, an expansion of each decision maker's concern, which contributes to agreement through, in the words of David Truman, "significant 'educative' and unifying effects throughout the political system." He goes on to say, "A group in need of alliances may have to accommodate as heterogeneous a collection of demands as does a political party."[3] Although Truman speaks only of interest groups, the same is true for all participants in mutual adjustment.

That building alliances makes a fundamental contribution to social agreement is now so familiar a point that it need not be elaborated further. But how are alliances formed? Negotiation is a commonplace device, for one. We have already referred, for another, to the role of prior decision in positioning decision makers so that their decision becomes an attractive point of agreement to other decision makers, as in the example from Chapter 8 of the dozens of groups who were attracted by prior decision of the Indian Commissioner on reorganization of the Bureau's work. Prior decision and its cousin, tacit bargaining, account for the formation of more wide-ranging alliances than negotiation can attend to. Deferential and calculated adaptation, as well as reciprocity, can also found alliances.

To be sure not all alliances are characterized by agreement among their members, for some may be built on manipulation of Y's by X's that leave the Y's prisoners rather than agreed members of the coalition. But this possibility does not gainsay the all-pervasive effect of the search for allies on the discovery—and actual invention, through reconsideration of prospects—of points of agreement.

(4) Agreement is also encouraged by the moderation imposed on demands in partisan mutual adjustment, by reason of the tasks and other responsibilities attached to making a demand.

In purely central coordination in which, by definition all decision-making power with respect to reconciliation of decisions is in the hands of one decision maker, the decision makers whose decisions are to be reconciled can make any demands on other decision makers they wish with little cost to themselves. They need not face up to the implications of their demands for others. It is the central coordinator's responsibility to make their demands effective if he rules in their favor; and it is his responsibility to consider implications for others.

By contrast, to make a demand in partisan mutual adjustment is to expend energy in winning what one asks for. The partisan decision maker does not present a case or file a claim; he typically makes his claim on another decision maker in the form of an attempt to manipulate the other decision maker. No one but himself or the allies he can arrange can make his demands effective; and it is costly in time, energy, and other resources to make them so. Moreover, since the costs of making his demands effective will depend on the other decision maker's resistance or other reaction, he cannot ignore the implications of a demand on any other decision maker on whom he makes it. Hence a participant in partisan mutual adjustment will, out of consideration of costs to himself, often carefully consider any demands he makes on another decision maker.

In the coordination of the work of the Recruiting and Manning Organization of the War Shipping Administration, to which we referred in Chapter 8, it may be remembered that the head of RMO spoke of desiring to transfer to his organization both the training and the licensing and inspection functions of the Coast Guard. We see how a point of conflict is dissipated by an estimate of the costs of attaining the objective. On the question of the training function,

. . . our natural allies were the maritime unions, the state maritime academies themselves, and the ship operators, all of whom might be expected to favor a civilian administration. . . .

As for the licensing and inspection functions,

Estimating the strength of our opponent, however, it did not seem that we could be successful in this and so, rather than fail on two fronts for lack of concentration, we worked on the transfer of the training program alone. . . .[4]

It might be argued that unconstrained demands put on each other by subordinates to a central coordinator do not undermine social agreement because they are finally reconciled by the centralist. Indeed they are, by definition, reconciled. But they are reconciled by fiat, not by agreement. And their reconciliation is consistent with continued lack of constraint in making demands. That is, in central coordination the final reconciliation is not part of a process that itself breeds dispositions to agree. By contrast, because of the caution with which demands are put in mutual adjustment, agreement is often encouraged. Real-world decision makers do not of course act so cavalierly as here described because they are in fact never highly centralized.

As with many of the attributes of partisan mutual adjustment, a contribution to agreement made by moderation of demands is common but not inevitable. Depending on circumstances, some of which are subject to systematic control and some not, this feature of the process will be present or absent. Moreover, there are some circumstances in which this attribute would be deplored, at least in some circles. In a situation in which decision-making processes were thought to be biased excessively toward preserving a status quo one might wish for unrestrained demands, for demands made without calculation of their costs to the demander and without consideration of their implications. Even in such a case, of course, one might, on the contrary, believe that action still required conciliation rather than unconstrained demands.

(5) *Because, in partisan mutual adjustment, decisions or outcomes of adjustment are tentative and can easily be altered, participants will agree where otherwise they would not.*

As we have seen partisan mutual adjustment is a serial and remedial policy-making procedure, and participants recognize it to be so. Hence any given state of affairs or combination of policies is viewed as only temporary. Features of the situation that would otherwise be undesirable, threatening, or even intolerable to some participants will often be accepted without alarm in the expectation that the features can be removed. We have said before, of course, that any given decision may completely ignore certain values, it being understood by participants that other decisions will attend to the neglected values. Here we are adding that the whole constellation of decisions may be accepted at any time, even if they are faulty in the eyes of many people, because further steps in the sequence of policy moves are expected to bring alteration.

One cannot dismiss this feature of partisan mutual adjustment on the ground that if participants tolerate the undesirable today they will insist on a showdown tomorrow. The showdown may never come. As long as the policy-making situation is fluid, as it always is in partisan mutual adjustment, there will always be a tomorrow where inequities can be righted, except in the eyes of those who believe that the decision-making system is given to irremediable chronic biases against their preferences.

The acceptance of the temporary is not irrational. For any given dissatisfied participant, his expectations of improvement tomorrow may be well founded. Moreover, many participants satisfied by today's situation are uncertain about their own future preferences; they wish, in their own interest, to hold open certain possibilities for the future. If all situations are tentative, they, too, are better satisfied.

Even if what is today acceptable were constrained, as is not actually the case, by a unanimously agreed set of weights prevailing generally, the serial and remedial character of partisan mutual adjustment would give enormous leeway to agreement on social states. Suppose that there existed unanimous agreement in a society on the weights to be attached to various conflicting values; that the agreement was stable; that it did not specify weights hour by hour or even month by month, but instead the weights that should be achieved by the policies of a few years taken together. Suppose also that the existing social state at any time did not correspond to the agreed ideal. In that case, over a wide range, any of many social states existing at any given time would, even in the light of the restrictive ideal of weights, be equally acceptable provided only that within a few years adjustment could be made to "average out" the weights in such a way as to satisfy the unanimous agreement on the long run ideal.

In the literature of economic theory there has been a long dispute over whether a state of affairs, B, can be said to be superior to an earlier state of affairs, A, if, although those who gained from the move to B profit so greatly that they could fully compensate those who lost in the move for their losses and still enjoy a net gain from the move, the gainers do not, however, compensate the losers.[5] The question has been thought to be important partly because it is believed that actual compensation is rare. The fact is, however, that through mutual adjustment many new states of affairs disadvantageous to some participants are accepted, even pronounced desirable, because the disadvantaged count confidently on a still subsequent set of moves to achieve the effect of compensation for their losses.

Thus it appears that some businessmen accepted the prospect of Presidential intervention in business price policy after President Kennedy's intervention in steel pricing in 1962 because they anticipated that the President could be induced to offer them tax relief to compensate them for having reduced the ease with which they could raise prices. In any case President Kennedy was quick to offer such compensation.[6]

There is, of course, a limit to the degree to which the remedial and serial character of partisan mutual adjustment makes value aggregations acceptable where they would otherwise be rejected. For millions of American Negroes, for example, no conceivable remedial sequence of decisions and reweighings will, in their lifetimes, raise the value of racial equality to an acceptable level. Even in this case, however, the most active of the discontented are to a degree mollified by their ability to keep a process of reform moving. Their own participation, and that of others, in partisan mutual adjustment gives them some confidence that the weight given the value of racial equality can be, even in their lifetimes, significantly increased.

Depending on the flexibility of a central coordinating system, it, too, can command some agreement because its decisions are viewed as temporary and remediable. But the more central the system, the more its power to effect a remedy is concentrated, and, to many decision makers, the less immediate appear the possibilities for making a remedial adjustment on their own initiative. When each of a multitude of decision makers can at his own initiative make, say, a deferential, parametric, or manipulated adjustment, propose a round of negotiations, or simply declare that last year's bargain is no longer binding, it is clear to all participants that what cannot be won today may be won tomorrow.

Widespread dispersion of decision-making responsibility in partisan mutual adjustment also so complicates decision making that the decision-making process is never finished and never can be. There are no closed cases; decision making is always open-ended. There is therefore no point, as there sometimes is in central systems, at which a decision is firmly fixed. Even where some firm commitments have been made in, say, negotiation, there are always marginal issues that remain open.

(6) *Participants find it to their advantage to make agreed concessions of specialized extra legal authority to each other, thus avoiding by prearrangement conflicts that would otherwise develop.*

In addition to grants or concessions of authority embodied in law, decision makers smooth the path of conflict resolution by conceding specialized authority to each other, subject to revocation but nevertheless relatively permanent. The President of the United States, for example, concedes certain authority to Senators on nominations for appointments to federal posts within their states. They in turn concede him authority, greater than the law requires them to do, to select his own Cabinet, an authority that accounts for the rarity of rejections by the Senate of Cabinet nominees.

The Tennessee Valley Authority, we saw in Chapter 3, concedes authority to the agricultural colleges and to the Extension Service in the Tennessee Valley on some matters of agricultural policy. The Treasury and the Federal Reserve Board work out and revise, from time to time, reciprocal concessions of authority. The Recruitment and Manning Organization of the War Shipping Administration concedes authority in hiring to union hiring halls in return for a union concession of RMO authority over labor supply to unorganized companies.[7] The appropriations subcommittees of the House concede authority in their respective fields to each other. The Economic Cooperation Administration was in its early months extraordinarily dependent on the assignment of jurisdiction to subdivisions through mutual adjustment.

Between April, 1948, when the agency was established, and about July 15, when it already had some six hundred employees, it operated without any formal plan for its internal structure even so elaborate as an organization chart showing its principal divisions. To be sure, certain formal organization decisions had been made by appointing and giving titles to key employees, and by specifying certain procedures for paper flow (which were frequently informally violated), and by settling certain disputes about self-assumed jurisdiction. But the real core of this organization, which was in full operation before May 1, lay in a complex set of behaviors and understandings that had grown up almost spontaneously. The formal plans that were finally issued in July and subsequently were in very large part ratifications of this informal scheme.[8]

The list of examples could be greatly lengthened, for the arrangements of spheres of authority through partisan mutual adjustment is a fundamental part of the coordination process; it is everywhere apparent.

Even where a central coordinator attempts to specify the jurisdictions of each of his subordinate agencies, the agencies themselves must often negotiate or otherwise arrange their respective authorities by reason of the centralist's failure to appreciate the intricacies of their relations. Of assignments to OPA branches,

. . . assignments were not made by the hierarchy because they could not be. The rationing branches had to make their own assignments. No one else knew what to assign. The branches planned implementations on their own initiative and presented them to the hierarchy for approval. The hierarchy rarely disapproved them because it did not have enough information (or superiority in problem-solving ability) to do so.[9]

Once such arrangements are made decision making can proceed by agreement among the participants. How are the arrangements made? By negotiation, in many cases, as, for example, in the arrangements between the RMO and the unions; by tacit bargaining often, as in the allocation of authority over appointments between the President and Congress; and by calculated or deferential adjustment, as in the case of TVA and the agricultural organizations. A decision maker might even successfully stake a claim to extra legal authority by unilateral manipulation, including prior decision.

Whatever type of adjustment is employed to achieve the concession of extra legal authority, once it is established it can provide for a new exercise of prescriptive authority by one decision maker over another. Or it can simply achieve, as an effect of the withdrawal from decision making in some area, an unchallenged exercise of decision-making power by the decision maker who receives the concession. In other words it can do either or both of two things: give X new prescriptive powers over Y or give X decision making jurisdiction no longer challenged by Y.

Where the concession of authority is agreed to by those who concede, it therefore replaces a conflict area with agreement. It does not, of course, magically convert points of conflict into agreement but represents an anticipation of those conflicts that, through a major strategic decision, hits on a formula such that thereafter the points are no longer in conflict.

(7) *In partisan discussion, in contrast to cooperative discussion, is to be found an important potential for agreement.*

Partisan discussion, being a form of discussion or persuasion, will certainly rank on anyone's continuum near the voluntary end of the scale of methods of influence or control. Any decision reached through partisan discussion is an agreed decision. We can understand its extraordinary potential if we contrast partisan discussion, as we did in Chapter 5, with the cooperative, common-value discussion so widely praised in democratic theory, where democracy is sometimes defined as "government by discussion," and where it is assumed that discussion is a cooperative venture in testing policies by commonly shared values adequate to distinguish between right and wrong, wise and foolish, good or bad decisions.

Cooperative discussion is often muddy where partisan discussion is clear headed; this is because it will often be the case that discussants can hold to an assumption that its members share common values only because they leave their values poorly understood, poorly defined, abstract rather than concrete, and general instead of marginal or incremental. A frank recognition (not necessarily a statement) of differences in principal objectives or, if not that, of inevitably remaining important differences in side conditions and secondary objective, permits and even encourages each participant in discussion to clarify his own position for himself.

To be sure it is not wholly certain that clarity promotes agreement; it may be that muddled heads agree faster than clear ones. Still, this is a feature of partisan discussion worth noting; and it can be suggested that sometimes a commitment to abstract formal values is a form of rigidity in thinking that militates against the adjustment of one's values to win agreement. This, in turn, suggests a second point.

Cooperative discussion is often hobbled by the discussants' commitments to the values presumably shared by the group. If one assumes he is part of a cooperative search for a solution in the light of commonly shared values, he is not free to shift his own values. Hence he and the other members tend to remain frozen on what each understands to be the shared values of the group. By contrast, a participant in partisan discussion is free to alter his values at any time; he is not a party to an implicit contract as to what his values are. Being free to shift, he can abandon values that stand in the way of agreement on policy; he can easily confess the inappropriateness of a value position he earlier thought he wished to take; generally, he can freely indulge in a fruitful interplay between fact and value, whereas the participant in cooperative discussion cannot, unless he slides over into becoming in effect a partisan.

Thirdly, in cooperative discussion the variety of appeals that can be made to others in the group is limited; one is supposed to appeal on the basis of empirical evidence that proposals do not, in fact, produce the consequences on which the group agrees it prefers. In partisan discussion no appeal is out of bounds; and certainly the appeal to another participant to reconsider his values is both proper and helpful in opening up new possibilities for agreement.

Fourthly, to repeat a point made in another connection, participants in cooperative discussion are paralyzed until they find the values on which they are willing to declare their agreement. By contrast, no such prior agreement is required in partisan mutual discussion. If partisans can agree on policy, their work is done, even if they disagree on the objectives or other values lying behind the policy in question. As we noted above it is easy for those who disagree on why they wish a particular policy nevertheless to agree on that policy.

Fifthly and lastly, cooperative discussion is often highly principled because the only way to state the basis of agreement on values is to lay out general propositions or principles. One cannot talk about shared values without describing them in some brief and systematic way. On the other hand, not having to articulate his values and remaining quite free to let his value position simply emerge as implicit in the policy proposals he makes, the partisan is not hobbled by formalizations of his position that cannot possibly reflect the subtlety of marginal or incremental evaluations, the actual and superficially inconsistent value choices he might make depending on the rate at which he has to sacrifice one value for another at the margin. Participants in cooperative discussion tend, therefore, to become somewhat rigid and peremptory, where no such difficulties block the partisans' path to agreement.[10]

The picture drawn here of cooperative discussion appears to put it in a worse light than the light of our own various experiences. But this is because the productive, presumably cooperative discussions all of us have heard or participated in are in fact usually partisan. This attempt to spell out the potential for agreement in partisan discussion is thus, in fact, an attempt to lay out features of discussion as commonly practiced and to take note of the difference between conventional concepts and actual practice rather than to contrast two actually practicable forms of discussion.

To be sure partisan discussants need some common experience, orientation, and values; otherwise discussion is fruitless and even only a way station to violence. These common elements are to be found in varying degrees in partisan discussion in such governmental systems as are being discussed. Given their presence partisan discussion is not the fruitless activity that might be supposed and, for the reasons indicated, is more productive of agreement than the conventionally endorsed cooperative kind of verbal interchange. That it is held in lower repute than cooperative discussion is perhaps due to a habit of thought that contrasts discussion in which participants have nothing in common with that in which what they have in common is sufficient to bring them to an agreed solution. The common situation for discussion—which is to say, for partisan discussion—is, of course, marked by some common elements, some agreement on values, but not sufficient value agreement to lead to a solution sanctioned by those values.

(8) *Compensation, bargained compensation, and partisan discussion are available as a means of testing whether a given state of affairs is a Pareto optimum for the potential negotiators and, if it is not, of moving to such an optimum.*

We took note in Chapter 13 of the possibilities for testing and moving toward consistency through partisan discussion, compensation, or bargained compensation. Having defined a consistent set of policies as a set that achieves a Pareto optimum, we were in effect saying that these three forms of mutual adjustment are capable of achieving agreement in the strict form of a Pareto optimum. The relation between the Pareto optimum and an agreed social state is close but not simple. A Pareto optimum is not necessarily, not even ordinarily, a social state on which all agree. It is, however, a social state, that (if one's preferences govern one's consent) is agreed to be superior to some other states. And, further, it is a social state such that there is no unanimous agreement on the preferability of any other social state.

It would be of some importance if a decision-making system were capable of moving to a Pareto optimum whenever the system was found not to be in one and yet one was available, even if the system never produced agreement on the desirability of any existing or potential social state. It is this possibility, to which compensation, bargained compensation, and partisan discussion lend themselves, that is now being identified. These three forms of adjustment provide strong motives, among a group of participants in decision making, to move to a new state of affairs whenever a new state of affairs is possible in which some gain and none lose.

Moreover, given any move once made through central decision making or any form of partisan mutual adjustment other than the three in question, there is always a possibility that in comparison with the new state of affairs, there is still another state of affairs of benefit to all of some given subset of decision makers or citizens. For subsets of decision makers not too large or not for some reason indisposed to negotiate with one another, the possibility is therefore open to work through to that further mutually advantageous social state. It is important to see these three methods in this supplementary role.

What of the case in which one state of affairs is not more immediately advantageous to all than another, but is such that if all moved to it, the gainers could afford to compensate the losers in such a way that all would be better off? This possibility for agreeing on a mutually advantageous policy can be explored through compensation, either unilateral or bargained. Compensating losers by subsequent benefits to them has already been noted as a method of encouraging agreement (see proposition (5) above); here we are identifying an even more immediate method of winning over decision makers who would otherwise be disadvantaged. The decision reached is a bargain that includes compensation; or, in unilateral compensation, X offers benefits to Y as a condition of Y's responding as desired. The examples of Roosevelt's compensations for support of his Court reform will be recalled.

(9) *Lastly, many of the partisans in mutual adjustment pursue a version of the public interest.*

They make their contribution to agreement because they do not pursue those values that they believe they do not share with citizens as a whole, and they stimulate others to take a less immediately and practically self-regarding view. As Schattschneider has written, the members of the American League to Abolish Capital Punishment are not active in that group's work because they expect to be hanged.[11]

There are many qualities of agreement, ranging from that reached by partisan discussants to that reached through "Your money or your life!" Because every demand one makes, every preference one feels, and every value one holds already reflects a compromise between individuals and circumstances—because, for that matter, we cannot conceive of a human personality that is not adapted to an environment—we cannot draw a nice line between "This I agree to" and "This I am under the circumstances going to accept." As a consequence the respects in which a social process produces agreement and the respects in which, while falling short of agreement, it nevertheless achieves a resolution of conflict, are not clearly separable. Having in this chapter specified how partisan mutual adjustment facilitates agreement, we proceed in the next chapter to identify noteworthy characteristics of the way in which the processes accomplish resolution in the absence of agreement. But the line between the content of the two chapters is somewhat arbitrary.

Finally, it ought to be noted that the agreement we have been explicitly discussing in this chapter is agreement among decision makers, including of course both interest-group leaders and government officials. Insofar as partisan mutual adjustment encourages agreement among decision makers it contributes to wide social agreement among citizens. The connection is not, however, logically necessary. Rather than claim a logical tie we instead allege the connection on the basis of the model of government set forth in Chapter 6, in which citizens and decision makers are closely linked, especially by competition for followings of interest-group leaders, as well as by elections and other devices. Even, however, if one were to reject the connection between agreement among decision makers and agreement among citizens, the points that have been made about agreement remain significant. For the decision-maker set, as we have defined it, is, of course, a critical one.

CONFLICTING VALUES

The Problem

IN THE IMMEDIATELY PRECED-
ing chapter the exploration of how partisan mutual adjustment
encourages agreement leaves us with a still unanswered question:
When agreement is impossible, what are the terms on which values
are reconciled in the decisions and states of affairs that result from
mutual adjustment? There being no criteria wholly adequate to
guide the coordination of decisions and, consequently, an unavoidable "arbitrary" element in complex decision making, one can
nevertheless ask whether the arbitrary elements might in some way
be more reasonably, judiciously, or "better" handled in central
decision making rather than in partisan mutual adjustment. Such
a question forces us to look into the way in which partisan mutual
adjustment achieves a weighing of conflicting values.

The question of how values are weighed into decisions or resultant states of affairs is central to the study of public decision making, because government can be regarded in large part as machinery for resolving value conflicts. One oversimplifies, however, by saying that "the kernel of all legislation does not lie in a work to be technically executed, but in a weighing of interests. . . ."[1] or that political problems are those of "devising ways and means to curb particular 'wills' or 'interests' and thus clear the track for the realization of other wills and interests in fuller measure."[2] For there is an enormous difference between weighing and choosing among given values or interests actually in conflict, on the one hand, and molding values or interests to reduce conflict, on the other. And both are fundamental political processes. Although the weighing of values or interests and the process of curbing some to "clear the track" for others is a large part of the governmental process, it represents only that part of the value aggregation process that remains when the possibilities of reconsidering, modifying, and reformulating values have been exhausted, possibilities already explored in the preceding chapter.

Coordination has been defined, it will be remembered, in the following way: *A set of decisions is coordinated if adjustments have been made in them such that the adverse consequences of any one decision for other decisions are to a degree and in some frequency avoided, reduced, or counterbalanced or overweighed.*

It would appear that there are three avenues to coordination. First is to achieve, with respect to any given set of values, a Pareto optimum—that is, a set of decisions such that no alternative set would benefit at least one decision maker and harm no other. To do this is to achieve one kind of consistency, discussed in Chapter 13. Second is to mold values so as to reduce the possibility that a decision desired by one decision maker carries adverse consequences for another. This possibility we have considered in the preceding chapter. Third is to weigh conflicting values against each other and appropriately sacrifice amounts of some to amounts of others. We are now about to explore how partisan mutual adjustment does this (though we are far from knowing what is "appropriate").

In setting down a series of propositions on how weighing and choosing is achieved through partisan mutual adjustment, we shall be mindful of widespread fears about the process, not all of which, however, will be explicitly considered in the present chapter. It is feared that the weights, hence the reconciliations, are arbitrary; that they do not follow any defensible rule or formula and specifically do not accord with any generally acceptable ethical formula; that the weightings are strikingly unequal; that the preferences of the strong smother those of the weak. Strength in partisan mutual adjustment, it is further alleged, depends on accidents of strategic position, on personalities, on good or bad fortune in finding allies, and on other elements and circumstances of unequal impact on various participants in partisan mutual adjustment. The power of the House of Representatives Rules Committee appears to be a case in point.

Still further, it is feared that the influence of minorities is unduly heavy in mutual adjustment processes, as evidenced by the often effective veto power of Southerners in the Senate. Similarly, well-established interests are alleged to be much more strongly represented than newly emerging interests—for example, rural interests more than urban. And lastly, it is often feared that partisan mutual adjustment processes themselves encourage participants to pursue excessively partisan interests to such an extent that the values finally aggregated are only the narrowest, while broader values or interests have been forgotten. It is a common criticism of the military services, for example, that in the relations of each with the others, the "enemy" comes to be not a foreign power but the other services, so that, as a consequence, a quite inappropriate set of values or interests determines the outcome of their mutual adjustments.

Weighing and Choosing

(1) *In the decisions and patterns of decisions reached through a system of partisan mutual adjustment the weight given to each of various conflicting values depends on and can systematically be made to depend on characteristics of that particular system, which is only one of many possible systems of partisan mutual adjustment; and even within a system the weight will vary and can be*

systematically varied to depend on factors to be specified in further propositions.

This proposition, which becomes unnecessary when more specific propositions are laid down later to specify the variability of weights, is introduced at this point to forestall the identification of partisan mutual adjustment with any one set of weights. If one were to think of systems of partisan mutual adjustment as specified by constitutional arrangements of power (the veto power of the President, for example, and the allocation of authority among executive, legislative, and judiciary), party organization and activity (defined by relatively stable characteristics of parties), and interest-group organization and activity (similarly defined), then it is clear that for each different system there would be a different weighting of conflicting values. Similarly, within one system weights would differ according to a variety of circumstances. A strong President, for example, achieves a heavier weighting for the kind of values that Presidents represent in the American political system than does a weak President. Common criticisms of mutual adjustment processes are, therefore, often in error. They should be directed to the weighting process in a particular situation, not to mutual adjustment as a process.

(2) *In partisan mutual adjustment in the United States and in the Western democracies almost any value that any even relatively small number of citizens moderately or strongly wishes to see weighed into the policy-making process will be weighed in at some value significantly above zero.*

This weak proposition follows from the propositions describing the governmental process in Chapter 6, especially those specifying a large number of interest groups and the freedom with which they can be organized, as well as those pertaining to the entrepreneurial role, with respect to values, of party leaders.

We do not mean by this proposition that every value of the kind referred to in the proposition achieves some minimum of effect on each decision taken, but only that it significantly affects some decisions. Typically, such a value is given a respectful hearing by important participants in policy making, including agencies, executives, and legislators, wherever its advocates wish. The number of interests to which every legislator and executive must give the most careful and respectful, even fearful, attention, is extremely large; it is all the larger when it is remembered that what he does not attend to in one decision situation he must typically attend to in some other. He may disregard the watchmakers in acting on tax reform, farm policy, reform of the judiciary, or military aid to Laos, but he must then attend to their requests for tariff protection. For many values an allocation of authority to an agency, sometimes the creation of a new agency, will assign specific responsibility for the protection or pursuit of that value, as, for example, when a concern for equality of job opportunity leads to the establishment of a Fair Employment Practices Commission. In all this we are briefly elaborating well-known characteristics of the American political system, which is conspicuously open to participation in decision making at an enormous number of points. In David Truman's language, partisan mutual adjustment permits multiple points of "access."[3]

Admittedly the proposition is very loosely stated. We do not claim that the most trivial values of citizens are weighted into policy making; on the other hand, we cannot specify just when a value is "moderately" or "strongly" urged rather than not. Hence the proposition is imprecise on that point, just as it is imprecise on the question of how large a group must be before it can count on its values being weighted in, and just as it is imprecise on the question of what "significantly above zero" means. In the United States some groups of half a dozen citizens, if they try with vigor, can count on influencing federal government policy; and, unless they can be dismissed as eccentric, or suffer from incompetent leadership, members of any group as large as a hundred can count, at least, on having some agency, executive, legislator, or party leader give careful regard to their wishes beyond politely listening to what they have to say. Still, it is impossible to be precise about their effect.

If one can imagine a highly centralized decision-making system, it would be easy to imagine important values consistently being neglected, as, for example, in Roosevelt's "centrally" prepared analysis of and decision on packing the Supreme Court. Central decision making harnesses no powerful motivations to insure that all important values are permitted to affect policy, just as, as we have seen, it is weak in motivation to collect and analyze information; indeed this is, in some opinions, one of the merits of centrality. By contrast, in partisan mutual adjustment every group, agency, party leader, executive, and legislator who finds a prized value neglected in decision making is motivated, because each is a participant in decision making, to see that it is weighted in. Moreover, while opponents of that value can resist its heavy influence on decisions, it is almost impossible to shut it out completely. To be sure, again, it can be shut out of any given decision among many; but it can always find its way into some other decision that is part of the pattern of decisions that constitutes policy.

If we imagine a central coordinator urging all interested parties to call their concerns to his attention prior to his authoritative and conclusive decision on their conflicts, he can still give zero weight to any given value even if it is deeply prized by an important segment of the society. He can do so through any one of a number of errors in his grasp of his complex problem; but he can also do so because, in his final and inevitably arbitrary resolution of the conflict in which he must inescapably suppress some values for the benefit of others, he may deliberately decide to give some value a zero weight. The veto may or may not appear in partisan mutual adjustment, but in centrality it is inescapably a potentially paralytic force.[4]

Because, on any given issue, only a few citizens are ordinarily politically active, through interest groups or otherwise, it is easy to believe that only a few interests are represented in policy making. There exists, however, in such a democracy as the United States, a representative function performed by citizens for each other, quite aside from the formal representation of citizens through legislators. On most issues most citizens "let John do it"; they are not practitioners of do-it-yourself in politics. And John does it. And, although there are differences in the pattern of preference or values between the politically inactive, on the one hand, and the active, on the other, the active in all their variety represent in policy making much of the pattern of interest or value of the inactive.

That there is such a process of representation or mirroring the values of inactive citizens is obvious enough; how accurate the representation or mirroring is, of course, is subject to some dispute. To the extent that feasibility considerations impose constraints on the variety of policy choices available and to the extent that differences in more ultimate values are reconcilable with agreement on policy positions among citizens—and these are both significant phenomena in American politics—the representation or mirroring is improved.

Finally, in the interpretation of this second proposition it is important not to conceive of preferences or values as exclusively segmental in contrast to widely, even nationally, shared values. Any values on which the political community as a whole is largely united make their influence felt, first, through the rules of the game binding on all participants in mutual adjustment, secondly through the interest of at least some participants in partisan mutual adjustment in the pursuit of these values, and thirdly in the particular interest of party leaders in capitalizing on the values on which a majority can be united.

(3) *On some counts partisan mutual adjustment, compared to central coordination, reduces the possibility that a set of decisions are so arranged as to constitute a gain for no one and a loss for some.*

This proposition is obviously a weak one but is nevertheless of some importance. Given the fallibility of central synopsis, it will often be the case that a complex enough central decision worsens, by its errors, the position of all concerned. There is in central decision making no highly motivated check to see that at least one interest is well served by a decision. A central coordinator may be a Jack of all values and master of none. He is not committed to any one of those values whose conflicts he is charged with resolving, but is committed to their compromise on some terms. If, in rearranging the relation among the values by a coordinating decision, it turns out that all interests lose, it is not necessarily apparent to him that this is the case. Different possible coordinating decisions produce different aggregations of values for each of which he expects some values to suffer (since in persistent conflict situations some values have to be sacrificed to others). If he finds that as a result of a contemplated decision a number of values suffer—even if he finds that all the values that he samples appear to have suffered—this is by no means evidence that his decision is a poor one, for he may assume that their losses are offset by gains for some other value. In comparing a state of conflict with the state of coordination he contemplates or achieves nothing requires him to make sure that some interest or value is advanced as an offset to those that are not.

It is, moreover, very easy for him to allow his preoccupation with the patterns of conflict and reconciliation to draw him away from an elementary test of his own work. When people speak of coordination their tendency to use loosely and abstractly such terms as integration, harmony, consistency, adjustment, reconciliation, equity, fairness, efficiency, and balance reveals some inclination to find justifications for coordinating decisions in abstract considerations of pattern rather than in a hard-headed examination of what values are advanced, on the one hand, and retarded, on the other.

In partisan mutual adjustment, on the contrary, no move is made unless it is believed to be advantageous to at least one decision maker who is highly motivated to understand and protect his own values. For in partisan mutual adjustment only partisans make moves; and partisans initiate moves only when they believe it to be to their advantage to do so.

One can easily make too much of this feature of partisan mutual adjustment. In both central and noncentral decision making, the decision maker may be incorrect in his perception of interests, the partisan even incorrect in the perception of his own interests. Hence some sources of error in all forms of decision making might account for losses to all values. Moreover, the dynamics of partisan mutual adjustment will sometimes produce a settlement of issues that no one wants. Mistaken interpretations of an adversary's moves in bargaining, whether due to his bluffing or for other reasons, can sometimes result in losses or no gain all around. This is not infrequent in two-party bargaining that ends in a contract, for in that kind of bargaining many moves are irreversible; but even in multiparty bargaining—typical of political bargaining, in which what is settled today can be reconsidered tomorrow, misinterpretation and bluff will sometimes result in loss or no gain all around. The proposition does not therefore allege any more than that "on some counts" partisan mutual adjustment, compared to central coordination, reduces the possibility of a gain for no one and a loss for some.

The character of the criticism of central and noncentral decision systems indicates that, cautiously as this last proposition has to be put, it may indicate an extremely significant difference between the two. Central decisions are often criticized for errors that cannot be defended by reference to anyone's interests; noncentral decisions are criticized for sacrificing someone's interests to someone else's. Central decisions, in short, are declared, when criticized, to be incompetent; noncentral decisions are declared to be exploitative.

Military decision systems, being highly centralized, illustrate the possibility that central decisions will not simply err in that they achieve a poor weighing of values in conflict, but will commit errors that sacrifice all the conflicting values. The Maginot Line, Pearl Harbor defense, and the employment of the Russian Fleet in the Russo–Japanese War are not criticized because they sacrificed too much of some values in order to achieve others, but because they were disastrous for all the values with which the decision makers were concerned.* By contrast, complaints against noncentral decision making—such as political bargaining over farm price supports—allege that values of the public at large are unnecessarily, unfairly, or unwisely sacrificed to those of a subgroup, such as farmers.

We are, of course, embarked on an examination of weighting in partisan mutual adjustment that will eventually bring us to an appraisal of this specific criticism of it; in the meantime we are simply taking account of the possible significance of the point that partisan mutual adjustment is only occasionally, and not typically, attacked for causing all-around losses. This is, possibly, a significant point of difference between the two systems, not, it should be noted, a point of superiority of either over the other. Large losses to the public at large coupled with small gains to farmers will be, by some standards, more regrettable than moderate losses all round.

* This is not an argument that military decisions ought not to be highly centralized, but simply an observation about a characteristic of centralized decision making.

(4) In some large part the weight given to a value depends on the authority held by the participants in partisan mutual adjustment who pursue or protect it and by their adversaries.

The proposition contradicts a careless assumption that influence over policy making in mutual adjustment processes is largely a product of accidents in the distribution of persuasive skill and other personal attributes on the one hand, and of strategic position in the informal structure of influence or power, on the other. Granting some strength to such factors, clearly the allocation of authority to legislators and executives and their allocation of it, in turn, to agencies determines in largest part who and what will influence policy.

Given that government decision making requires authoritative acts of politicians and agencies, it ought to be considered a truism, even a mere redundancy, that weights depend on the specific authority of those participants who take a position on the policy at issue. If one argues, to the contrary, that it is, for example, pressure groups rather than those in authority who determine the weights given to various interests, we reply that these groups influence the weights, indeed and heavily, but do so in large part through their influence on other participants in mutual adjustment to whom authority has been allocated. We need not argue about "ultimate" sources of influence; we wish only to make the point that policies go through authorities whose grants of authority proximately determine the weights given various preferences.

Authority determines weights not only where partisan mutual adjustment takes the form of authoritative prescription, for authority appears in partisan mutual adjustment in a variety of forms. In unconditional manipulation, for example, authority may be used to weaken or strengthen a decision maker, as when Congressional authority is employed to reduce an agency's budget. Also, we have seen that any bargainer who enjoys authority can threaten to use it on his adversary, in which case authority becomes influential in negotiation quite apart from its use when actually exercised. Moreover, authority is given extended employment through indirection. We have seen that where X cannot employ his authority on Y, he can often employ it on Z, who in turn can authoritatively prescribe to Y. In adaptive forms of adjustment the location of authority will greatly influence decisions to defer or not to defer, to calculate or not to calculate. And, of course, X's own grant of authority, if he has one, is a determinant of his capacity to satisfy himself with no more than parametric adjustment. However reviewed, authority is a pervasive influence on weights.

The significance of this fourth proposition appears in connection with a fifth proposition, to which it leads.

(5) *Within very wide margins weights given to values can be systematically altered by systematic reallocations of authority.*

This proposition seems most persuasive at the agency level. For any neglected value it is in principle possible to create a new agency or reassign function and authority to existing agencies in order to give the neglected value any given weight. Whatever the pressures explaining the weight given a particular value at any time, some reassignment of authority is sufficient to alter it. The authority of legislators and executives, or of high-ranking agencies, is sufficient for the task.

But if it is clear that to raise the weight of the value given to, say, civilian defense, a civil defense agency can be established with certain authority, and if it is clear that in order to raise the weight further its authority can be enlarged, it is not clear that any reallocation of authority to the legislature can raise the value of civil defense within the legislative process. Here the possibilities of raising weight by reallocating authority are much more crude, to be sure, but they exist. If the President of the United States were allocated the authority of an item veto on Congressional legislation, the kinds of values for which the President stands—and typically Presidential values are somewhat different from Congressional values—would be more highly weighted. Or if the authority of the House Rules Committee were reduced, certain predictable consequences for the weighting of values would ensue simply because the Rules Committee typically, through its authority, gives a relatively high weight to what might be called traditional or conservative values. If Senators were to be deprived of the authority to filibuster, certain values espoused chiefly by the South would decline in weight. One can imagine more fanciful reconstructions of authority—giving Representatives from urban areas exclusive authority over, say, housing legislation—that would achieve quite specific changes in the weights accorded to certain values.

One reason for making the point is not because we wish to suggest that any deficiencies in weighting can or should be easily remedied by appropriate reallocations of authority. Obviously, some reallocations of authority—for example, that to urban Representatives for housing legislation—would not be worth their cost even if practicable. And many are not practicable given the present distribution of political preference and power. Our reason, instead, is to make clear, by an additional line of argument, that weights are variable over time and from one system of partisan mutual adjustment to another, that they are not God-given or "natural" in some sense that denies their manipulability, that they are systematically manipulated by participants in government, and that a principal method of doing so is by reallocation of authority. Nothing is being said at this point about what conditions and circumstances actually constrain the reallocation of authority, a question to be investigated in a later chapter.

(6) *By reason of the preceding two propositions and for other reasons as well, in any system of partisan mutual adjustment the weights given various values vary from one decision-making situation to another, and the weights in one situation will often correct deficiencies in earlier weights.*

It is a mistake to think that certain interests, preferences, or values are garrisoned in such a way that they fixedly enter into all policy determinations with invariable strength. We have already referred to the impotence of watchmakers on questions of farm policy and, contrariwise, to their strength when the tariff is under deliberation. Variations in influence, of course, are not simply at the option of the interested parties concerned, as that example might indicate. Against their will, trade unions, for example, probably affect monetary policy in the United States substantially less than they do wage and hour policies.

The subtleties of weighting are achieved in various ways. As we have just seen, the allocation of authority together with prescription of function to an agency in a prescribed field is a device for adjusting the weighting process to circumstances and issues. In the regulation of railroad rates, for example, the authority and pre-scribed function of the Interstate Commerce Commission is presumably designed to bring certain values, preferences, and interests to bear—consumer interests in low prices, for example, or small businessmen's interests in nondiscriminatory pricing—with a strength that would be quite out of place if brought to bear on another policy issue such as space research, to which both the general interests and the named interests of these groups are, however, still to some degree pertinent. Indirectly, too, allocation of authority by politicians to agencies will give certain preferences extremely high weight along some lines and low weight along others, as is illustrated by the heavy weight given to local agricultural and business interests in programs of the Army Engineers and the low weight in effect given to the preferences of the same parties in national security policy making.

Variability is also achieved because any given participant adjusts the values he himself brings to bear on that adjustment in which he participates. The shift in dominating values from, say, full employment and price stability for considering policy on taxation, to, say, equity, in dealing with minimum wage legislation is accomplished not simply because the two policy areas call on different groups of participants in partisan mutual adjustment, but also because some of the participants common to the two situations shift their standards of relevance. No one, it has already been shown, achieves satisfactory skill in bringing all his value to bear in important ways on any one decision or area of decision making; hence an essential prerequisite for making evaluative tasks manageable is to be selective in values made pertinent to any one decision or group of decisions. In our political system we shift values both by shifting participants and by shifting the attention of given participants. Many legislators and executives have to shift their attention simply because they take part in extremely large numbers of widely different kinds of decisions.

One of the most conspicuous subtleties in partisan mutual adjustment as practiced in the United States is that preferences are so variable in weight as to count heavily when effecting a veto on a policy proposal and less heavily when generating momentum for a policy. This variability in weighting, of course, is written into the

Constitution itself, and is also deeply embedded in traditions such as the two-thirds rule on some issues put to a vote and in the filibuster, both of which immensely strengthen the hand of a partisan who wishes to stop rather than start a new line of policy. Nevertheless, partisan mutual adjustment can throw advantage either way, even though for a most conspicuous example of the opposite extreme we turn to the economic system rather than government, where partisan adjusters (there called businessmen or entrepreneurs) have extraordinary powers to innovate, that is, to initiate, new products, new methods, or the capture of new markets, but extraordinarily weak powers to block similar initiative taken by others.

We have already seen that shifting weights from one decision to another in a sequence is a self-corrective coordinating process. What is neglected at one point in decision making is attended to at a next. Moreover, in building up outcomes from combinations of decisions in which weights are not all the same, decision making is exploratory and tentative. We have also seen how information is mobilized in partisan mutual adjustment; much of the information throws new light on appropriate values and weights, as well as on the strictly empirical aspects of the decision problem at hand.

(7) *In policy choices partisan mutual adjustment will often so weigh values as to achieve, after the decision, a wide endorsement of the value weights implicit in the decision, despite the absence of any criteria that would call for such weights in advance of the decision and in the absence of prior agreement on weights.*

Given failure of agreement on values, it is of course not a mark of failure of mutual adjustment that after policies have been set there is no widespread agreement on the value combination implicit in those policies. On the other hand, where, after a policy has been set, subsequent agreement emerges on the value mix implicit in the policy, the achievement of that agreement is noteworthy.

Partisan mutual adjustment is adapted to a situation in which there is conflict of values. This calls to mind the difference between synoptic central coordination and partisan mutual adjustment. In the face of unresolved value conflict we cannot specify how central coordination is conceived as operating; but, since partisan mutual adjustment is an adjustment among partisans each of whom pursues his own values, coping with value conflicts is built into the very model of the process. In the face of conflicts over the proper weights to be given values the various devices of partisan mutual adjustment nevertheless bring participants to decisions or resultant policies. Negotiators, for example, find a way to agree on a decision, even if all negotiators hold to different value weights; or if X unilaterally manipulates Y, X and Y are coordinated to a degree despite their value conflicts; or if X defers to Y, they are coordinated without agreement on values.

Thus, as is not the case in central coordination, unresolved value conflict is no barrier to decision in partisan mutual adjustment. And once the decision is reached or a resultant state of affairs is reached as a result of various partisan moves, the weights on values implicit in that decision or state of affairs will then often and only then be very widely endorsed.

Why are the decisions widely endorsed *ex post* if not *ex ante?* One reason is that actually reaching the agreement or resultant state of affairs through partisan mutual adjustment will often legitimize what has been reached and the value implicit in it. Parallel legitimizations are those given to many decisions reached by voting, by tossing a coin, or, say, by delegating the decision arbitrarily to one of the parties in conflict. Whatever decision follows from any one of such as these processes will often be widely endorsed in the absence of any other more appealing basis for judgment.

To be sure, we sometimes vote, toss a coin, or delegate and yet say about the resulting decision that it is unfortunate, wrong, or foolish, as when, for example, although sanctioning the choice of a public official by election, we nevertheless regret the victory of the candidate we did not vote for. That is to say, we sometimes endorse the use of a process for reaching a decision without endorsing the resulting decision itself. On the other hand, for some choices we have no basis of criticism or endorsement other than that the choice is a product of an accepted process.

If partisan mutual adjustment took the form of a conflict of naked power, the participants thus attacking each other unrestrained by conventions, it would hardly be an accepted process. But the process is highly conventionalized, as is indicated not only by the heavy dependence of power on authority, but also by the participants' acceptance of various rules of the game that have the effect of civilizing the conflict. Hence there will be some decisions widely endorsed simply because they emerge from partisan mutual adjustment. Many of us will endorse both the decision and the values implicit in the decision—say, to increase the benefits of old age insurance, believing that the decision is an outcome of a process that we find acceptable. Some of us may be equalitarians, others inequalitarians, some advocates of the welfare state, others advocates of a tight rein on government expenditure; but on the specific problem of how to reconcile values in conflict over a specific issue of how much and when old age benefits should be liberalized, we will endorse the value resolution implicit in the decision taken, lacking any ground for complaint in view of the process by which the decision was reached.

In such cases one might wish to say that rather than a wide endorsement there is to be found a wide indifference to the value aggregation achieved implicitly in the decision. That is, the implicit set of values are endorsed in the sense that they are as good as any alternative set that might have been chosen. The difference between the two views is of no consequence; the point is that out of the process of partisan mutual adjustment itself comes a decision the implicit values of which are taken as acceptable.

Widespread endorsement of the value reconciliation implicit in a state of affairs reached through partisan mutual adjustment is not attributable solely, however, to such a process of legitimization as we have been discussing. The *ex post* endorsement of value aggregation implicit in policy choices may in fact represent discriminating judgment. For, as we have seen, we often learn our value preferences from experience with concrete and real policy choices, drawing from such choices insight into preferences that we do not gain when choices are generalized or when they are only hypothetical. Thus, it is highly possible that a group of policy makers incapable of prior agreement on values might quickly find reason to appreciate those values that lie implicitly in a policy on which they could and did in fact negotiate an agreement, or in a policy arrived at through, say, parametric, deferential, or unilateral manipulated processes. Bargainers, for example, having tediously worked their way to a settlement of a dispute posed by their prior attachment to conflicting values, will often see in the aggregation of values finally achieved a merit to which they had earlier been blind.

Sometimes a given policy or state of affairs is consistent with each of a number of different value mixes and will be endorsed by various observers for quite different reasons, each of the observers finding his values satisfied by it. In such cases we cannot say that there is a single set of values and weights implicit in the decision that has, in effect, been endorsed by those who endorse the policy; but we can still conclude that however differently observers view the implicit weights, to the extent that all observers are in agreement on the policy chosen, all are satisfied with the implicit weights.

(8) *Other things being equal, the more widely shared a value, interest, or preference, the heavier its weight in partisan mutual adjustment.*

This proposition is intended to assert a significant dependence of the weight given a value on the number of people who share it. Because it does not deny other factors in weights, it is not a very controversial proposition and needs only brief discussion.

All participant decision makers in partisan mutual adjustment are greatly influenced by the numbers of people advocating any given value. For legislators and executives this follows from their selection through elections. For agencies it follows from the authorized responsibilities of the agencies laid upon them by legislators and executives. For party leaders it follows from their desire to win elections. For interest-group leaders it follows from their competition for followings.

If this is plain enough, it can be suggested as an hypothesis that all decision makers in government accept a convention or rule of the game according to which the numbers of citizens supporting a value is accepted, other things being equal, as a valid consideration in weighting.[5] To some degree it appears that any participant in the process will acknowledge through deference, calculated adjustment, negotiation—and generally through his response to manipulated adjustment—some right of any other decision maker to prevail to the extent that he is taken as "speaking for" large numbers of citizens.

Given that numbers count in the espousal of various values by different decision makers, numbers count again through the importance of alliances in determining outcomes and decisions. This hardly needs developing, for we have already explained both how decisions and outcomes are greatly influenced by the formation of alliances and how the process of forming them brings about a reconsideration of interests from which, to varying degrees, agreement on common-denominator values emerges. Thus, values widely shared are those on which decision makers are allied, and those on which they are allied are those that can be effectively pushed.

The proposition does not deny that citizens often vote and join interest groups according to intensely held segmental values rather than according to less intensely held but more widely shared values, which is widely alleged to be the case. We shall, in fact in the next proposition, acknowledge intensity as an important determinant of the weight given a value in mutual adjustment. However, in a two-party system, for example, both parties will respond heavily to mere numbers, as will be indicated by the similarity of their candidates and platforms. If, then, in choosing between two candidates or parties, a voter lets that decision be governed by the narrowly rather than widely shared values he holds, widely shared values have nevertheless already put their definitive stamp on the candidates and positions of each party, and will have their effect on decisions no matter which party wins. Similarly, intensely held, narrowly shared values that motivate citizens to associate themselves with interest groups do not deny the effect of widely shared values in determining the way in which alliances will form, and in determining, even before alliance is formed, the position that executives, legislators, and agencies will take in policy making. Again, we do not deny that other factors than the number who share a common value are powerful determinants of value weights; we want only to make a place for widespread sharing as one of these factors.

(9) *Other things being equal, the more intensely held a value, interest, or preference, the heavier its weight in partisan mutual adjustment.*

Again, the proposition is hardly controversial. To bypass the argument that intensities cannot be interpersonally compared, the proposition can be read to mean that an individual's more intense preferences will count for more in influencing governmental decisions than will his less intense preferences, and that if two individuals, A and B, have preferences with respect to value x that weigh equally, then a changed and more intense preference of A with respect to x will count for more than B's preference with respect to x.

Intensity is an important determinant of weight because, other things being equal, decision makers will be activated on those questions on which citizens feel intensely. Their intensity of feeling will be represented in their voting behavior and in their commitment to interest-group leaders.[6] A system of partisan mutual adjustment is, of course, one in which citizens and decision makers, responding to intensity of feeling on a value, can influence the decision making process at many points. And since indication of intensity is willingness to expend energy to realize the value in question (though other factors influence the expenditure of energy too), it is almost impossible to deny, in a system of partisan mutual adjustment, as it could be denied for a highly centralized system, that intensity does not necessarily, other things being equal, result in heavier weight to the intensely prized value.

To be sure, heightened intensity sometimes follows from rather than leads to heightened espousal of a value in partisan mutual adjustment.[7] And one's *generalized* intensity of dissatisfaction with the political order does not increase the weights given to one's values. On the contrary it appears, although from quite inconclusive evidence, that "American politics tend to express the needs and wishes of the more contented and satisfied citizens at every level in society, rather than the discontent and alienation of the dissatisfied."[8]

Intensity is weighted into partisan mutual adjustment not only, of course, in its dircet effect on the vigor with which a decision maker pursues a value, but also in the resistance he meets since intensely held values stimulate, others things being equal, more resistance. Since in partisan mutual adjustment any decision maker typically has a choice of strategies or tactics before him, and since, for reasons already explained, he habitually reconsiders his values in the light of the possibilities of attaining them, expected resistance stemming from intensely held values comes to be a determinant of decisions and outcomes even when the resistance is only anticipated. That is to say the intense values that Y seeks to protect come to be respected by X.

(10) *In partisan mutual adjustment authority and other powers are often allocated in such a way as to give, other things being equal, special weight to the values of persons having a special concern with or interest in a decision, quite aside from the intensity with which they hold various values or preferences.*

In the United States only certain classes of farmers are polled in order to decide whether certain forms of price support are to be put into effect. And it is common to give special weight, sometimes through formally established advisory boards, to the wishes of businessmen in establishing policies with respect to business. Special interest or concern sometimes overlaps heightened intensity, but the two do not necessarily run parallel.

Nothing about these features of partisan mutual adjustment disqualifies the process as a possibly acceptable method of coordination, and for most people each will be taken as a merit. Of the propositions, the first and the fifth are especially critical to the evaluation of partisan mutual adjustment. For they draw a distinction between the merits of any particular distribution of weights in a system of mutual adjustment. They therefore turn aside those criticisms which are ostensibly of partisan mutual adjustment itself but are in fact criticism of particular distributions of weights. Other propositions in the chapter lay down some counstraints on the kinds of distributions of weights that are possible, but they are not troublesome constraints; on the contrary, they support favorable evaluations of partisan adjustment.

To be sure, we have not yet shown that in actual practice the distribution of weights can be controlled so that where weights are intolerable it is possible to alter them without abandoning mutual adjustment. This we will look into in a later chapter.

EQUALITY

AS A

CRITERION

Critical Allegations about Value Aggregation

WE HAVE SAID THAT HOWEVER
values are perceived or formulated, there is an arbitrary element
(as "arbitrary" was defined in Chapter 12) in the weighing of conflicting values in any decision-making system. Hence the way in
which the aggregation of conflicting values is accomplished in
partisan mutual adjustment cannot be attacked simply because it is
to a degree arbitrary. We have also shown, in Chapter 14, that for
many reasons partisan mutual adjustment so influences the perception and formulation of values that the scope and significance
of value conflict is reduced, thus reducing the arbitrary element in
aggregation weighing. And we have shown in Chapter 15 that
weighting in partisan mutual adjustment is marked by specific features, such as the responsiveness of weights to numbers of persons

holding a value, or responsiveness to intensity of feeling about a value, that bear in obviously significant ways on an appraisal of the weighting process. We are now ready to examine specific allegations that can be brought against value weighing in partisan mutual adjustment.

The virtue of taking this next step in the analysis is simply that the examination permits us to continue relevant comment on the process of partisan mutual adjustment despite the absence of adequate criteria by which the process could be more systematically evaluated. Not knowing exactly what we want from partisan mutual adjustment, we can at least consider critical allegations about it. Where the allegations imply criteria, as they often do, we will be in a position to analyze those proposed criteria, even if we cannot formulate satisfactory ones ourselves.

This chapter will be taken up entirely with the first of several critical allegations about conflicting values in partisan mutual adjustment: that they are in some unacceptable sense unequally weighted. Although we argued in the preceding chapter that weights in mutual adjustment can follow various patterns, our claim that the patterns are variable does not go so far as to assert the possibility of complete equality. Hence the allegation of inequality needs to be treated as a serious one. We shall treat the allegation at great length, out of respect for the importance of issues regarding equality and inequality in democratic government.

Forms of the Allegation about Inequality

A very careless allegation is that values are not weighted equally in partisan mutual adjustment. Certainly in observable systems of mutual adjustment they are not, nor can one think of any reason why they should be. Trivial values ought not to count so heavily as more important values; every one agrees to this, even if people disagree on which values are important and which trivial. A stronger but still ill-considered allegation is that there is inequality among the various groups who engage in partisan mutual adjustment. For example, the parties to bargaining, it will be alleged, do not enjoy equal bargaining power. Again, why should they? Should a bargainer who speaks for a group of ten people enjoy equality with one who speaks for ten thousand? Should the President of the United States bargain on terms of equality with the president of United States Steel? An alternative form of substantially the same allegation is that the groups who participate in mutual adjustment do not equally divide the values to be shared. But, again, no one proposes that a group of ten members should divide among themselves the same share of a sharable value that must be divided among ten thousand in another group.

Where Congressional leaders, the President, the Budget Bureau, the Secretary of Commerce, representatives of the Chamber of Commerce and other business interests, and representatives of farm organizations engage in partisan mutual adjustments on, say, tariff adjustments, the distinctive role of each in the decision to be reached will, by anyone's standards, both call for different powers to each and deny the desirability of treating the wishes of each participant equally. In such an instance some people would hope for the dominance of the values spoken for by the President and Budget Bureau, others for those spoken for by Congressional leaders, others for an amalgamation without dominance by any participant. But no one can make a case for equality of powers in adjustment or for equality in the weight given the values represented by each participant.

To be taken seriously an allegation against partisan mutual adjustment on the ground of inequality in weights must allege that the way in which values are weighed somehow violates the principle of equal regard for or equal weighting of the preferences or values of each citizen. This is the nub of the allegation: that some citizens count for more than others when their conflicting preferences are weighed into public decision through partisan mutual adjustment. Stated this way the allegation, like the others, is a true one. Nothing we have said about partisan mutual adjustment assures equal treatment; and several things we have said about it— among others, its responsiveness to intensity of feelings about issues—deny equal treatment.

The allegation, however, appeals to the same criterion of equality that we have had reason to reject as an adequate criterion for decisions in Chapter 9, where we asked whether any adequate agreed criteria were available to a synoptic decision maker.

How, then, are we to take into account a suggestion, implicit in the critical allegation that values are unequally weighted, that after all equality is an agreed criterion? Apparently what is being suggested is that despite the failure of participants in partisan mutual adjustment to acknowledge the equality principle as a criterion, anyone in our culture who can rise above partisan involvement in the decision-making process itself will agree on the criterion. Scholars, or any dispassionate competent observers of the process, it is suggested, will agree on it. This is the view or proposal to be analyzed.

We, as presumed dispassionate observers of mutual adjustment, can of course very quickly reject the equality criterion if it is offered as an exclusive criterion for all occasions. Suppose I held that it was a mistake to reelect President Eisenhower despite the evidence—an overwhelming vote—that an equal regard for each citizen's preference called for a second term for him. My opinion is not necessarily foolish or irrelevant. Moreover, it does not necessarily even challenge the equality principle in its appropriate form. If I say that the decision to continue Eisenhower in office was the wrong decision and then go on to say that the correct way to decide the Presidency is to hold an election, I will be understood. I will be understood to have criteria of my own by which I disapprove of the decision to reelect Eisenhower but also to share a widespread agreement that, in the face of disagreement on who should be President, a good practical political rule that I propose to accept is equal weighting of votes. From my two different standpoints, between which I shift rapidly and frequently, the decision on Eisenhower was a good one and a bad one.

Equality is ordinarily offered as a criterion for a practical political rule to people who, having accepted it, are not constrained from holding to other criteria as well for other purposes. It might be acceptable to a philosophical inegalitarian as well as to an egalitarian. For in his commitment to a practical political rule the inegalitarian might prefer equal weights to any pattern of inequality of weights that he thought achievable, believing, as might be appropriate to our age, that an inequality of the kind that would

support an aristocracy is unattainable. So that, in asking whether
the equality criterion is an acceptable one for appraising value
weighing in partisan mutual adjustment, we need ask only whether
an observer of the process should endorse it as a criterion for a
practical rule for making political decisions even if he, on other
grounds, continues to criticize the decisions. Would we as appraisers
of mutual adjustment want any other practical political rule or
rules in its place?

The ensuing analysis will raise questions about the equality
criterion that will make clear that it is not an obviously useful
standard for appraising mutual adjustment, although the analysis
necessarily leaves the choice of whether to use it and in what form,
if any, to use it, to each reader.

Ambiguity in the Equality Criterion

A first objection to the criterion, already alluded to, is that it is
in fact a number of related conflicting criteria. If ambiguity is
sorted out so that one derives unambiguously applicable criteria,
then no one of the resulting criteria is obviously superior to another. It may mean counting each person as equal in the weighing
of known (to citizens themselves) preferences; but it may mean, on
the other hand, counting them as equal in the weighing of those
preferences they would presumably have if they had the opportunity to inform themselves. Or it may mean—and this is something different again—that any elected official should, on any issue
on which he thinks his constituents do not have significant preferences, discharge his decision-making responsibility in such a way as
to avoid favoritism.

On such a question, for example, as the level of price support
for wheat, these three interpretations of the equality criterion
would point to three different decisions. It could easily be argued
that equal attention to the perceived values of an electorate with a
large proportion of wheat growers would point to a high price support. Yet one can call on a great body of evidence and competent
opinion that, taking the larger implications of high price supports
into account, a lower price support should follow from an equal

weighing of the "real" values of that electorate. What the third interpretation would point to is unclear: it would presumably require an equal regard for the general welfare of all citizens (again: as citizens see welfare or as the official sees it?); it would not bind decision makers to an equal regard for existing or imaginable preferences on the specific issues at hand.

Other ambiguities can be suggested. Suppose that on three issues the population divides into two preference groups—the same division roughly for each of the three issues. Suppose the decision accords with the wishes of the larger group in each of the three issues. Does equal regard for citizens now require that on a fourth issue the preferences of the smaller number of people, three times deprived, be gratified? Certainly "He's had his way this time; you'll have your way next time," is a common interpretation of equal treatment; the indoctrination in it begins with parental allocation of conflicting values among small children. But it contradicts the majoritarian interpretation of the principle of equality, according to which the larger group wins each issue without exception. What decision is sanctioned then by the principle of equality?

Surely, one might reply, in the United States and some other countries the majoritarian form of equality is the appropriate one. Each decision should follow majority preference. In fact, however, the majority principle itself is ambiguous and inconclusive. It has merits when applied to simple situations in which it is clear and conclusive. But what can be made of this criterion when applied to decisions reached by those whom we have defined in this study as decision makers?

DEFICIENCIES IN THE MAJORITY CRITERION EVEN WHEN IT IS ACCEPTED

Suppose the Army and the Air Force are in conflict in the Joint Chiefs of Staff over the military budget. If they both attempt to defend their proposed budgetary allocations as being in the public interest, as they do, and if they both allege that they seek to advance the values of a majority—even an overwhelming majority of citizens, as they do, and if any observer or critic can do more conclusively demonstrate what is in the interests of a majority than can the Army or Air Force, what reconciliation of conflicting values does or does not satisfy the majority principle? What are in conflict in such a case are alternative reconciliations of conflict each of which can be argued to satisfy the majority principle.

There are still other ambiguities beyond those already noted. For whatever position is taken as to what kind of preference is to be counted equally—perceived, for example, or hypothetically informed, the facts are rarely conclusive as to what the preference is. That is, even if we all could agree that we should weigh equally from person to person those preferences he would presumably have if he were informed, we cannot usually know what they are. To determine conclusively what values people have or what values they would have if better informed would require for any observer or evaluator heroic synoptic intellectual capacity and mountains of data. To make reasoned estimates is not impossibly difficult, but the estimates differ.

If one wished to follow expressed preferences, the difficulty is that preferences are usually not expressed; any proposal to weigh expressed preferences runs into the difficulty that citizens express their preferences only on a tiny minority of all the decisions that must be taken in the daily run of government. On the rediscount rate, tariffs on particular commodities, location of highways, administrative organization of a department or bureau, grants to municipalities for urban renewal and the like, only an exceedingly small number of citizens express or know values.

In fact, of course, no one really believes that a direct appeal to a majority principle is appropriate for appraising the settlement of the countless specific questions which are the daily business of decision makers. Most of us would say that most decisions ought to be evaluated "logically," "on their merits," and in the context of a large number of related decisions. Only about the whole complex of interrelated decisions might one ask whether preferences are equally regarded.

As a vivid case in point consider a World War II policy decision on whether gas rations were to be provided for transporting athletic teams to interscholastic competitions, a policy question consequential for what many people considered to be important values. In favor of the gas ration it was argued that interscholastic sports aided physical development, mental alertness, and self reliance, all important qualities in men soon to be inducted into the military services. Lives would be saved if inductees had inter-scholastic competitive experience. Intramural contests offered in-adequate incentives to participation in sports. On the other hand it was argued both that intramural sports involved much larger numbers of youth than did interscholastic, the latter providing for participation for only a very small number, and that even without the gas ration interscholastic competition would somehow continue.[1]

There is no way to appraise the settlement of such a question by a direct appeal to the equality–majority principle. If the prin-ciple were invoked as a criterion, the observer or appraiser would have to work his way carefully from such specific criteria as are cited in the arguments, through intermediate criteria to, at last, his evidence that a decision would, in fact, respect the majority's values. Moreover, for most specific government decisions values cited on any side of the issue will typically be alleged to be values of almost everyone. In this particular decision mental alertness and physical fitness are assumed to be so; and, on the other side participation by many instead of a few is also assumed to be nearly a universal value. In conflicts between price-level stability and full employ-ment, between aiding Latin America and restricting public expendi-tures, between more liberal unemployment compensation and strengthening incentives to drive the unemployed back to work, everyone is assumed to value both of the conflicting values. Hence the value conflict does not appear as an interpersonal or intergroup conflict to which the equality principle is directly applicable.

If the principle is applicable at all, it is because one assumes that with respect to the final reconciliation of pairs or sets of con-flicting values, even though everyone esteems both or all of the conflicting values, individuals will finally differ as to their prefer-ences for how the conflict is resolved; some may wish, for example, relatively more price-level stability, and others may wish relatively more employment. But the usefulness of the equality criterion is drastically reduced when issues are pushed back to a question of preferences on exchange ratios between values—how much unem-ployment is it worth suffering to avoid how much price inflation—for on such an issue anyone can claim almost anything he wants as to the fact of whether this or that value is desired by this or that number of citizens. No one can know the facts about that subtle kind of value or preference.

To be sure, in some cases the justification of a decision by reference to values almost everyone shares is so transparent that the appeal is discredited. For example, during World War II deer hunters asked for special gas rations so that they could contribute to the nation's limited supply of meat. Yet even in cases like that we cannot always apply the equality criterion directly.

If fishermen want streams stocked with fish, motorists more thruways, nature lovers more wilderness areas, music lovers more tax-supported concerts, farmers better rural roads, the equality principle does not tell us that each of these minorities should be denied. What, then, does it indicate? It indicates that decisions to indulge these minorities should be taken to the extent that a majority approves. But who can say he knows to what extent expenditures for these minority purposes are sanctioned by majorities?

If no one knows just what the values are that are to be equally regarded, another fundamental obstacle to the application of the majority criterion, directly or indirectly, is that on most issues that come before government decision makers citizens' preferences are, in fact, unformed. As was indicated in Chapters 6 and 14, citizens do not know what they value except in interchange with leaders on whom they are dependent for information and advice. In a complex process of interchange in which leaders respond to some vague preferences of the citizenry, meanwhile guiding and forming specific decision preferences of the citizenry, it will never be clear whether a decision followed majority preference or majority preference followed the decision. It will be easy to claim or deny the sanction of the majority principle for any decision to be evaluated.

It might be thought that there is a solution to all these ambiguities and uncertainties. One need only take note of those major expressions of majority preference that occur in elections. Accepting the majority criterion, an observer could then pronounce a decision or outcome of mutual adjustment defective if on an issue on which voters had expressed their preferences the decision or outcome did not correspond to those preferences. In addition, many specific decisions not entering into the election campaign could be evaluated in the light of the expressed preferences, at least more easily than in the light of inferred or hypothetically informed preferences.

In actual fact the number of issues that are raised during a campaign limits the applicability of this evaluative device. For most public decisions—even for most major decisions—there is no recent election in which a majority opinion on the issue has been expressed. To go further, elections—other than referenda—permit the expression of majority sentiment on no issue other than which candidate should take office. It seems now clearly established that a majority vote for a candidate favoring, say, generous Western reclamation projects is quite consistent with overwhelming majority sentiment against that policy. Elections are often won by the votes of a collection of minorities, each gathered around one issue.[2]

OBJECTIONS TO THE MAJORITY–EQUALITY
PRINCIPLE ITSELF

If the majority criterion is deficient on grounds of obscurity and inapplicability even for those who accept it, it is also disabled because there is, even among the most detached observers of decision making who might be expected to accept it as a criterion for a practical rule, uncertainty on how far to follow it, even where it is not obscure and inapplicable. Some will object to it, of course, because they want to establish a political aristocracy, because they believe the educated or the rich should count for more than the uneducated or the poor, or for other fundamentally inegalitarian reasons. In addition, however, those favorably disposed toward political equality will depart from equal weight for various reasons and in varying degree. Here we can return to some of the points on the inadequacy of the equality principle briefly introduced in Chapter 9.

To begin with, the view that at least in some cases the weight given preferences should be adjusted to take account of intensity of feeling about them contradicts the majority principle. We need not take a position on whether intensity should count; our point is only that equality as a criterion is seriously compromised by a regard for intensity. Some competent appraisers of mutual adjustment would argue that a majority preference for racial desegregation is not enough to justify desegregation policies; the policies must be tempered by consideration for the intensity of minority opposition to them. Some would say that a majority preference for segregation is similarly not enough. Many would say that a passionate desire of a minority for a municipal park and playground should prevail over a moderate disclination of a majority to finance the venture.

Consider the hypothesis that in principle intensity should be weighed into a decision only insofar as each equally weighted citizen wishes to take them, his and others' intensity, into account in deciding his own preference on an issue. If intensity were so handled, and citizens did in fact considerately regard each other's intensity, then strict equality in weighting individual preferences would result in an incorporation of regard for intensity. Whether, if it were possible, intensity should be taken account of in that way and only in that way, is not easy to decide. There is no evidence that such a possibility has ever been widely considered. We have introduced the possibility not because it is a real one but because it clarifies the variety of ways in which it might be argued that intensity should be allowed to influence decisions.

Secondly, those who might wish to use such a criterion as equality for evaluating mutual adjustment will also disagree over how far to depart from the criteria in order to endorse the guarantee of certain minimum values to everyone. Many will say, for example, that no matter how overwhelming the majority, no decision or outcome that arbitrarily takes property from a minority for the benefit of a majority can be condoned. Strictly speaking the majority principle permits such a decision or outcome.

To be sure, it might be argued that as a practical matter there is a majority opinion in American and other societies that such decisions are intolerable; hence one does not depart from the majority principle in deploring a system that permits such a decision. Logically, however, a majority can, and sometimes does, take advantage of its power to act in ways that some observers think are abusive of the minimum values of minorities. In contemplation of that possibility one might conceivably decide that he wants no constitutional constraints on the majority, although he remains greatly troubled on the question that is relevant to the present inquiry: In appraising mutual adjustment how far does one want to depart from the criterion of the majority principle to include, as another criterion, protection of the minimum values of each and every person?

Thirdly, there will be other departures from the equality–majority principle on the ground that some values, being more carefully considered, should be more heavily weighted than others. This is not necessarily a departure from equality, but is so when the more carefully considered values are those of one set of individuals and the less well-considered those of another set. What is here referred to as a more carefully considered value is sometimes referred to as a more genuine or high-quality value. Whatever the terminology, many of us draw a distinction between a value that is not hastily considered and one that is.

We took note above, following the exposition in Chapter 6, of the degree to which values or preferences are formed only in interchanges between citizens and their leaders. Some observers attach no importance to political preferences hastily expressed outside such a process of interchange, as when in reply to an opinion poll a citizen declares that he is in favor of a piece of legislation about which he in fact knows nothing. They do not believe in interpersonal equality in regard for preferences of that quality so carelessly considered. On the other hand, a citizen's opinion on an issue that has been much debated, or on one on which some leader in whom the citizen has confidence has taken a position known to that citizen, is to be taken seriously.

Fourthly, as a practical recourse most of us depart from equality in varying degrees in order to acknowledge the claims of a special interest in a policy area. We assume that the values of the citizens of New Haven should be weighted more heavily than the values of residents of other cities in decisions on the control of traffic in New Haven; hence we sanction, as a matter of fact, a monopoly of control over New Haven traffic decisions, with few exceptions, to the city of New Haven. If we consider New Haven citizens to feel more intensely about traffic than non-New Haveners, this point adds nothing to the point earlier made. It seems possible, however, that we often depart from equality in the direction of conceding special weight to citizens with a special stake in some body of decisions without considering whether they feel more intensely. We assume that the frequency of their involvement with the questions at issue or the other objective evidence of their higher rate of involvement is sufficient to justify special weights for them. The argument for special weights in such cases can be made formally without reference to intensity of preference.

Fifthly, some observers will also justify departures from equal weighting because they want to motivate active participation in politics. In varying degrees they believe it desirable that at least some citizens write their Congressmen, participate in political campaigns, take part in interest groups, and play the traditional role of the "good citizen." People who do these things win larger weight for their own preferences, and inequality in their favor can be argued to be a necessary incentive for them. To be sure, some of them may participate actively because they like the activity itself; but not certain that this is sufficient motivation, some observers want the additional incentive of greater weight held out to participants. As a practical matter there is not much open choice as to whether the incentives are to be offered, because, as already recognized, participation does increase one's weight. The point is, however, that the resulting inequalities are not to be regretted, are not to be suppressed even if it were possible to do so.

Lastly, an objection to the majority-equality criterion is that it conflicts with the criterion of consent. So important is this conflict that we must give it special prominence.

Equality versus Consent

The strong appeal of the equality criterion lies in its close association with democratic government. If we wish to discuss methods of decision making appropriate to political democracy, it seems at first blush difficult to escape from a commitment to the equality–majority principle. Yet in actual fact we escape in a variety of ways. Any real-world government called democratic departs from the equality principle not only in ways dismissed as regrettable aberrations, but also in ways sanctioned by very large numbers of thoughtful observers. In the United States we sanction, but not by reference to the equality principle, the unequal representation of citizens from large and small states in the Senate and, to some degree, unequal representation in state legislatures.

In opposition to the equality principle are some constraints on the weighting of values that cannot be disregarded without crippling what is called democratic government. We cannot specify precisely what they are, we can only say that some allocations of conflicting values undermine the consent that citizens give to be governed in what we call a democratic manner. By one view, in which democracy is defined as government by consent, if citizens do not consent then democracy is to that degree curtailed. By another view, in which consent is conceived of as facilitating democratic government, if they do not consent they make democratic government more difficult to operate. By either view some resolutions of value conflict are, because of their consequences for consent, inimical to democratic government. Such a belief does not deny, of course, that other factors also influence consent.

That no one knows precisely what allocations do and do not undermine that consent is not evidence that resolutions of value conflict can disregard the problem of assuring continuing consent, but instead encourages a generous regard for demands that might turn out to be the price that has to be paid for the continuing consent of those citizens who make the demands.

Consent plays a role in supporting any government. Presumably a Khrushchev remains in power because, in addition to the devices of repression he can call upon, his rule is consented to by other powerful participants in the governmental process. When they withdraw their consent he is deposed. In democracies, however, consent takes the place of other bonds for large numbers of persons, perhaps including all but an insignificant number of citizens. Even if the distinction between that to which one consents and that which one is forced to do is obscure and at best only a matter of degree, there is a difference between a chief executive who consents to step down when he hears the election returns and one who will not do so unless his life is threatened, a difference between citizens who consent to obeying the laws of their country and those who mix reluctant partial obedience with nights given to sabotage, between party leaders who consent to accept the election of the candidate they opposed and those who promote riots in the streets when defeated, and between taxpayers who pay, even if grumbling, and those who illegally but effectively refuse. But consent is not mere obedience to the law, for the citizen who obeys only under immediate threat of violence or imprisonment is not consenting to be governed as does a citizen who obeys by easily borne habit.

A disinclination of citizens to consent to their government shows itself in a variety of forms ranging from tax evasion through aggravated problems of law enforcement, riots and other forms of overt and conspicuous disobedience to the law, and *coups d'état*, to revolution. To most citizens of a democracy and to their leaders the practical advantages of encouraging consent are therefore conspicuous.

In some societies, like that of the United States, each of many citizens will consent because he believes his values will be counted for no less than those of any other citizen. To that degree the requirement that citizens be encouraged to consent to their government does not challenge the criterion of equal weight. But there are also many demands made upon the government for special treatment, and the satisfaction of these demands is often the price asked for consent. Hence the principle that values should be reconciled on such terms as encourage consent and the principle that they should be reconciled on the basis of interpersonal equality are to some degree competing principles in democratic government.

The consent principle in a sense takes precedence over the other. This is admittedly a loose statement, yet it carries some meaning. Most of us in the Western tradition would, if faced with a practical choice, probably sanction any degree of inequality necessary to maintain a government based on consent rather than a high degree of repression. We might doubt that a highly inequalitarian government could command consent; but if it could we would prefer it to a repressive egalitarianism. We are, it might be noted, fairly consistently recommending inequality plus consent over repressive egalitarianism to underdeveloped nations, where the Communists appear to be offering the latter over the former.

One might also argue that precedence was given to consent over equality in the writing of the Constitution of the United States. As the political leaders and citizens of that time appear to have seen the issue before them, their task was to win, by any necessary concession of special consideration to those who demanded it, the consent of all the colonies to the new venture in government. To be sure, there were some demands that if pressed would have blocked the establishment of the new government; that is to say, not every kind of inequality would be tolerated as the price of winning consent. But the urgent and fundamental need was for consent up to the degree that was won, and inequalitarian concessions to small states and to the minority of Southerners were willingly granted. That the Founding Fathers may well have estimated how much consent they needed is indicated by the history of the Whisky Rebellion. That it took place indicates that consent was limited; that it was dissipated so easily and that similar rebellions did not occur indicate the strength and pervasiveness of the consent that was granted to the new government.

Whatever the priority or rate of exchange between the two principles, the point is that they are often in conflict. And when in conflict, every thoughtful observer is troubled about how the two principles should be reconciled. To what extent, for example, should filibusters be accepted as necessary to consent? To what extent should inequalities be granted in favor of rural and small-town voters, or, for another example, to what extent should a variety of devices for overweighting the values of various minorities in the Senate and House be permitted?

In Constitutional provisions for inequality in order to gain consent—specifically the provision for representation in the Senate by states rather than by population—the price of consent is an inequality firmly lodged in the system that may persist after it is no longer necessary to win continuing consent. Such a provision may be protected by Constitutional provisions that make its removal difficult or impossible. But apparently some people will argue that inequalitarian commitments made in one generation to win consent should be perpetuated whether necessary for continuing consent or not; the commitment establishes a permanent moral obligation. Here again, then, is a conflict between the two principles of consent and inequality. In 1962, for example, a committee of fifteen scholars commenting on legislative apportionment unanimously declared:

The United States was created by thirteen sovereign states, and the Constitution embodies a theory of federalism which divides sovereign power between the nation and the states. A key device for protecting their residual sovereignty was the equal state voice in the Senate. Thus the Senate was a condition of union among a group of states which *the Federal Government created by that union has no power to destroy.* Counties, by contrast, were never independent or sovereign. They did not create the states but were created by them. They are wholly creatures of the states and may at any time be merged, divided or abolished by state governments [italics mine].

What is the relation between the requirement that weights given to values encourage consent and a requirement that they take account of the varying intensity with which values are held? To anyone who denies the significance of differences in intensity except as they can be made objective through the behavior of citizens, taking account of consent takes account of intensity. He might believe that if the frustration of intense desires does not show itself in disobedience or revolution, it can be disregarded. On the other hand, he might acknowledge that intensity can be proved by forms of behavior—petitions, peaceful demonstrations, and the like—that by no means imply a withdrawal of consent, in which case he can distinguish a problem of intensity from one of consent. Others less fastidious in their demands for evidence of differences in intensity, too, will often draw a distinction. On many issues they might propose a difference in weights to take account of different intensities even if they were persuaded that the withdrawal of consent was not at all at issue. Then, too, one can distinguish consent and intensity as separate problems in weighting if one believes that citizens may demand special favor in weights—and insist on them as a price for their consent—even though they do not intensely feel the preferences for which they demand special consideration. Their demands may be rooted not in intensity of feeling but in, say, a tradition of belief that they are entitled to favor on certain issues.

The Equality Criterion and the Democratic Faith

Does our deprecation of the equality principle as a criterion for appraising decision making clash with the apparent evidence that there exists in such societies as the United States a nearly unanimous citizen commitment to democratic government? Granted that there is such a commitment, there need not be a comparable commitment to an equalitarian principle specific enough to be useful for appraisal of decisions or decision systems. To be sure, political scientists have commonly alleged that a prerequisite for political democracy is a consensus on certain values and rules of the game. But the consensus need be only a very loose one, as seems to be the case with the equality principle. One might ask why consensus has been thought to be necessary anyway. Presumably because, unless citizens agree on certain values and rules, government by consent is not possible. In the absence of such consensus one imagines only the possibility of a highly coercive or repressive government. But Carl Friedrich has argued skillfully that consent takes the form of common behavior rather than agreement on principles.[4] Certainly proximate threats to the viability of democracy come from behavior other than verbal, from unrest, disobedience, and revolution; hence it would appear that commitment to verbal principle is, in any case, less important than commitment to certain acceptable forms of political behavior.

It might be suggested, then, that the overwhelming commitment to democracy of, say, American citizens takes the form of verbal commitment to loose and abstract principles that are quite inadequate for application,[5] and of habits of political behavior that proximately support democratic government. Given the habits, repression is at a minimum, and government is consented to even in the absence of consensus on less loose and abstract principles.

If this is so our deprecation of equality as a criterion for evaluating decisions and decision systems is not in conflict with evidence of a near unanimous citizen commitment to political democracy. Moreover, it is now possible to suggest that the endorsement by habitual political behavior, though not by consensus on principles, of dispersion of power, of widespread participation in decision making, of interest groups, of partisanship among agencies and elected officials, of negotiation, and of all other means of partisan mutual adjustment, the ubiquity of which is evidence of their endorsement, may make it possible to argue that these aspects of government are more firm and meaningful points of near unanimous commitment than any loose formulation of the majority or equality principle capable of commanding an equally widespread commitment. That is to say, we are now in a position to consider the possibility that the weighting of values in a decision or decision system might be evaluated as acceptable not because it can be shown to respect equality but because it is controlled by the very features of political behavior that constitute partisan mutual adjustment. But this runs ahead of our story.

In any case, the allegation that the values of different persons are unequally weighted in partisan mutual adjustment is now seen to be an allegation of very dubious relevance, for we have seen that the allegation appeals to a criterion of equality that is not at all suitable for appraising decision systems like partisan mutual adjustment.

Chapter

17

INEQUALITY AND

MUTUAL ADJUSTMENT

THE DISCUSSION IN THE PRE-
ceding chapter of deficiencies in the equality criterion illuminated
features of decision making that would presumably enter into any
thoughtful person's appraisal of decision systems. We can, therefore, now ask to what extent the weighing of conflicting values in
partisan mutual adjustment departs from equality randomly or
in some sense perversely or, on the contrary, in ways that might in
fact be sanctioned in the light of the foregoing discussion of deficiencies in the equality criterion.

Points of Correspondence Between Sanctioned Inequality and the Inequality of Partisan Mutual Adjustment

Partisan mutual adjustment is egalitarian in the extremely loose way in which the egalitarian principle is agreed to and is inegalitarian in the various ways in which the egalitarian principle is often qualified. It is in a very loose and rough sense egalitarian because, as we saw in Chapter 15, other things being equal, the more widely a value is shared the higher its weight (proposition 8 of Chapter 15). This follows from the characteristics of elected officials and party leaders for whom mere numbers of voters count, and from the characteristics of interest-group leaders, who gain in influence, other things being equal, according to the numbers of citizens for whom they speak, and from the role of alliances in mutual adjustment by which widely shared values receive the support of a variety of allied decision makers. Moreover, all the propositions of Chapter 14 on agreement explain how partisan mutual adjustment both follows lines of agreement and encourages the development of agreement.

Partisan mutual adjustment is, on the other hand, inegalitarian in that values that stimulate citizens to participate in voting, in interest groups, and in other political activity gain higher weights than values that do not. But this inequality provides an incentive to political participation, and incentives of that kind have just been seen to justify a qualification of a strict equality–majority principle. Moreover, in mutual adjustment intensely held values are weighted higher than those less intensely held (proposition 9 of Chapter 15); on this point, too, there is a correspondence between a desired qualification of the equality–majority principle and a feature of mutual adjustment.

Partisan mutual adjustment is also inegalitarian—at least as we know it in the United States and some other countries—in that it permits an extraordinarily large and varied number of agencies, groups, elected officials, and party leaders to influence policy out of proportion to the number of citizens for whom they might be presumed to act (proposition 2 of Chapter 15). On almost any issue very small groups can count on being heard; on some issues very small groups or their representatives have a veto power; and on very many issues these small groups can insist on prolonging problem settlement and on having an influence on the terms of settlement—witness the influence of antivivisectionists, of nuclear disarmament groups, or of die-hard segregationists in national politics. But, again, this feature of mutual adjustment corresponds to another respectable dissent from equality: that to some degree equal weighting shall not be allowed to violate a guarantee of certain minimum values to everyone. Clearly the characteristic inequality of partisan mutual adjustment on this score goes beyond the guarantee of the right to speak and other civil liberties; it permits minorities to have influence on policy disproportionate to their numbers. But, correspondingly, the endorsement of departures from inequality to guarantee minimum values to everyone seems to go beyond the endorsement of civil liberties, so that this feature of partisan mutual adjustment and a persuasive qualification of the equality rule appear to match each other at least roughly. (We shall, however, have more to say in a later chapter about the role of the minority veto in partisan mutual adjustment.)

Again, partisan mutual adjustment is inegalitarian in the disproportionate weight sometimes given to the values of those who are conceded a special interest in or concern with a decision or issue (proposition 10 of Chapter 15). But, again, this feature corresponds to a widely sanctioned qualification of the rule of equality, as we have just seen.

This rough point-by-point correspondence between characteristics of the value weighting process in partisan mutual adjustment and agreed qualifications of the equality–majority rule would, if necessary, be worth dwelling on for a number of pages because it is an extremely important fact about partisan mutual adjustment. But the rough correspondence is on most points obvious, and we shall not labor it. There remains, of course, the difficulty that one may believe the correspondence to be too loose.

EQUALITY, BUT NOT MAJORITARIAN EQUALITY

There is a point of correspondence between a widely sanctioned qualification of the majority principle and a feature of partisan mutual adjustment not so quickly perceived; it arises in those situations in which equality calls for some other form of the principle than the majority principle. We have taken note of egalitarianism in the form of "They got what they wanted the last time; now it's our turn to have our way." Egalitarianism in that form can be construed as demanding that those outvoted by a majority on one issue be allowed, because they were outvoted, to prevail on another issue. This is a principle applied selectively rather than universally, and we noted that when it should be applied is not a question on which competent appraisers would agree. One might seek to assimilate it into the majority principle by claiming that it should be applied only when a majority wishes to apply it, but it is not clear that the majority principle is the appropriate rule for governing its applications. It seems quite possible that it is a principle in competition in many people's minds with the straightforward majority principle, as though people wished to hold that equality means more than letting a majority decide issues, that in addition it sometimes calls for allocating *some* values to those whose values at issue were denied them by the majority vote.

Strategic decision making in partisan mutual adjustment, because it is remedial, serial, and fragmented, is consistent with this stream in egalitarian thought. As we have seen it is a method of decision making in which very little justification is attempted for any single decision taken alone. One can claim that by this method decisions are democratic, respectful of the equality principle, and are deserving of endorsement because any one decision offsets other decisions to which it is related. Thus the wartime decision to impose a legal maximum on wages was defended on the egalitarian ground that ceilings would also be imposed on prices; that is to say, policy proposed to deprive wage earners along one line and gratify them along another. Or, as we noted, President Kennedy held out tax reform as an exchange for his attack on a steel price increase in 1962; or a policy may give special consideration to fishermen and hunters, a small minority, because it also gives special consideration to other minorities.

Partisan mutual adjustment, as a form of strategic decision making, enlarges, through the multiplication of decision makers, the opportunities to practice remedially the egalitarian rule of

"Since it was your turn on that point, it is my turn on this one." The practice of the rule through partisan mutual adjustment makes it possible to discover many alternative ways of allocating values widely, where, in the absence of mutual adjustment, remedial equalizing moves would be much more restricted. In calculated adjustment, for example, or in approximations to deferential adjustment, X can be indulged on some points where he is frustrated on others. Reciprocity too is an equalizer; the norm of reciprocity itself is, for those who accept it, a kind of egalitarian rule. Unfortunately for the appraisal of partisan mutual adjustment, the practice of this form of the equality rule is often characterized as logrolling, which is indeed one of the ways it can be practiced. On this form of the practice, sometimes alleged to be degenerate, we shall have more to say in a later chapter.

The Quality of Values

In the preceding chapter we noted the demand, qualifying equality, that more carefully considered values should count more heavily than less well-considered values; this is a demand to which partisan mutual adjustment responds in important respects not immediately obvious. It follows from a number of the propositions in Chapter 14 (on agreement) that partisan mutual adjustment encourages a never-ending reconsideration of values. Generally, we saw, motives to push toward agreement are powerful in partisan mutual adjustment (proposition 2, Chapter 14), and this fact in itself accounts for reconsidering what one demands. But the need for allies reinforces a reconsideration and modification of demands (proposition 3, Chapter 14); so also do the costs of attaining demands constitute a moderating influence (proposition 4, Chapter 14). Moreover, because decision making is open ended, commitments are tentative and demands can be accommodating where they would otherwise be intransigent (proposition 5, Chapter 14). And, of course, in partisan discussion as one form of mutual adjustment, a carefully considered demand will survive the test of critical discussion better than one that is hastily considered.

These are impressive reasons for believing that values in

partisan mutual adjustment are indeed often carefully considered and that, other things being equal, the careful consideration given to a value is a source of strength on its behalf. The values or demands that remain to be reconciled when the possibilities of agreement are exhausted are largely those that have survived the processing through which the search for agreement passes the values in dispute. These considerations would suggest that hastily considered values tend to be driven out of the political arena.

There is, however, another attribute of partisan mutual adjustment that is significant for the quality of the values represented in decision making. As we have seen in the preceding chapter, a "good" decision requires some clarification of more or less stable values held by the citizen—or, if not of stable values, at least of those key values that are consequential for a variety of decisions. It also requires a careful linking of those values with the decision to be preferred, which is an empirical task of extraordinary complexity. Now if we mean by a well-considered value a relatively immediate and specific demand, preference, or valued course of action that has been carefully tied to a clarified set of key values, it becomes clear that such a well-considered value will not be formulated unless leadership is available both to clarify the key values and to establish the chain of connection between them and the policy position.

The required role for leadership is twofold: it is empirical and evaluative. For the empirical work of establishing the chain of connection, it might appear that decision makers in a central system and in a system of partisan mutual adjustment would be equally capable. For the work of clarifying key values, however, the partisan mutual adjuster might be argued to be more competent. For he enters into, as we saw in the model of the governmental process, a continuing interchange with citizens for whom he attempts both to articulate and to mold their values, the latter through the superior information he commands. As a leader with loyalties and other affiliations to a segment of the citizenry or to a segment of the interests of all citizens, he can, without denying the arbitrary element in citizen selection of key values, raise the level of sophistication at which they are considered. By contrast, the ostensibly unattached decision maker in the central system does not participate in such an intimate interchange that both allows himself to be influenced by his followers' views and, at the same time, changes his followers' perceptions of their views. If we could imagine a pure case of central decision making, the divorce in this respect between decision maker and citizen would be striking.

Consent

Consent requires inequality, we have seen; and consent in earlier periods of history required inequalitarian concessions in nearly ineradicable forms, so that today's inequalities are partly the price of yesterday's consent. It should be obvious that many (but not all) of the inequalities too quickly objected to in partisan mutual adjustment—some of the heavy weights, for example, given to Southern whites—are those necessary to gain consent. The simple correspondence between the sanctioned qualification of equality and this feature of partisan mutual adjustment hardly needs developing.

One might wish to ask, however, whether a central system could so allocate weights as to satisfy the requirement of consent, as that requirement was spelled out earlier in the chapter. The actual historical fact is, of course, that in the period of the Constitutional Convention in America, certain minorities could not distinguish between disproportionate *weights* for their values and disproportionate *power* to protect those values. No highly centralized system could guarantee the weight to their values they demanded as the price of their consent to the Constitution; certainly no centralized system could assure the continuation of the weight they demanded. As a practical choice unusual weight called for unusual power; hence, for example, the special attention that policy making must give to the preferences of citizens of small states is provided for in their grant of power in the Senate.

Moreover, the price of consent often is not that disproportionate weight be attached to preferences generally at issue, but that the consenting group be able to call for disproportionate weight on certain kinds of issues or in a certain way. This, we can see, requires the dispersal of power that gives rise to partisan mutual adjustment and shuts out the possibility of a high degree of centrality.

If one could meet the needs of consent simply by allocating two or more votes to certain classes of citizens, thus giving them a generalized superiority in weighting, one could easily imagine a highly centralized system consistent with that equality. But such a generalized inequality is intolerable to many citizens; in effect it would buy the consent of some only at the price of the withdrawal of others. Moreover, it is a greater inequality than is demanded by those whose consent is sought. Citizens of states with small populations demand not a general disproportion but a disproportion in the form of representation in one house by state rather than by population. Rural citizens demand not a general disproportion but one that takes the form of discrimination in state affairs in favor of the preferences of citizens of already established communities. Southern senators demand not two votes for their constituents but the right to filibuster.

The intolerability of general inequality and the acceptability and mutual compatibility of highly specialized kinds of inequality as a price for consent thus results in a distribution of power that does not permit a high degree of centrality. At an extreme veto powers may be widely distributed; but short of that various decision makers possess special powers that vary according to the kind of decision at issue. In a system in which, on one issue, the preferences of citizens of Connecticut small towns and rural areas are most heavily weighted, while, on another issue, the preferences of white Southerners are most heavily weighted, while, on still a third issue, those interests that find their chief spokesman in the President take priority, central coordination is crippled.

The conclusion is therefore not only that partisan mutual adjustment is consistent with the requirement of consent but that the requirements of consent will, depending on demands made as the price for consent, be inconsistent with the possibility of central coordination. This is, although in different language, a familiar observation on American government; but where the inference is often drawn that the need for central coordination requires the suppression of the obstructing special concessions of weight and power, a no less appropriate inference might be that consent requires an alternative to central coordination.

If partisan mutual adjustment is consistent with the requirements of consent, it is also worth adding that the propositions of Chapter 14 on agreement can be marshalled to show that partisan mutual adjustment makes a contribution to the ease with which consent is granted. For the propositions that characterize the ways in which partisan mutual adjustment encourages agreement and exploits fully such agreement as exists are at the same time descriptions of processes that avoid challenges to consent, that reduce the reasons for withholding consent, and that reduce the possible losses of granting consent.

Our controlling concern, however, is how departures from the equality principle in partisan mutual adjustment fit or do not fit the requirements of consent. If we were to go beyond that limited inquiry into the subject of consent, there would be no end of discussion. For one can question, to take up a line of inquiry about central coordination that lies outside the scope of this book, whether, quite aside from various minorites wishing disproportionate weights, a majority would consent to an extreme of centralism in government decision making. Or, for another example of a line of possible inquiry, we might ask whether partisan mutual adjustment is not, in fact, a system of decision making in which minor withdrawals of consent are not made part of the accepted game, so that such withdrawals become moves in the adjustment process rather than challenges to a coordinator.

Let us be clear, therefore, that our intention is not to raise the question of which of the two coordinating systems is more likely to be consented to; it is only to examine consent in its connection with the allegation that weights are unequally assigned in partisan mutual adjustment and with the defense against that allegation: that indeed they are, and for many reasons among which is that inequality is necessary to consent. We have not claimed, it might also be noted, that there is any agreement as to how far the need for consent sanctions inequalities, nor that we know which of various claims for special weight as a price of consent are genuine or spurious.

Chapter 18

PUBLIC INTEREST

AND

GROUP INTERESTS

Alternative Concepts of Public Interest

WE HAVE DISTINGUISHED BE-
tween defects of partisan mutual adjustment and defects of a particular distribution of weights in a system of adjustment, showing
that since weights are variable in such a system, a criticism of any
particular set of weights is not necessarily a criticism of the fundamental adjustment process. Hence, one may be outraged, say, by
the weights given to the preferences of pharmaceutical firms in
their negotiations with the Food and Drug Administration and yet
not conclude that partisan mutual adjustment is inappropriate in
that relationship.

What remaining objections can nevertheless be raised to the
process? One is that although in principle undesirable weights can
be altered, in practice they cannot. We shall consider that possi-

bility in the immediately following chapter. Another is that despite the variability of possible weights in a system, there is some inherent tendency in it to betray the "public" interest, in particular a tendency to the pursuit of narrowly held rather than broadly shared values. Since it has been shown that weights among values can be altered at least in principle, it might be thought that this challenge has been met; for if widely shared or "public" values are underweighted, they can be given greater weight, especially through reallocation of authority to governmental participants in the process. For those, however, who suspect some underlying disposition of participants in mutual adjustment to preoccupy themselves with narrow values to the exclusion of "public" values, we shall here undertake a further investigation of the allegation that the public interest somehow evaporates from partisan mutual adjustment.

THE INFLATED CONCEPT

We need to analyze the allegation at once in order to see what new issues are raised. At one extreme, the terms "public interest," "general welfare," and "common good" can be taken to refer to a general aggregate denoting what is on balance good for the citizenry. The pursuit of the public interest, general welfare, or common good is, then, a comprehensive consideration in public policy making; and these terms refer to the most general and supreme goal of public policy. To say that partisan mutual adjustment does or does not serve the public interest is to assert nothing specific about it other than that taking everything into account it has features that lead one on balance to endorse it or condemn it.

The evaluation of partisan mutual adjustment pursued in the preceding chapters has raised a variety of questions about the consequences of a policy-making and coordinating system in which partisans pursue partisan interests. We have therefore asked a variety of questions about grounds on which the pursuit of partisan interests might be expected to achieve or fail to achieve acceptable results. The chapter can therefore be read as having explored the extent to which partisan mutual adjustment serves the public interest, general welfare, or common good. The allegation that the process does not serve it poses no new issue and asserts no new fact or hypothesis, if "public interest," "general welfare," and "common good" are defined in this first summary and comprehensive sense.

To be sure, we have not completed the analysis, in the eyes of anyone who believes he knows much more precisely than we have claimed to know what, in this large sense, is in the public interest, and who is therefore willing and able to lay down some firm principles about the character of the public interest. For our analysis of partisan mutual adjustment has made a variety of points that are presumably relevant to anyone's general evaluation of the process, yet has shrunk from attempting a final evaluation in the light of some social ideal or set of comprehensive principles. In shrinking from such an attempt, I am both acknowledging that those to whom this work is addressed do not agree on any such ideal and that I have no such set even for myself. And it is, of course, widespread political disagreement on ideals or criteria that constitutes one of the principle political problems to which partisan mutual adjustment can be considered a response.

THE DEFLATED CONCEPT

The allegation that the public interest is neglected can also be read as a more modest and specific criticism.[1] Here the public interest refers specifically to values thought by their sponsors to be of value to almost everyone. They will be either values in fact widely shared or values which partisan advocates can and do honestly recommend to those citizens who do not yet appreciate them. They stand in contrast to objectives or policies that can benefit only a few. Whether a value is a shareable or a narrow value turns not on the state of preference of the citizenry or the potential state of preference (though these may be relevant pieces of evidence), but on whether some objective or policy is conceived of as benefiting almost everyone or only a few. The question, then, is whether participants in mutual adjustment promote, deliberately or otherwise, shareable values, so defined. In this reduced form the allegation that partisan mutual adjustment sacrifices the public interest to group interests is understandable. But, again, it turns out to raise no new issue. For this is a possibility on which a great deal has already been said in preceding chapters, going beyond the point that value weights can be altered where unsatisfactory.

In Chapter 14, on social agreement, we explored a variety of reasons for expecting partisan mutual adjustment to move participants toward agreement, hence toward values they believe shareable. Some of the reasons given—in the form of the numbered propositions on which the chapter was built—bear directly on the question of whether widely shared values are given heavy weight:

(2) *Participants in partisan mutual adjustment have stronger motives than do central coordinators to find an agreed decision or outcome.*

(3) *The need for allies is an especially powerful motivation toward agreement in partisan mutual adjustment.*

(4) *Agreement is also encouraged by the moderation imposed on demands in partisan mutual adjustment, by reason of the tasks and other responsibilities attached to making a demand.*

(7) *In partisan discussion, in contrast to cooperative discussion, is to be found an important potential for agreement.*

(8) *Compensation, bargained compensation, and partisan discussion are available as a means of testing whether a given state of affairs is a Pareto optimum for the potential negotiators and, if it is not, of moving to such an optimum.*

The pursuit of agreement is not on every count a pursuit of shared values rather than values peculiar to a subgroup; but these propositions selected from the earlier discussion may recall our discussion of the many ways in which partisan mutual discussion becomes, on some counts, a never-ending search for the values in a society that can be widely shared. Each proposition identifies a specific feature of the pursuit of agreement that makes that pursuit simultaneously a pursuit of shared values.

That the pursuit of agreement turns participants to the pursuit of shared values does not, of course, offer sufficient assurance that the values will be those so widely shared or shareable as to constitute, by the present definition of the term, the public interest. But other chapters offer a good deal more on that point. In Chapter 15, on conflicting values, proposition 2 stated: *Other things being equal, the more widely shared a value, interest, or preference, the heavier its weight in partisan mutual adjustment.* The supporting argument, it will be remembered, rests first on the support given by all participants in partisan mutual adjustment to those values they share, even if those values are not the major objectives of any of them; and, secondly, on the special authority and other powers given those participants who have as their responsibilities the pursuit of widely shared values. It needs further to be said that it is obvious—and the term is deliberate—that many important participants in partisan mutual adjustment have as a principal concern or interest, steadily or at intervals, some shareable value. The military arms of government pursue national security; the Antitrust Division, the maintenance of more or less competitive markets; the Securities and Exchange Commission, the protection of the investor against a variety of practices declared to be not in the public interest; the President, a variety of shared interests too numerous to list; and the League of Women Voters, the Foreign Policy Association, the Committee to Defend America by Aiding the Allies, America First, the Planned Parenthood Federation, the Navy League, the Farm Bureau Federation, the AFL–CIO, and the Chamber of Commerce of the United States all pursue characteristic shareable values the character of which is often clear from the name of the organization. To be sure, all of these organizations pursue some narrow values, and at a given time one of them may be pursuing a narrow value to the exclusion of a shareable value. But even the greatest of the acknowledged pressure groups are deeply committed to the pursuit of shared values, as is the AFL–CIO in its pursuit of rights and procedures often referred to as industrial democracy, and as is any businessman's organization in its attempts to restrict the regulatory scope of government.

That you or I might not regard, say, industrial democracy or constraints on government economic regulation as valuable does not, of course, deny that those participants in partisan mutual adjustment hold them to be values or that they are genuinely shareable. For some shareable values pursued by one or another group we will, of course, take note of a mixture of shareable and narrow values that appear to govern the policy of the group, and we may even be confident that the assertion of a shareable value is window dressing for the pursuit of a narrow value. Still, let us not deny that, for one reason or another, many participants in partisan mutual adjustment vigorously and explicitly espouse shareable values. Nor should we deny that many participants, like the National Wildlife Federation, the American Civil Liberties Union, the National Committee for Mental Hygiene, as well, of course, as many legislators, executives, and agencies, are deeply committed to shareable values that are not at all masks for narrow values.

Collective Values

To find a new issue in the allegation that the public interest, general welfare, or common good are sacrificed to group interests in partisan mutual adjustment it is necessary to give these terms a still more restricted meaning. If these terms are taken to refer not simply to shareable values generally but only to those shareable values that are in some sense collective or indivisible, the allegation indeed becomes a more specific one than has yet been considered.

The distinction is this: A value is collective to the degree that a benefit from it cannot accrue to one member of the citizenry without accruing in some significant amount to many others, and cannot be withheld from one member without being in some significant amount withheld from others. By contrast, a private or particular value is any other value, specifically a value whose benefit can accrue to one or a few alone, including a value whose benefit to one is at the expense of benefit to another.

Thus both national defense and language, in addition to being shareable values, are collective values to the extent that benefits to one citizen are simultaneously benefits to many others. So also is public education to the extent that education is an asset to all or many rather than merely an advantage to those who receive the education. To the extent that any of us benefit from living in a society of educated citizens, public education is a collective value.

Other collective values include law and order, the maintenance of markets, and any valuable rule for the distribution of particular values.

To conceive of these two kinds of values it need not be assumed that all members of a group regard the collective values as a value, or its benefits as benefits. I may, for example, as an observer of a society composed largely of pacifists, consider national defense arrangements to be a value, of benefit to each member of the society despite their opposition to them. Hence, to draw a distinction easily overlooked, collective values are not necessarily agreed values. Nor, for that matter, are agreed values necessarily collective; in a society in which everyone agrees that electric refrigeration is a value, its value can nevertheless remain almost wholly particular.

Given this distinction, the criticism of partisan mutual adjustment that appears to follow is that since decisions will be evaluated and made by partisans, and since partisans are concerned with their particular values (hence insensitive to collective values), collective values will suffer. The possibility that all or nearly all can simultaneously benefit when X benefits from a value is, it might be feared, a matter of indifference to X. His partisanship gives him habits of thought that lead him to look for particular values rather than collective; and, when the benefits *to him* of a collective value are smaller than those of a particular value, it will be to his advantage to neglect the former in favor of the latter despite the gains to many or all that would follow if only he would pursue the former.

In many governmental systems inattention to the value of national security promises an end to the system; so also does inattention to the value of law and order. In more or less democratic systems neglect of the value of literacy and other forms of knowledge is not consistent with the viability of democracy. In almost any governmental system in a large industrialized society, for example, neglect of the values of a more or less stable monetary system and a system of markets is so damaging to the welfare of the citizenry as to constitute a source of revolutionary unrest.

In addition, however, to collective values that are well recognized there are others only imperfectly perceived—in some cases, perhaps, wholly missed. If one were to regard all values as preferences, one would say that in addition to recognized collective preferences there are others that would emerge from a more informed and thoughtful inspection by each individual of his own and others' preferences. It is not hard to believe, for example, that there is a yet unclarified collective value in certain reforms of agriculture price-support programs in the United States. Appropriate weight to collective values, therefore, calls for attention to their discovery, clarification, and formation; hence we recognize a problem more complicated than finding appropriate weights for collective values already recognized.

Because collective values often evaporate from pluralist and group theories of politics, we want here to acknowledge their existence and importance. Their obvious importance in the examples above hardly does justice to the claims that can be made on their behalf. There is, for example, a long tradition of belief, beginning in classical Greece, that the good life lies in the pursuit of the common good, according to which tradition it could be claimed that a preoccupation with collective values is the mark of the most fully developed, and therefore happiest, human being. In a younger tradition one can argue that collective values provide the basis of that fundamental prerequisite of political democracy: agreement on the desirability of certain political mechanisms and on certain fundamental policies or policy dispositions. In any case, by their very defined characteristic that if one citizen enjoys them others must also do so because their benefits spill over, they are especially gratifying values to pursue. To neglect values whose benefits spill over from one citizen to another would be to waste human opportunities.

Granted then that the allegation that collective values are sacrificed to particular values is a significant issue not already discussed, it now needs to be said that we can find no reason for believing that these values will be any more neglected than any other kind of shareable values. Everything we have just said about shareable values appears to hold for this subgroup of them. For example, that partisans explicitly pursue collective values as their principal goals seems as true as that they do so for other shareable values. Each of the above examples of partisan pursuit of a share-able value is, in fact, also an example of the pursuit of a collective value, as an inspection of the list of examples will quickly show.

Might there, however, be more agreement among participants on particular values than on collective values, hence on that ground a neglect of the latter? This seems hardly possible. It is in the very character of collective values that they stimulate agreement. For, by definition, they are those values that accrue to many if to anyone at all, and that are denied to many if to anyone at all. That is to say, no one can describe a value as collective without pointing to benefits to a large group, hence to a basis for agreement. Of course it is not therefore guaranteed that agreement is inevitable. Even though antivivisectionists believe that vivisection is generally dam-aging to the society and not merely to the members of their own group, they do not necessarily convince others. Still, leaving other considerations aside, the collective character itself of a value would seem to promise more rather than less agreement than on particu-lar values. One would expect more widespread agreement on the value of soil conservation, if conservation is presented as a policy of protecting national resources, than on the value of one or an-other of a variety of possible income distributions, each distribu-tion representing a different allocation of conflicting particular values.

When a given collective value does come to command wide-spread agreement, how do we explain that outcome? In some cases a de Gaulle, a Churchill, or a Lincoln finds, on an overview of his country's problems, a proposed collective interest on which he then wins the agreement of a vast segment of the citizenry. But such a feat is rare—these are not the daily occurrences of politics—and nearly impossible. If Churchill succeeded in moulding a collective interest in stubborn resistance to Nazism, de Gaulle succeeded with one large group only by failing with an extremely large minority; and Lincoln succeeded in making political equality a widely agreed political value by running the risks of civil war.

The more usual and successful process by which a collective value comes to command agreement is through partisan mutual adjustment. The collective interest in foreign aid that developed in

America after World War II, or the interest in exploring outer space, or the growing American interest in free international trade —all collective values—are the result of complex maneuvering to explore areas of agreement that were detailed in Chapter 14 in our discussion of social agreement.

Contemporary agreement on the value of foreign aid is, for example, a result of such factors as Secretary of State Marshall's dramatic public commitment to it in the form of the Marshall Plan, of earlier ventures into foreign aid in occupied territories in Europe, of continuing concern among the military with the survival of certain kinds of regimes abroad, of trade-union humanitarianism matched by some concern for a level of government spending suffi-cient to maintain high employment, and so on. All those who have participated in making the great variety of American public policies that together constitute American foreign aid have pursued partisan objectives—some collective and some not; and the result of their conflicts, mutual reinforcements, and bargains struck has been to create a nearly unanimous agreement on the collective value of at least some flow of foreign aid.

If collective values are explicitly pursued by many participants in partisan mutual adjustment, and if there seems little reason to believe in the existence of any special obstacles to agreement on them that underweigh them relative to particular values, it might nevertheless be objected that no participant in partisan mutual adjustment pursues an overriding aggregate of collective value, something that might be called "the" public interest, rather than "a" (hence one of many) public collective interest. Such an alle-gation would be true, for it is extraordinarily rare for anyone to try to formulate let alone pursue such an aggregate; at the same time the allegation may not be significant, or even valid, as a criticism of partisan mutual adjustment.

To propose that anyone formulate such an aggregate is to pro-pose an extreme of synoptic analysis. It is to suppose that the mind can—and to propose that the mind ought to—undertake a com-prehensive analysis of all policy questions taking full account of their interrelationships and aggregating all conflicting values at issue. It is to propose not such a collective value as law and order, national security, administrative efficiency, civil liberties, or economic growth but to substitute for these specifics one overriding aggregative goal so formulated as to take all of them into account. It is, in short, to propose to ignore again the very difficulties of problem solving with which this book is concerned and to which strategic decision making and partisan mutual adjustment are adapted. None of this proves the proposal to be wrongheaded; it is clear, however, that such a proposal (and its accompanying criticism: that in partisan mutual adjustment no one proposes such an attack on policy problems) does not constitute a specific new criticism of partisan mutual adjustment but instead represents a summary, implied restatement of all the claims for synoptic central decision making and claims against partisan mutual adjustment that have already been discussed. In short, to ask that "the public interest" as an aggregate of all collective values be explicitly pursued is to ask generally for an extreme of central synoptic decision making.

Still another fear about collective values is: granted that many of them will indeed be pursued, those pursued will be those poorly considered and formulated. Almost any, and perhaps all, particular interests can be formulated as collective interests. If, for example, organized farmers want to make a play for higher money incomes, they will not neglect to pursue this particular value as though they were in fact pursuing such collective values as maintenance of the stability of the economy, protecting the nation's supply of food and fibres, and preserving, through continuing to make farming attractive, the basic social and political configuration of American society. The possible allegation against partisan mutual adjustment is that collective values well worth considering will be pressed less vigorously than will those ill-considered, even fraudulently presented, collective values that mask the pursuit of particular values.

What is the distinction between the acceptable and criticized kind of collective values? It is presumably that some proposed collective values can be seriously regarded as values of widespread benefit to the citizenry, while others are only alleged to be of widespread benefit. If this is so, however, this distinction is the already familiar one between widely shared values, on the one hand, and the values of a subgroup, on the other. This is a distinction we have earlier discussed in this chapter and in the chapter on social agreement, and we have indicated that there are powerful forces in partisan mutual adjustment pushing toward attention to widely shared values. This last criticism, therefore, has only returned us to an old issue, on which the analysis need not be repeated.

To be sure, the fact that there are powerful forces pushing toward agreement and toward a cultivation of widely shared values in partisan mutual adjustment is not a guarantee that the forces will be powerful enough. On the basis of the argument of this study taken as a whole one would expect that in some circumstances they would be, in others not. If synoptic analytical capacity were great enough—but it is a major argument of this study that it is not—one could systematically indicate the circumstances in which we need have no fear or need have fear of excessively narrowly conceived collective values.

Clearly one can find in American politics examples of scandalously formulated collective values—and such a harsh judgment of them will be agreed upon by competent observers. But it is important to draw a distinction between features of partisan mutual adjustment and its features in the least favorable circumstances. Without doubt collective values receive enormous attention in partisan mutual adjustment, and without doubt they are not always poorly formulated. What inferences should be drawn from the cases in which they are poorly formulated is a question that will be considered, among others, in the immediately following chapter. But it should already be clear that the preferred and achievable alternative to poorly formulated collective values in partisan mutual adjustment will often be better formulated values rather than an attempt to move from partisan mutual adjustment to central decision making and coordination.

The Structure of Interests

With respect both to shared values in general and to collective values, the decision-making system—whether partisan mutual adjustment or centrality—is of only limited, even if large, influence on the formulation of interests to be pursued. If, then, one is concerned with the extraordinary attention given in the United States, say, to only narrowly shared and particular values, one cannot simply attribute the phenomenon to the practice of partisan mutual adjustment. It ought to be clear from our earlier discussion of the impossibility of synoptic problem solving that the necessity for strategic decision making and for partisan mutual adjustment stems, in some large part, from an underlying heterogeneity on some values, preferences, or interests and from rivalry on other interests —which latter, once partisan mutual adjustment is established, are then mistakenly attributed to the adjustment process. Clearly, causation at least works from heterogeneity and rivalry to partisan mutual adjustment, and it is not at all clear whether it works in the other direction. In our examination of allegations of causation running in the second direction it is easy to forget the first and clearly established line of causation. This point is no less important for being briefly made.

In short, what this chapter has had to say up to this point on the conflict between widely shared and collective values, on the one hand, and narrowly shared and particular values, on the other, can be summarized roughly as follows: The conflict is posed, in some large part, by certain forms of heterogeneity and rivalry among individuals and groups, and no form of political organization is without the problem. In the United States, it could be added, heterogeneity appears to pose a more serious problem of conflict between these kinds of values than is posed in some other countries with which we are often tempted to draw instructive comparisons. Partisan mutual adjustment has been shown—the demonstration drawing on Chapters 14, 15, 16, and 17 on social agreement, weighing of conflicting values, and inequality—to encompass powerful forces making for a heavy weight to widely shared and collective values. But it is visible to the naked eye that in partisan mutual adjustment values pursued are not always those widely shared and not always well formulated collective values; and we are at this point in our thinking left with a problem of whether partisan mutual adjustment can itself be molded to exploit the best of it and to avoid the worst of it.

Protection of Group and Particular Values

At this point the analysis needs a fundamental readjustment. If one fears that widely shared and collective values will be neglected, public interest sacrificed to group interests, might one also fear that group and particular values may be neglected?

The narrow, the particular, and the private need to be given their due, first, because they exist. By any reasonable standard farmers need different governmental services than do businessmen or wage earners. The aged need services different from those for school children. "Need" aside it is desirable, by any reasonable standard, for governments to provide, say, national parks for some of its citizens, even if most citizens were never to enter one. And if citizens are rivals for shares of money income or other scarce but widely sought values, it would be, by any reasonable standard, folly to disregard these interests; they are private values well worth attending to.

Sometimes well-formulated particular interests are not even in conflict with one another, in which case it would be the height of folly to neglect their satisfaction. Nor need they necessarily be in conflict with widely shared or collective values. If, then, they are "free," it would be wasteful of values not to attend carefully to them. Simply to assign hunting and fishing rights in a wilderness area to sportsmen is to confer a benefit on a tiny minority at no cost to others individually or collectively. On the other hand, even where narrow and particular values are in conflict with widely shared and collective values, by any reasonable standard the former should sometimes dominate the latter at the margins where choices have to be made. Not every magnitude of sacrifice of a particular value, for example, is worth making for a small gain in a collective value; we do not employ the right of eminent domain to claim private homes for inconsequential collective purposes.

A deep respect for narrow and particular values is not, of course, wholly dependent on the most obvious and tangible interests of individuals and subgroups. In a society in which most people believe that the whole and final truth has not yet been discovered there is such a thing as too much political agreement, too much conformity of preference, interest, or value, even too much for the collective value. Hence many thoughtful people will endorse the pursuit of some narrow and particular values without regard, within some range, for the character of the values themselves.

Where narrow and particular values are in conflict or are in conflict with widely shared and collective values, there are two specific further reasons for giving them great attention in decision making. On the one hand, the only way to avoid unnecessarily harmful conflict is to face up to the existence of it rather than sweep the conflict under the rug of public interest. There may be no solution of the conflict other than one that promises an allocation of the values in conflict; a solution that proposes that the citizens in conflict simply fix their eyes on some widely shared or collective value may fail. The more interesting second reason is that inadequate respect for the narrow and particular values in conflict achieves a poorer aggregation of these values than would otherwise be possible. One way to aggregate values in conflict is to gloss over points of difference or mechanically compromise them rather than reconsider their possible mutually consistent features. Another way is to consider their points of difference with great care, to explore what lies behind those points of difference, to see whether, in that light, there exist possibilities of reconciliation, to look for secondary issues with the use of which the conflicting parties might be brought into consonance without mechanical compromise. The merits of the latter method, which depends for its success on giving each narrow and particular value respectful attention, are persuasive.

On this last point our purpose here is to enter a reminder that narrow and particular values need to be treated with careful attention if aggregates or reconciliations are to win agreement or, failing that, to avoid unnecessary sacrifice of one value to another. The fuller argument on this point and the attendant argument that partisan mutual adjustment meets this need better than does central decision making was presented in Chapters 14, 15, and 16, and especially in the section entitled "The Quality of Values," in Chapter 17.

All this may seem unnecessary in a study devoted to the exploration of the adjustment of partisan interests. It is conceivable, however, that a system of partisan mutual adjustment might neglect narrow and particular interests. If all partisans, governmental and private, pursue either a widely shared interest or a collective interest (and there is nothing in our concept of partisanship that denies the possibility), then the whole system is a method for winning agreement, or making adjustment in the face of conflict, among a set of values all espoused by partisans, but none of which is the self-serving interest of any subgroup. Every partisan is pursuing either his version of a collective value or some widely shared value.

For any known political system we know that the values pursued are a combination of the wide and narrow, and of the collective and particular. The possibilities that partisan mutual adjustment will neglect the wide and collective rather than the narrow and particular would superficially seem to be more obvious, but the opposite possibility is a real one. The possibility that attempts to diminish partisan mutual adjustment in favor of central decision making and coordination will give inadequate attention to the narrow and particular is great, especially in the light of tendencies toward premature and mechanical aggregation of narrow and particular values in central systems. The earlier discussion of the quality of values, in Chapter 17, provides a contrast between these tendencies in central decision making and many tendencies in partisan mutual adjustment to uncover, discover, reconsider, and reformulate values so that they are neither glossed over or unnecessarily sacrificed one to another.

A reasonable fear that the narrow and particular can be underplayed as well as overplayed is illustrated in this perceptive statement about complementary relations between political parties and pressure groups.

In certain political systems, therefore—especially two-party systems —pressure groups may be said to have still a second general function alongside their integrative function: a "disjunctive" function. Two-party systems (perhaps any party system other than the most splintered of multi-party systems) tend perhaps to integrate political opinions all too well. In attempting to win mass support, necessarily from a large variety of groups, they do not so much aggregate opinions as reduce them to their lowest and vaguest denominators, sometimes distorting the perspectives and goals they seek to mobilize out of all recognition. One may doubt whether such systems could persist if groups did not have readily available outlets other than the parties through which to pursue their political goals.

The integrative function of parties in two-party systems is certainly important for the existence of stable governments and the simplification of issues at elections, so that easy choices may be made by the electors. The disjunctive function of pressure groups is equally important to prevent the alienation of groups from systems which persistently distort their goals; in that sense they are an indispensable element of stability in such systems.[2]

Part
6

Policy Toward
Mutual Adjustment

CHOICE

AMONG

POLICY-MAKING

METHODS

Appraisal and Choice in Specific Circumstances

IT SEEMS IMPOSSIBLE TO ESCAPE
the conclusion that the unbiquitous processes here called partisan
mutual adjustment are helpful to decision making and policy
making. It has not been shown that they are in some general sense
superior to central decision making, but the claims made for the
rationality of central decision making have been to some degree
deflated. The issue of general superiority or inferiority is in any case
a spurious one, for questions about the merits of alternative methods arise in various specific contexts; hence it is in these contexts
that one needs finally to evaluate them. What has been said about
partisan mutual adjustment in this study is enough to suggest that

in an enormously wide variety of circumstances it will be an appropriate policy-making method, superior to attempts at central decision making. Conversely, in an enormously wide variety of circumstances it will not.

But how does one decide when it is appropriate and when it is not? In what circumstances is it appropriate? for what functions?

One way to decide is by escape routes. One can endorse partisan mutual adjustment indiscriminately because of its merits in dispersing otherwise dangerously concentrated political power. This is a familiar and to many persons a conclusive argument for decentralization of decision making of the form here called partisan mutual adjustment. Similarly, one might indiscriminately endorse it for its merits in encouraging, even requiring, widespread participation in the political process, participation being taken as a value in its own right or as a means to social stability.[1] Or, again, one might indiscriminately endorse it because it produces action rather than inaction where central decision making is often inhibited. Although deadlock is a common phenomena in two-party negotiation, as in labor relations, multiparty negotiations, as well as the many other forms of partisan mutual adjustment, do not display this tendency. On the contrary, the relative autonomy of many participants in partisan mutual adjustment holds out promise, as we have already seen, for initiative rather than delay. To be sure, action is not everywhere agreed to be preferable to inaction; nevertheless, a widespread belief that governments should have the initiative to cope, even if not too judiciously, with fast moving events in a dangerous world confers some merit on this indiscriminate endorsement of partisan mutual adjustment.

The concern of this study has been, however, with partisan mutual adjustment as a method for calculated, reasonable, rational, intelligent, wise—the exact term does not matter—policy making. The merits of mutual adjustment to disperse power we have consistently passed over as an issue that, although no less important than the issue of the intelligence of policy making, is well worked out in many other studies.* And its merits for such values as participation or initiative are, in our eyes, only peripheral to its funda-

---

* The relation between the present study and pluralist studies of the virtues of dispersed power was discussed in Chapter 1.

mental merits for intelligent decision making. Hence, we do not want to take any of the escape routes. Moreover, most of those who are impressed with partisan mutual adjustment on grounds of dispersal of power, participation, initiative—or for any other merit it might have—would presumably not endorse it indiscriminately but would instead appraise it in specific circumstance with those considerations in mind.

The alternatives among which one can choose should be familiar at this point in the analysis. First, there are alternative combinations of central decision making and partisan mutual adjustment. These were developed in detail in Chapters 7 and 8, on mixed systems. Secondly, there are the variety of alternative forms, pure and mixed, of partisan mutual adjustment itself, the variety having been laid out in Chapters 3, 4, and 5, on adaptive adjustments and manipulated adjustments. Thirdly, there is the particular choice between private and governmental participants in the process. Especially since allocations of authority to governmental participants can specify in considerable detail the character of participation in mutual adjustment in this or that specific situation, an imaginative reconsideration of the role of governmental participants in the process is almost always an appropriate approach to remedying a deficiency in the process. Fourth, there is the specific choice between participants who pursue narrowly held values and those who pursue widely shared ones. The cure for excessive partisanship in the process is often not the abandonment of mutual adjustment but the moderation of the excess, or the displacement, of one kind of participant by another.

Finally, a fundamental set of alternatives in every problem situation is *alternative distributions of power to the participants,* a point to which we have returned again and again.

The Approach to the Choice

We have not been able to lay down in this book a set of criteria for the evaluation of partisan mutual adjustment that would appeal to a wide group of readers nor even, for that matter, to formulate a systematic set of criteria that could be recommended to any single reader. For that reason alone, even if there were no other complexities that also frustrate us, we have been unable to approach the analysis of partisan mutual adjustment synoptically. Nor, we now suggest, can the choice among alternative methods for policy making in particular contexts be approached synoptically.

We have shown that one of the merits of partisan mutual adjustment is that it is adapted to situations in which there are no criteria adequate for resolution of a policy problem by a central decision maker.* That there often are no such criteria, that the majority–equality principle is itself not acceptable, and that this state of affairs is to be expected—these points have all been discussed. In appraising the equality criterion we went on to explain why readers of this book will presumably lack adequate formal criteria for choosing in particular contexts one policy-making method over another and why we cannot formulate a set of formal criteria to recommend.

An additional reason why we cannot formulate formal criteria —and are reduced to quite inconclusive evaluation of partisan mutual adjustment both generally and in particular situations—is that what we have been saying about the process raises questions, which remain for the time being unsettled, about the adequacy of our existing appraisals of other aspects of political organization from which a standard of evaluation might be derived. One might, for example, confidently employ an understanding of the requirements of democracy to appraise partisan mutual adjustment were it not that the analysis of some aspects of mutual adjustment, as in the chapters on equality, for example, requires one to reconsider the democratic requirements themselves. In the immediately following chapter, in which is developed an illustrative analysis of the process of choice among policy-making systems in a given context, the analysis of the appropriateness of partisan mutual adjustment goes far to raise fundamental questions about principles that would otherwise serve as stable points in evaluation. In short, one cannot at this time make the choice between partisan mutual adjustment and centrality by reference to one's concepts of good government

---

* But, it will be remembered, this is only one of its merits, for complexities of problem solving make a case for partisan mutual adjustment even where there is political agreement on adequate criteria for policy choices.

because the analysis up to this point has asked for revision of such concepts.

Moreover, on the strength of the argument so far one will sometimes take partisan mutual adjustment itself as the standard for evaluation, asking no more of a decision than that it be a product of partisan mutual adjustment, or some particular form of it. Consider, analogously, our attitudes toward the majority principle in those cases in which we think it may be applicable. On the one hand, we may appraise it by analyzing the qualities—which are important to us—of such decisions as might be reached by it. But for many decisions we have no concern other than that it be a majoritarian decision; that is to say, any qualities of the decision other than its majoritarian quality are a matter of indifference to us. Similarly, one's general evaluation of partisan mutual adjustment may lead one to endorse, for some category of decisions, any decision reached through the process. For such a category we will in effect not ask whether partisan mutual adjustment serves the public interest, but will declare that whatever emerges from partisan mutual adjustment, or some particular form of it, is in the public interest.

This is not at all surprising or unreasonable. If partisan mutual discussion takes place in the political context of the model set forth in Chapter 6, participants in it will have not violated certain agreed rules of the game; hence they will not have practiced certain forms of deceit, coercion, and violence. Moreover participants will have drawn their principal powers from grants of authority. Partisan mutual adjustment will have produced policy not from a wild struggle of partisans who have gone to almost any length to impose their wills on others but instead from a highly ritualized process of mutual influence.

Lacking adequate formal criteria for choice of method in a specific context, we can, of course, ask questions that are suggested by the earlier chapters. These will be questions that raise relevant considerations without implying formal criteria. For many of them it will not be clear *a priori* whether an affirmative answer or a negative answer points toward the desirability of partisan mutual adjustment. Some examples are: Is a policy problem in this area or category (for which a choice of policy-making method is to be made) typically well defined? technical? amorphous? Is there a clear concept of a solution to the policy problem, or is defining a solution a large part of the policy problem itself? (For some amorphous problems in which the solution itself is undefined, partisan adjustment may be greatly superior to centrality.) Are potential participants in mutual adjustment well informed? narrow or broad in their evaluations? governmental or private? intransigent or conciliatory? (Here the importance of the questions is apparent, but one cannot generalize on which answers point to which methods of policy making.) Are policy mistakes remediable? in what ways? Is a sequence of incremental moves possible? Are various interested individuals, public officials, and groups all represented as participants? If not, are their values or interests mirrored by other participants? Is participation open? Do participants share any common values? Do they agree to rules of the game? Are the rules acceptable? What forms of mutual control, other than the use of authority, do they practice? How coercive are the controls? Would the decision process chosen be thereafter alterable without excessive difficulty? Does the process have any self-corrective tendencies?

This is only an illustrative list of some of the simplest questions that represent relevant considerations. In an actual appraisal questions will multiply. Moreover, as the next chapter will show, choice of a policy-making method may raise extremely complex issues that cannot be represented usefully in such questions as these.

The general formula for choice of method turns out to be, not surprisingly, this: Anyone choosing among alternative methods of policy making is driven to the same strategic problem solving that has been practiced in this book with respect to the general evaluation of the process and that was described in Chapter 9, "Strategy in Problem Solving."[2] He will be required to make specific incremental comparisons of possible alternatives, proceeding to ascertain what he believes to be the critical facts, bringing to bear on his problem those values that he finds pertinent and manageable, and terminating inconclusively.

He will have to be especially wary of assuming that a defect in observed mutual adjustment constitutes a case for centrality. That at a particular time a form of partisan mutual adjustment produces a poor mixture of values, for example, signifies an ill to be corrected but not necessarily a reason for shifting to centrality. It may call instead for reallocations of authority or for restraints on certain individuals, agencies, or groups so that mutual adjustment can continue with improved weights. Similarly, excessive partisanship may call for measures that reduce it so that mutual adjustment can continue rather than be displaced. Or, again, a conservative bias built into partisan mutual adjustment by the grant of veto powers to some of the participants may call for curbing the veto powers rather than shifting marginally to centrality.

An illustration of an apparently quite persuasive case for moving toward central decision making would appear to be that in which a long chain of serious disturbances follows in the path of parametric adjustment. A gets what he wants only at heavy cost to B, B then moves to get what he wants but only at heavy cost to C, C then moves to get what he wants but only at heavy cost to D, and so on, with no tendency toward abatement of the disturbances. But one has to be wary in finding an argument here for centrality, for it is quite possible that a shift, say, from parametric adjustment to negotiation would be sufficient to bring an end to the disturbances.

It must never be forgotten that we have collected under the name partisan mutual adjustment a group of adjustive devices which offer a variety of policy-making possibilities and which can be combined in a rich variety of ways. One may not wish to endorse deferential adjustment where a policy of deference would leave the deferring participant in mutual adjustment without "space" in which to move; nor would one wish to endorse the method of prior decision where there are simply no policy positions a participant can take that suggest a point of juxtaposition with the policy of another participant; nor would one endorse parametric or manipulated adjustment where either the costs of the decision passed on to others are heavy and cannot again be shifted, or where a potentially dangerous policy move is irremediable; nor would one endorse negotiation where it breeds intransigence. But each of these methods has its place, and in particular situations some are candidates for replacing others where the others have reached their limit of usefulness.

We have said that analysis of alternative policy-making methods will inevitably be inconclusive for the analyst. What concludes it, if anything? The answer is in part that the analysis is indeed never concluded. Beyond that, however, take note that *the analyst will be a participant in a process of partisan mutual adjustment from which a final choice of method will emerge.*[3] If he himself actually understands that, insofar as his opinion has any effect on the choice, he is a participant in partisan mutual adjustment, at the very least in partisan discussion as one form of the process, he may wish to tailor his role to increase his effectiveness, if that is what he desires. And, incidentally, he will come to accept certain divergence between his preferred choice of method and actual choices made as appropriate, not necessarily evidence of the foolishness of political choice.

Open Choices

When one form of partisan adjustment seems preferable to another, or when one distribution of weights seems preferable to another, is it actually possible to achieve an alteration? Or in actual practice are these choices closed? At best, might the country drift from one to the other but never achieve deliberate choice? These choices are as open as any ordinary political choice. Why, then, might it be thought otherwise? Because, at least in the United States, one is struck by evidence of entrenched powers. Is it possible to overcome, for example, the resistence to reform of Congressional committee procedures that are constituted by the power of the committees themselves? To propose to reallocate weights in partisan mutual adjustment appears to call for striking against those participants most able to resist the reallocation.

The most strongly entrenched interests, it is some surprise to note, are not private individuals and groups but government officials, agencies, and committees. An intense business opposition to the growth of government regulation has not been able to stop it, nor has labor opposition prevented the growth of trade-union regulation. Private groups have power to delay, no doubt; but no veto power in their hands matches that, say, of a Congressional committee or even of its chairman.[4]

Formally, the possibilities of reorganizing partisan mutual adjustment or, more specifically, of reallocating weights to values in conflict are great. As we saw in the model of government presented in Chapter 6, partisan adjustment rests heavily on allocations of authority to governmental and private participants, and these allocations are, formally, easily alterable. Nor does the existence of partisan mutual adjustment itself impose any obvious barriers to change, although one can imagine both a distribution of authority and other power in mutual adjustment that preserves the status quo and one that innovates rapidly.

If there is any reason to believe that reforms of particular decision-making methods are impossible, it must be that there exists some underlying distribution of power that is impervious to attempts at social control or at least a status quo distribution that cannot be altered because the real, as against the formal, allocation is such that those who have power can maintain it against any proposed change. Yet the pace of political change in the United States, distressingly slow as it sometimes appears to be, is evidence that there is no such rigidity in the distribution of power. But if there was, it needs to be noted immediately that this is no more an objection to partisan mutual adjustment than to central decision making.

One is easily drawn into a fallacy on this point. If it is true that there is very little possibility for deliberate change in the distribution of power in partisan mutual adjustment, and if it is also true that those who are able to suppress change do so through the exercise of their power in contemporary partisan mutual adjustment, then it indeed appears to be the case that partisan mutual adjustment cannot be much reformed. This conclusion is, however, fallacious. For on these assumptions it is not the case that partisan mutual adjustment cannot be much reformed; it is only the case that the particular form of partisan mutual adjustment present in the United States today cannot be much reformed. Now if this, if true, would be a damning feature of contemporary American partisan mutual adjustment, what is its significance for choice between mutual adjustment and centrality? The answer is that it closes off the potential for centrality quite as tightly as for mutual adjustment, for almost nothing is possible except the status quo. Hence this hypothetical feature of contemporary American mutual adjustment does not support a devaluation of partisan mutual adjustment relative to centrality.

To make anything of the argument that the use of partisan mutual adjustment itself closes off possibilities for choosing intelligently among policy-making methods, one has to show that mutual adjustment has tendencies to preserve rigidly its existing forms and distributions of power in ways that central policy-making systems do not. But beginning with some propositions in Chapter 6, (propositions 24, 25, and 26) we have offered abundant evidence of tendencies in mutual adjustment that at least hold open, and more commonly impose constant change on, the very structure of partisan mutual adjustment in any sequence of situations.

It is a crucial point that partisan mutual adjustment is a principle method for making choices about itself. A habit of thought tempts one to believe that policy on partisan mutual adjustment itself must necessarily be made centrally. The habit is revealed in one of its manifestations in such a statement as, "How and how far a more general interest can utilize, discipline, or curb these special interests in the governmental process is a supreme test of a people's economic and political genius."[5] In actual fact the special interests can utilize, discipline, and curb each other to achieve, among other things, a more general interest. Their so doing is perhaps a greater demonstration of a people's genius. Obviously, partisan mutual adjustment in large part determines policy on itself; and we have already noted how an appraiser of the process himself becomes a participant in it.

It might be objected that central decision making is a kind of button to press where reform is needed while, by contrast, the diffusion of policy-making responsibility in mutual adjustment means that there is no point on which to move in reform. Clearly, however, if there were anything analogous to a button to press in a central system, almost no one would be allowed to press it. And, conversely, in partisan mutual adjustment anyone can press at least one button, anyone can enter into policy making; it is a feasible system of transmitting impulses from any of us to those whose consent to or participation in reform is required.

Illustrative Problem Areas

Partisan mutual adjustment is an issue in every area of government; we can illustrate how questions arise in several. On the organization of the administrative branch of American government, for example, dominant patterns of thought suggest that the potential of partisan mutual adjustment for intelligent policy making has not been fully considered, despite, again, the acknowledgment of the virtues of dispersion of power as a democratic safeguard.

Although pluralist views of public administration are common, improved mutual adjustment is hardly recognized as a systematic alternative to improved central coordination in public administration. That it is at least a logical possibility is often denied by omitting it from lists of possibilities; and, beyond that, its practical possibilities are hardly analyzed. Gulick, we saw in Chapter 1, has limited the possibilities of coordination to two: centrality, on the one hand, and singleness of purpose, on the other.[6] Friedrich quite correctly finds in size and complexity a clear call for central coordination; but he gives little thought to mutual adjustment as, perhaps, as necessary as centrality. "As soon as an organization grows to any size the large number of officials who exercise partly conflicting functions stand in constant need of integrating and coordinating leadership. . . . The semimilitary, authoritarian nature of a government service is by no means a gratuitous invention of petty autocrats, but is inherent in the very nature of the processes which form the essence of all administrative services."[7] Harris finds central coordination the apparently exclusive required method, and finds competition and conflict among partisans, which are essential elements of partisan mutual adjustment, categorically disruptive: "Government is notoriously plagued by a rank spirit of departmentalism, which frequently leads to internal squabbles and lack of effective cooperation. . . . More and more it is necessary for several departments or agencies to join in a co-ordinated effort, if the work of government is to be performed effectively and economically. It is the function of overhead management to secure team work and coordination."[8]

An even more categorical denial, we saw, of the possibilities of coordination by mutual adjustment is W. Y. Elliott's, "If a government is ever to be coordinated, it must be coordinated in the minds of the people who authorize it and those who operate it, from the top to the bottom of the structure."[9] Nor does more recent thinking indicate that the possibilities of partisan mutual adjustment are well explored. Simon, Smithburg, and Thompson enumerate ways, beyond familiar executive, legislative, and hierarchical formal controls, for increasing administrative accountability; they are parliamentary democracy, strengthening the chief executive, independent regulatory commissions, governmental corporations, and consultative arrangements. The possibilities of increasing accountability by a better structuring of mutual adjustment are not mentioned.[10] Thompson has suggested cooperative activity based on recognized mutual interdependence as a coordinating alternative to command and to group identifications; again, however, the list slips over the possibilities that we have called partisan mutual adjustment.[11]

That there are, therefore, a host of issues in public administration that have not yet been analyzed simply because an entire array of possible forms of improved organization have been missed seems likely. We can see, for example, that the possibility that discordant values can produce good results is simply overlooked. Gulick, for example, has just been seen to stake the possibilities of coordination, if not on central management, on an overriding common value, simply neglecting the possibility that partisan values may be harnessed to policy making and coordinating in administration. Elsewhere he has written, "Truly effective action in administration arises from singleness of purpose and clarity of policy, ardently believed in both by the leaders and by the public in all parts of the country and in all strata of society."[12] In the light of even the minimum case for mutual adjustment this is an extraordinary statement! Thompson's third alternative method of coordination, cooperation in the light of recognized mutual interdependence, similarly rests coordination heavily on shared values, without thought of the possibility that discordant values can be harnessed.

Similarly, possibilities for employing conflict, although now increasingly explored for public administration, are still looked upon with suspicion born out of insensitivity to the useful role of conflict in mutual adjustment. Simon, Smithburg, and Thompson, for example, do not so much explore its possibilities as indicate their unease about it: "If we know under what circumstances conflict is likely to emerge, we will know also what conditions must be satisfied to produce cooperation." This is because "to understand the conditions of war is to understand the conditions of peace." And again, "We should also warn the reader not to regard conflict as necessarily or inherently bad." Why should they, at the end of a chapter on conflict, feel such a warning necessary? They go on to acknowledge the possible merits of conflict: it "may be a means for bringing to bear on individual decisions a wide range of specialized competences," and it is possibly valuable on still other counts. But these concessions to its virtues are concluding qualifications in a chapter given over to its problems rather than its potential.[13]

We go so far as to suggest that even among those political scientists whose work is of such a character as would appear to lead them into a sympathetic appraisal of the possibilities of administrative organization through such devices as we have collected under the name of partisan mutual adjustment, these devices are only peripherally explored. Key, for example, reveals an overriding disposition toward centrality in his comments on administrative reform. Recognizing, to be sure, that "in the initiation and formation of public policy, the power of group and class drives . . . is fundamental," and that "the legislative programs of administrative agencies, however, tend to incorporate the objectives of private groups and to temper and to modify them in the public interest," the possibilities of improving on the situation appear to him to rest in improving the directing skills of high-level administrators; the alternative of mutual adjustment is not considered.

A possible line of development, then, would be the direction and harnessing of the power, knowledge, and skills of the administrative services so that they might constitute a force in the initiation of public policies calculated to promote the common weal. The development of an administrative corps of this character depends in large measure on the further development of techniques of organization and supervision whereby the political heads of administrative services may better overcome the parochialism of the permanent staffs and liberate their talents. This problem of the overhead organization of governmental departments and of the government as a whole is of prime importance in the determination of the direction in which the powers of the bureaucracy will be exerted. Politically responsible officials in collaboration with Congress have the task of orienting public policy, but in the absence of effective techniques for organizing and directing the administration their efforts are likely to be either obstructed or ineffectively carried out by the administrative services. Recent years have seen much attention give to the organization of administration for policy planning.[14]

David Truman has, of course, as sympathetically as anyone explored the functioning of conflicting groups, private and public, in government. Even he, however, has not taken the mutual adjustment of various partisan participants in government as a major alternative for administrative reform. In part this is because his questions about group behavior do not ask about possibilities of achieving rationality or coordination; they more simply ask, as we saw in Chapter 1, whether and how interests are represented. Moreover, his work is largely descriptively analytic rather than evaluative. It is significant, however, that he considers his analysis to be a necessary preface to an evaluation. Of what? of the usefulness of mutual adjustment for intelligent policy making or administration? His answer is, instead, it will be remembered, that it "is essential to a reliable evaluation of the alleged mischiefs of faction."[15] The same concern is indicated in his final chapter, where, again, he does not evaluate the possibilities that mutual adjustment offers for intelligent policy making but instead evaluates its potential danger—and, to be sure, some off-setting gains—to representative democracy. Latham alone, in his *Group Basis of Politics,* seems to have brought himself to the point at which an inquiry into the potential of partisan mutual adjustment for administration and administrative coordination might successfully be launched.[16]

If one cannot conceive of administration without centrality and hierarchy, one can easily conceive of freer departures from hierarchical norms than at present exist. One can, for example, entertain the notion that overlapping administrative jurisdictions can be deliberately created to activate negotiation rather than be deplored as *prima facie* evidence of organizational confusion. And one can reconsider established ideas of the appropriate function for ostensibly central coordinators, if, for example, their role is seen less as achieving an approximation to synoptic coordination than as intervening from time to time in a highly selective way in a process of partisan adjustment. Many practicing coordinators, in fact, see their role in precisely that way, but theoretical discussion of coordination and management is not fully adapted to the possibility.

An appreciation of partisan mutual adjustment also opens up possibilities for structuring administration so that some major social objectives are achieved as a by-product of the assigned objectives of an organization. Where economic theory is fully sensitive to the possibilities of achieving such objectives as a desirable resource allocation through the decisions of business managers none of whom have such an objective in mind, administrative theory, and especially organization theory, still largely assumes that organizations accomplish at best no more than they intend. Organizations are, in fact, often defined as groups of men or interactions united by a common purpose, with the result that the very concept of an organization tends to obscure its role, as in partisan mutual adjustment, in achieving policies other than those intended by its members. It was a central point early in this study that the mutual adjustment process systematically achieves, and can be deliberately structured to achieve, policy objectives other than those intended by participants.

Possibilities of partisan mutual adjustment also make complexity of administration a more critical variable in the design of appropriate organization. As complexity increases, the case for partisan mutual adjustment, rather than centrality, becomes stronger. And some problems, it would appear to follow from this study, are complex beyond any significant possibility for central coordination, a conclusion hardly hinted at in the literature of public administration.

For an example of another area in which questions about mutual adjustment arise, consider the national budgetary process, both administrative and legislative, in the United States. It is the product of a fairly consistent line of development, at least since the Taft Commission on Economy and Efficiency in 1912, in which central management, unification of decisions, and synopsis have been principal aspirations.

Such prescriptions as the following for budgetary reform are taken as axiomatic; they simply assume that centrality is a cure for budgetary ills.

Congress should be made a more responsible body. Because of the dispersion of authority, the large powers exercised by individual members and committees which are only partially subject to control by Congress itself, and a set of rules which defeats rather than facilitates responsible legislative action, responsibility is dissipated and no man or group of men can be held accountable for any action of Congress or for its failure to act.[17]

In order that Congress may consider and adopt a definite fiscal policy for the government, which becomes effective and binding, more fundamental changes in procedure are necessary. The budget will have to be considered in its entirety and in relation to revenues, public debt, and the economic outlook; a single appropriation act will have to supplant the numerous separate appropriations now voted; and the present review and action on the detailed estimates without information on or regard to the over-all fiscal situation and program will have to be changed.[18]

A more recent illustrative commitment to a centrally coordinated, hopefully synoptic, budgetary process, with inadequate attention to the possibilities of intelligence through partisan mutual adjustment, is seen in such prescriptions as these: Clear and explicit formulation of governmental objectives before allocations are made; deliberate coordination of revenue and expenditure decisions; no expenditure decisions until all claims on the budget can be considered together; unified policy making and unified budgeting; legislature should avoid a segmented view of the budget; decisions should be made on the basis of a cooperative division of function between legislature and executive.[19]

Appealing as these prescriptions are, the increasing size and complexity of the budget surely call them into question, even as ideals.[20] In an earlier chapter we noted the failure of the omnibus appropriations bill; there is now a reasonable case for decentralizing Congressional committee study of budgetary proposals even beyond present decentralization. With aggregates of authorized expenditures, obligations, and cash flows running in different directions and problems of allocation within each aggregate, the case for a unified presentation of the budget and for a kind of central Congressional response is by no means any longer persuasive. Partisan adjustment among relatively independent (in the sense that they do not even formally exchange views with each other) Congressional committees needs careful exploration as an alternative to proposals to increase the centrality of Congressional budgetary action.

Even so relatively well contained a process as technological research and development for a specific governmental service may be better organized by a mixture of mutual adjustment and central management than by the latter alone. Klein and Meckling have found that the development of military weapons systems is less costly and more rapid when it is not well centrally coordinated. They found by an empirical study of actual developmental sequences that some kinds of duplication, cross purposes, and even confusion produce good results, while central management of the process is inevitably excessively constraining.[21]

Still other problem areas can be mentioned as illustrative of those in which choice among forms of mutual adjustment or between mutual adjustment and central decision making is at issue: relations between national and state governments, relations among national governments, relations between the President and other top leaders in crises, for example. For more concrete examples consider the relation of Army Engineers to Congress, President, and interest groups; decision making by the Joint Chiefs of Staff and service unification more generally; and independent regulatory commissions. The relative merits of mutual adjustment as against centrality are even at issue in present tendencies for the American government to drive underdeveloped countries, as a condition of receiving aid, to the use of schemes for economic planning that rest heavily on central plans rather than on strategies appropriate to partisan mutual adjustment in those countries.

The general analysis of mutual adjustment no more specifies particular features of governmental organization as needing reform than the familiar case for central and hierarchical forms of organization specifies. Hence, although we have indicated illustrative issues, we have not been able to illustrate precisely how an understanding of mutual adjustment leads to a specific conclusion. We can go a little further than we have gone, however. In the immediately following and final chapter we shall illustrate at length the way in which, in a particular context, questions about mutual adjustment arise and can be discussed. It is an illustrative analysis of a question that goes to the heart of the governmental process, the question of party discipline.

Chapter
20

AN ILLUSTRATIVE

APPLICATION

OF THE

ANALYSIS

The Question of Party Discipline

IN THIS CHAPTER WE SHALL
undertake a prolonged illustration of how problems about the
appropriate use of partisan mutual adjustment in a specific context
arise and can be discussed. Considering some aspects of the controversy over the merits of national party discipline in the United
States, we shall see how the case for party discipline raises
questions about partisan mutual adjustment in various possible
governmental loci, and how our analysis can be brought to bear
on them. We could choose other issues, such as administrative reform, federalism, congressional organization, the budgetary process,
even international organization; but the party system is as good as

any illustrative issue and better than some. A little more than a decade ago the appointment by the American Political Science Association of a committee on party discipline indicated the importance the profession attaches to this question, just as, subsequently, the committee's recommendations indicated the strength of professional support for more party discipline.[1] Quite aside from the flurry of articles stirred up by the committee's report, the question is of continuing interest, both to the profession and to politicians. Moreover, one cannot explore it without raising questions about the fundamentals of American government.

A synoptic competence on the issue is not possible. We shall proceed strategically, asking whether, over some range of incremental alterations in our national party system, we might expect net advantage or disadvantage from some strengthening of party discipline. In certain circumstances some alternatives are foreclosed: for example, there are some characteristics of citizen opinion on public issues—exclusive preoccupation with local issues, perhaps—that make discipline impossible, and other characteristics—extraordinary national homogeneity of political opinion, perhaps—that make it inevitable. For the United States, however, a variety of choices are open. On the one hand, American national parties are not wholly without discipline.[2] On the other hand, there appear to be a variety of possible reforms to increase discipline that lie within the political leadership's power to inaugurate.

Party discipline is a very big and complicated issue. The discussion here is only a sketch of a beginning of an analysis designed, to repeat, only to illustrate how questions about the appropriate use of partisan mutual adjustment arise and how one might deal with them in a specific context.

The Marks of Discipline

By comparison with the present state of affairs in American national parties an increase in discipline would be marked by at least the following attributes, ranging from the obvious to the less so. They are definitional.

1. Members of any one party in the national legislature are more disposed toward voting alike, and they differ in their voting

from members of the other party, who also vote alike. In the legislature, insofar as they influence policy through means other than legislative voting, they similarly group themselves.

2. Each party presents, more than at present, the same face in all electoral districts in which it competes; candidates affiliated with the party are greatly constrained to suppress appeals to voters that are different from appeals made by other candidates of the same party in other districts.

3. The party's (hence, the legislator's) interest in and endorsement of local and other only narrowly shared values that cannot be made part of a standardized national party position are muted.

4. Local and narrow interests of this kind being muted, the party and each legislator are more committed than presently to policies and values of potential common or very widely shared interest to the citizenry.

5. Some of the strengthened common or shared values are those on which there is no significant disagreement within the party; they are relatively neglected, in the absence of party discipline, not because of internal party disagreement on them but because of the legislator's preoccupation with local and sectional values.

6. On many other issues on which the party chooses to take a position disagreement among the party's legislative members is resolved by partisan mutual adjustment within the party.

7. Hence there is a substitution of partisan mutual adjustment within the party for partisan mutual adjustment in the legislature itself.

8. The party in power can carry many legislative votes without any votes from the opposition; hence members of the opposition party are removed in great degree from participation in the partisan mutual adjustment that proximately and near proximately determines policy.

9. Between elections a kind of contractual and fixed relationship develops between the "government," that is, the party in power, and the citizenry, for in policy making legislators are constrained to follow the party's pledges and intimations given during the campaign.

10. Not all the partisan mutual adjustments of local and other narrow interests is transferred from legislature to party; some evaporate. For some interests are simply dropped, as explained above, and some others are reconciled not through partisan mutual adjustment but cooperatively in the light of widely shared national values or interests that provide criteria for their reconciliation.

11. Within each party, there emerges a better defined central leadership or leader with great influence over specific issues through its or his acknowledged responsibility for the making and coordinating of party policy. The proximate determinant of party policy is, in large part, the leadership's decision. A variety of circumstances, not necessary to specify here, induces party members in the legislature to waive many of their claims to immediate participation in the determination of party position on every policy issue on which the party takes a position.

12. At the same time party members in the legislature can remove party leadership and replace it. With or without formal procedures for doing so, they achieve this control over leadership because the party remains a voluntary organization in which leadership leads only if followers follow.

13. Hence, despite the degree of central determination and coordination of party policy, partisan mutual adjustment between leadership and legislative members of the party continues to determine party policy in large part. The determination of party policy is an extremely complex process that we will not, however, detail.

14. Interest-group leaders are diverted to a degree from partisan mutual adjustment with legislators to partisan mutual adjustment with agencies.

15. Interest-group leaders also engage in partisan mutual adjustment with party leaders and legislative members in the determination of party policy to be brought to the legislature.[3]

16. Party position serves more than presently to establish a set of criteria for the determination of such policies as fall to agencies to decide. For the legislature and party leadership speak to agencies more in one voice than in many conflicting voices.

Alternative Aggregations

Given these defining features of party discipline, the choice between the more and the less disciplined party offers, of course, a choice between two partial methods of aggregating values (including both objectives and policies) in a society. Here aggregation means a good deal more than counting preferences, noting commonly shared preferences, and resolving differences by some such rule as that the social decision shall follow a plurality of preferences. It refers, as it has also in earlier chapters, to processes by which values of participants in a political system are discovered, invented, formed, reformed, considered, reconsidered, and where conflicting, reconciled with or weighed against each other and finally brought to bear on public decisions. It is a complex social process embracing social indoctrination in the home and in small groups, as well as specific governmental processes like representation through a legislative. And it includes processes for calculating relations between ends and means. As we have noted in an early chapter, parties play a large role in such a process of aggregation.

Certain features of the process make it so complex that everyone flounders in the attempt to deal categorically with the merits and demerits of alternative systems of aggregation unless they are, like tyranny and democracy, starkly different from each other. Part of the difficulty is that it is, as just noted, a process in which values are not *given,* to be thereafter reconciled by rules such as the "greatest good for the greatest number" or by the majority principle. Clearly it is, as we have said, a process by which values are themselves formed. Moreover, a rule or procedure applied to the reconciliation of given values itself has a powerful effect on the formation of the values themselves: a democratic political system is one in which values are in some sense democratic and is not simply one in which values are democratically reconciled.

Aggregation is, again, complex and therefore difficult to evaluate because citizens delegate choices among values. On most issues citizens turn over their proxies to interest-group leaders, to agencies, to legislators, and to executives. They do not simply ask these delegates to represent the values that citizens hold; they as often ask them to represent whatever values that the delegates believe the citizens would hold if better informed. Hence an appraisal of alternative methods of aggregation requires an appraisal of the processes of interchange of information and attitudes between leaders and citizens, processes described in earlier chapters.

Evaluation is further complicated because, both in party politics of the present style and in a more disciplined party system, the party system would presumably continue to play its intricate, historic, twofold aggregating role. First, it would offer alternative policies to the citizenry. To be sure, it might, on one hand, offer alternatives largely on local issues and then only indirectly through the proximate offer of alternative candidates at elections. Or, on the other hand, it might offer alternative policies on national issues somewhat more directly through alternative candidates tightly bound to party programs at each election. But these are two complex ways of discharging the same function.

Secondly, it would play its role, which is major, in uncovering as well as producing the national synthesis, consensus, or overwhelming majority that fundamentally directs policy in the United States. Much of the work of political parties is finished before the election is held. Well before the time of election arrives both parties have committed themselves to such policies as promise that, no matter who wins the election, majority opinion on many fundamentals will prevail. Hence both parties will usually be committed to roughly the same program of national defense, social security, urban redevelopment and housing, desegregation, antitrust, public health, and so on. That their rivalry drives them to offer slightly different—yet significantly different—programs in each of these areas does not deny that the mere threat of elections has usually also driven both of them before election time to follow the overwhelming majority on the many points on which one exists. If undisciplined and disciplined parties perform this synthesizing role somewhat differently, our point is that they both perform it in complex ways difficult to evaluate.[4]

Consequently, as between the present level of party discipline in national politics in the United States and the greater degree of discipline with which we compare it, there is no simple formula that tells us that the one level of discipline is more rational than the other, or more democratic, or more majoritarian, or more sensitive to important values, or on any other account better.

More Discipline Or Not?

Unable to deal synoptically with the merits of discipline, we can nevertheless make some headway. Unable to develop systematic criteria for a choice between more or less discipline, we can nevertheless make points essential to evaluation.

Consider, first, the contractual and fixed relationship that develops in a system of party discipline between the party in power and the citizenry (point 9 above). It is endorsed as the foundation of responsible government. Such a relationship is necessary, it is alleged, if voters are to know what they are voting for, if they are to be able to count on getting what they express a preference for, if they are to be presented with meaningful alternatives to which they can say "yes" or "no," and if they are to be able to hold someone to account if they do not get that for which they express a preference. These are some of the major themes in the case for more disciplined parties.[5]

But responsible parties or responsible government so characterized may not be desirable. The fixity of the contractual relation is a source of rigidity in the aggregation process. More specifically, it contrains or terminates partisan mutual adjustment in areas in which such adjustment would otherwise be performing a useful aggregating function.

For one thing it reduces the possibilities of sequential learning and revising, of which much has been made in earlier chapters. Secondly, it severely constrains the shifting from one decision to another in the weights accorded to different conflicting values, shifting, it was argued in Chapter 13, that is essential for the representation at some point in the decision-making process of values that cannot all be represented, given the limits on man's intellectual capacities, in any one of a few decisions. Thirdly, it compels policy makers to deal with complex and fluid situations under the constraint of fairly simple systems of generalization or declarations of concrete policy, for no party platform can ever be more than that. At their worst, these paralyzing factors are displayed in the inability of the British Labour Party to free itself, not only in an interelection period but over a long period of years, from the contractual fixity of its commitment to nationalization of key industries, a commitment regretted by dominant leadership in the party but nevertheless constraining.

Fourth, the fixity of the contractual relation undercuts the educative role of legislator and party leader. In Chapter 17 in a section entitled "The Quality of Values," we drew together much of the argument of the book with respect to ways in which interchange between leader and citizen in partisan mutual adjustment permits leadership to play a venturing, innovative, educative role. We need note here only that discipline within the party constrains the interchange of information and attitude between leaders and citizenry, for at any given time each legislator and other party leader is committed to a program which he cannot, therefore, appraise, let alone attack, without danger to himself and party.

Fifth, discipline reduces the possibility of regrouping supporting individuals and groups in new coalitions on new issues. Therefore it throws away possibilities for agreement that legislative partisan mutual adjustment might uncover were it not suppressed. And even with respect to partisan mutual adjustment within the party, discipline turns the members' attention to stable coalitions of individuals and groups with the result that party members miss possibilities of discovering a variety of coalitions, one on each of a variety of different issues. If one large, even overwhelming, majority wants certain reforms in public education and another equally large majority, composed however of different elements from those of the first majority, wants price-level stability, it will not be possible for a disciplined party to accommodate both if an electoral appeal established a contractual relationship with one but not the other of the two majorities.[6]

The preceding point throws light, of course, on the claim that disciplined parties give the voter a definite set of alternatives to which he can say "yes" or "no" at an election. He is given alternative combinations, alternative packages of policies, between which he must choose. He is unable, however, to speak his mind on each of the component parts of the package. By contrast, in a system of undisciplined parties, although he cannot speak on each part at election time, subsequent possibilities for him to engage in inter-action with individual legslators not bound to a party position open up some possibilities for him to declare himself on specific issues.

But on the other hand, it is not an unquestionable merit of a system that it permits the citizen to speak a clear affirmative or negative on policy issues and thereafter hold certain leaders account-able on specifics. To permit him to do so, at least in such form as very tightly to constrain his delegated leaders, is to permit him to undercut the function they can usefully perform for him, which is, to consider with some discretion what "good" policy is, even if, in this case, we mean nothing more by "good policy" than that policy the citizen would choose if he were better informed. It is to permit the citizen to paralyze to a degree that partisan mutual adjustment within the party and especially within the legislature out of which agreements and acceptable aggregations are laboriously fashioned.

In summary, the argument that party discipline achieves re-sponsibility is in large part an argument against discipline, an argument for permitting legislators and executives to act flexibly and intelligently toward each other and in interchange with the citizenry in order to explore through partisan mutual adjustment, within the legislature as well as elsewhere, all possible opportuni-ties for agreement and acceptable aggregation. The fixity of the contractual relation between leadership and citizenry gives us, on one hand, something called responsibility and, on the other hand, paralyzes to a degree the learning, correcting, weighing, educating, and synthesizing functions of partisan mutual adjustment. One's considered choice in the face of such a conflict will, of course, de-pend in part on still other features of party discipline.

A feature closely related to one already discussed is the packag-ing of policies for party members in the legislature by the party leader or the coterie of top leadership. Party leadership proximately sets policy for the party, we have said; and the legislative members of the party who are not among the party's top leadership exercise a variety of controls over leadership, including the threat to re-move the leadership or the threat to resign from the party. But the members are not necessarily able to exercise a heavy influence on specific pieces of the party program. A member is often constrained in exercising his powers because he knows that in a system of party discipline his only alternative is another leadership that will offer him another package of policies some elements of which he may dislike no less than the policies to which is already opposed.

This perhaps unhappy feature of party discipline is the other side of the coin of central coordination of party policy, about which we shall say more presently. It is not a feature of discipline that can be denied by the assertion that each party is itself internally democratic. Disciplined parties are not necessarily democratic in the ordinary sense of the term; though they may be called democratic by reason of the kind of controls just described that legislative members hold over party leadership, the very controls that permit central leadership in the party to package party policies for legislative members.

Not far removed from either of the two proceeding evaluative points is the tendency in a system of party discipline for the problem-solving activity of party leaders and members to become superficial. (Having already obliquely alluded to some tendencies in this direction arising from the fixity of the contractual element in a system of party discipline, we here develop the point more explicitly and with reference to features of party discipline other than the contractual relation.)

Throwing responsibility for making party policy to relatively few leaders in the party is to reduce the number of active participants in specifically *political* problem solving. To be sure, party leadership can hire a large research staff and can incorporate party members in a subsidiary way through party committees on various problems. But the kind of problem solving that requires interchange with other leaders and with the citizenry rather than research and committee work is diminished. In elaborating the relation between strategic problem solving, the fragmentation of decision making, and the mutual adjustment of partisan participants in the process in Chapters 9 and 10, we called attention to the particular respects in which problem solving goes beyond purely intellectual activity to include certain political processes. For example, sometimes one learns how to solve a problem by negotiating on it; there may be no substitute for the information, bearing on a feasible settlement, that emerges from the negotiation process itself.

Moreover, the case for concentrating problem-solving responsibility on party leadership to the degree called for by party discipline runs against all those points, running like a theme through this entire study, that argue the discrepancy between man's intellectual capacities and the complexity of his political problems. Just as partisan mutual adjustment in the political system as a whole has been shown to be an alternative to central synoptic attempts at competence on problems, so partisan mutual adjustment within a party, if not too weakened by party discipline, is an alternative to overburdening a central problem-solving group within the party. Within some organizations central competence is sufficient for the organization's problems, even if it is not sufficient for the larger problems of the society. But the problems facing party leadership are the larger problems of the society.

One might reasonably expect, therefore, than an overburdened central problem solver or team might easily drift into formulating its problems so that they become less demanding. One way to do this is to play down the question: "How can we solve this problem?" and give increased attention to "How can we satisfy the electorate on this problem?" To be sure, these are not wholly separate questions, but they differ greatly in the profoundity or superficiality of problem solving they suggest.

For reasons given in earlier chapters participants in partisan mutual adjustment fairly closely linked to the citizenry are highly motivated to find real solutions to real problems. The pressures on them to do so are heavy. By contrast, central party leadership is driven in the direction more of formula than of solutions, driven by the need to develop a communicable standard party program on which all candidates can run. It is also motivated to gloss over difficulties that peril party unity and, at the extreme, it is tempted to use its control of the party to manipulate the electorate rather than to solve economic and social problems.

That British party discipline has gone to that extreme is indicated in two opinions, one encapsulated in the other.

Even more important, the framework of public thinking about policy, the voters' sense of the alternatives, is in large degree fixed from above. "The effect of party management today," Nigel Nicolson writes, is "to use all modern means of mass-communication to create a mass mind which does not require to think and therefore ceases to discriminate." Radio, television, popular newspapers and general education, he says, instead of facilitating the process of discovering, instructing and expressing the public's point-of-view, have "merely served to stamp it out from two huge rounded moulds." Thus the attitudes that divide the parties "are themselves the product of constant party warfare." The danger is that popular sovereignty in the polity may be modified by the same technique of manipulation that modifies consumer sovereignty in the economy.

To talk of public opinion being manipulated or manufactured irresistibly conjures up the notion of dark, designing "power elites" cleverly controlling the masses, perhaps by tapping deep springs of irrationalism in the "crowd." That would be a caricature of reality. Yet we cannot fail to sense in Britain the extent to which the classical function of party has been reversed. That function is, of course, to transmit the wishes of the voter to the centers of authority. But the modern party also performs another function: it makes what the state is doing acceptable to the voter.[7]

It might be countered, of course, that even if undisciplined parties deal less superficially with problems than do disciplined, they pay a high price for that advantage. For, it might be argued, problem solving through partisan mutual adjustment within the party, uncoordinated by party leadership, engages so many diverse problem-solving energies as to promise incoherence and inconsistency in policy making.

Indeed, the claim for the superiority of disciplined parties on the grounds of consistency and coherence is one of the major points to be found in the literature and is well worth considering.[8] There is at least a kind of superficial coherence and consistency in a disciplined party's program; on conspicuous points one would hardly expect a centrally formulated program to contradict itself or lack the possibility of defense as a more or less unified whole. The contractual element in a system of party discipline would account in part for the appearance of consistency; so also would the tendency of parties to deal in formulae or principles capable of representing the party's position in an election campaign.

When in Chapter 13 we looked into inconsistency as an allegation against partisan mutual adjustment, consistency turned out to be an illusive concept. Depending on policy objectives, two or more policies can be viewed as consistent or inconsistent: crop restriction and land reclamation are or are not inconsistent depending on objectives. If consistency is taken to mean that policies bear such a relation to each other that a Pareto optimum is achieved, it is not at all clear that disciplined parties produce more consistent sets of policies than do undisciplined. For we looked into the special difficulties of achieving Pareto optima by central synopsis and into the special motivations toward their achievement through partisan mutual adjustment. Free play to intraparty negotiation and to compensation offer opportunities not so freely exploited under central coordination.

If, on the other hand, consistency refers to stability over time in the pattern of choice among policies, we have some reason to fear it, on the same ground that we indicated fear of the fixed element in the contractual relation between party and citizen in a system of party discipline. To say that a party is consistent in this sense is to raise the possibility that it is not learning and reconsidering in sequential moves, and that it is not coping with changing events. And it is to doubt that party policy is shifting its weighing of conflicting values from decision to decision as is necessary for reasons now familiar from earlier argument.

Consistency on conspicuous points is not, of course, consistency on important but less conspicuous points in any sense of the term. The British Labour Party's consistent fixation on nationalization for some years after World War II was inconsistent with its desires to maintain full employment, stimulate investment, and husband its reformist energies and competence along lines of greatest potential gain. Nor, in another sense, was it consistent to hold to a fixed policy on nationalization as it became apparent that at least some circumstances for which nationalization had been thought appropriate had changed. But we need not recapitulate the entire discussion of consistency that was set forth in the earlier chapter; it should be enough to suggest its relevance to the consistency and coherence argument for disciplined parties.

Another principal argument for discipline is the alleged desirability of raising the weight given to very widely shared values and reducing the weight given to local and certain other narrowly shared values. That such a shift in weight follows from an increase in discipline seems fairly clear, and we specified such a shift in defining party discipline (points 3, 4 and 5 in the list of identifying features, above). It is achieved by neglecting in policy making any local or other sectional values exclusive to the opposition party, as would not be the case where discipline is absent (see point 8 in the same list) and by suppressing partisan mutual adjustment within the legislature.

Whether the shift is to be endorsed depends on several factors. Some of the most disturbing subgroup values are not those that discipline will curb. The protection of monopoly, for example, is a value to a subgroup. But the value is respected in all Congressional districts, and is not at all like a local interest in harbor improvement or one locality's interest in the watch, shoe, or hat industry.[9] Nationally distributed narrowly shared values are not necessarily reduced in weight by party discipline; at least our explanation of the shift in weight does not apply to them. On the other hand, all values peculiar to a geographical area lose, and among these are values worth very great weight.

As the preceding chapter argued there is such a thing as too little weight to subgroup values, and clearly discrimination is required in de-emphasizing any of them. Here is where the superficiality of problem solving under a system of discipline is especially troublesome, for what is often required to a high degree is a skillful aggregation of subnational values into widely shared values. Any shift of emphasis away from local values that makes their aggregation no longer worth the legislator's time and energy is potentially dangerous to the political system. Local values do not deserve neglect; they do deserve reformulation into more widely shareable values. It is not at all clear that party discipline has much to offer on the reformulation. The whole argument of this book indicates that partisan mutual adjustment in party and legislature has something to offer.

There is some danger that party discipline reduces public scrutiny of public policy making. In any case it is a point of some interest that partisan mutual adjustment can be open to inspection in varying degrees, a system of party discipline providing an example of foreclosure of public adjustment in the legislature in favor of private adjustment within the party. In addition, to the extent that discipline turns interest groups from legislator to agency (point 14 in the list of marks of party discipline, above), their role in partisan mutual adjustment is less publicized. The extent to which, for example, British interest groups quietly and inconspicuously remake public policy in cooperation with the bureaucracy has been much speculated on.[10]

As between the failure of public scrutiny of partisan mutual adjustment within the party and its failure in the relations between agency and interest group, the former is probably more serious. A disciplined party, better than an undisciplined one, can lay down guidelines, even strong and relatively enforceable directives, to agencies as an offset to the increased attention given the agencies by interest groups. It is harder to find a compensating advantage for the relative secrecy of policy determination by private partisan mutual adjustment within the party.

Finally, is it true that a disciplined party has a superior capacity to initiate, to act rather than not act, in policy making? Given the authority within the party of the party's leadership and the party's majority in the legislature, it would appear so. But the legislative member of the party can, we have seen, in a general way control the party leadership. *A priori* it would appear that party leadership might or might not choose to maintain its position and party solidarity by timidity in policy making. Insofar as it lays down strong control over the bureaucracy it may weaken agency initiative. There seems to be no reason to count securely on the disciplined party for strong initiative.

On the other hand, a relatively undisciplined party has many decision-making participants within it, each free of discipline and free to take the initiative. In the United States, to be sure, we have so allocated power within the legislature as to make the power to veto much more apparent than the power to initiate. But this is not an essential feature of an undisciplined party system. Considering the range of possible distributions of power possible for Congressional partisan mutual adjustment, one can easily imagine the present capacities for initiative, which are considerable, let loose from the heavy constraining force of informal veto from committee chairman and other decision centers within Congress.

In the market mechanism we see the possibilities of initiative at an extreme. The market is, of course, a system of partisan mutual adjustment; and one of its noteworthy features is entrepreneurial freedom to innovate without veto of any kind. Given the prospect of at least some customers, a potential seller cannot, in an unregulated competitive market, for example, be constrained by the indifference or opposition to his product of other consumers, by the opposition of his employees, or by his competitors. It seems unlikely that we should want initiative in political decision making to be so unconstrained; but the comparison shows that strong initiative is reconcilable with partisan mutual adjustment and is perhaps in no other way achievable.

To be sure, there are reasons for hesitancy in innovating within any decision system, including partisan mutual adjustment.[11] The question is, however, whether there is reason for believing hesitancy to be more marked a problem in the absence of discipline.

Through Which Can The Majority Rule?

We have already said that there is no simple formula that will tell us which of the two methods of aggregation, that of the more- and that of the less-disciplined party, will best respond to majority preferences. Some of the points just made can be brought to bear, however, on some further inquiry into that question. Summarizing, and in part endorsing, a line of analysis of A. Lawrence Lowell, Austin Ranney has written, "A responsible party system, in short, is indispensable to a system of 'unlimited' majority rule."[12] Ranney goes on to question whether unlimited majority rule is desirable; but the question to be raised here is whether in fact disciplined parties are more majoritarian than undisciplined parties.

That two different aggregations of values can both be defended as majoritarian follows from the complexity of the aggregation process.[13] Ordinary tests for the presence or absence of majority rule are quite inadequate for testing these complex processes. That all adults vote, that their votes are equally weighted, that those candidates who win a plurality of votes take office in the legislature, that legislators cast equally weighted votes in the legislature, that legislative issues are settled by a majority vote, that any adult can run for elective office—these and other similar provisions are not at all sufficient to prove majority rule. It is not surprising, then, that differences in party systems are not clear evidence for the presence or absence of majority rule. The difficulty is not simply that we are uncertain about the facts on any system we might empirically observe, but also that we are not wholly clear as to what we wish to mean by "majority rule" for an extremely complex system of aggregation.

Disciplined parties would appear, for example, to permit a clear expression of majority sentiment on electoral choice between the two-party packages or combinations of proposed dispositions and policies. But, following our argument above, by the same token they do not permit an expression of majority opinion on each, even each major, element in the package; and they may be less able to detect and respond to majority wishes on particular elements than can an undisciplined party. Hence, on this score one might associate the disciplined party with majority rule on combinations and the undisciplined party with majority rule on specifics.

Moreover, electoral wishes are translated into policy via the legislature, and here we contrast the majoritarian feature of the contract between party and electorate that marks a disciplined party—the majority has spoken and the party is bound to its wishes—with the potential or actual sensitivity of the undisciplined party both to *ad hoc* legislature majorities and to changing majority opinion in interelection periods. Again, which is majority rule?

Taking note, too, that both parties, in both disciplined and undisciplined party systems, approximate an overwhelming majority view on issues therefore not disputed between the parties, we can also question whether the freer play in an undisciplined party for a wide ranging partisan mutual adjustment does or does not more correctly formulate the national synthesis or overwhelming majority, and whether the disciplined party does or does not manipulate this great majority more than help it to articulate its preferences. Again, in drawing this distinction between what might be called the petty majority—that which wins an election—and the grand majority—that which prevails regardless of who wins the election —we are simply drawing attention to points of evaluation already made but are making the points now relevant to the question of majority rule. In particular the earlier points made on the quality of values formulated through partisan mutual adjustment are relevant to the question of which system best forms and responds to the grand majority.

On the petty majority, of course, it has been shown that discipline may turn the choice of policies over to no more than a small majority of a party supported by only a small majority of the electorate, thus, in effect, to a minority.[14] And where party leadership sets party, hence legislative, policy with only generalized power in the hands of legislative members of the party, it is even less clear that disciplined parties implement the rule of the petty majority.

Conclusion

We leave the discussion of party discipline at this point, somewhat abruptly. For our purpose is not to complete an analysis of the question but only to illustrate the form in which questions about the appropriate role of partisan mutual adjustment arise and the application to those questions of what we have had to say in this study about partisan mutual adjustment. It is indicative of how much analysis remains to be done that we have hardly begun an examination of the relation between different particular forms of partisan mutual adjustment and party discipline.*

* Moreover, in playing up connections between the party discipline issue and partisan mutual adjustment the analysis has given undue attention, as the argument has turned out, to grounds for doubting the desirability of discipline. For what it is worth as a corrective—and a way of underlining the incomplete and only illustrative character of the analysis— I think a case for somewhat more party discipline than exists in the United States today is persuasive, even if the case generally made for party discipline is typically overdone because insufficiently attentive to points such as these made in this discussion.

With this illustration of how issues concerning partisan mutual adjustment arise and can be analyzed we complete not a demonstration of the superiority of partisan mutual adjustment over central policy making—for that is not the issue—but a nonsynoptic analysis indicating that certain ubiquitous forms of noncentral decision making and coordination are useful and undervalued procedures. They do not serve merely to disperse power, believed to be dangerous when concentrated, although that function has always been conceded to them. They are powerful instruments for intelligent policy making—this has been our theme.

Appendix

Summary of
Analysis

LEAVING ASIDE THE ORIENTING
comments of Chapter 1 and the illustrative application of the
analysis of the final chapter, the main lines of the analysis can be
set out in summary form.

I. Interdependent (21f)* partisan (28ff) decision makers can be
coordinated (154) in the following ways, without a central
(25ff) coordinator (Chapter 2).

A. Adaptive (X seeks no response from Y.)
1. *Parametric,* in which the decision maker X adapts to Y's
decisions without regard for consequences for Y (37).
2. *Deferential,* in which X seeks to avoid adverse consequences for Y (45).
3. *Calculated,* in which X does not wholly avoid adverse consequences for Y but nevertheless adjusts his decision out of
consideration for adverse effects for Y (52).

B. Manipulated (X, as a condition of making his decision, induces a response from Y.)

* Numbers in parentheses refer to relevant definitions or explanations
in the text.

330

1. *Negotiation,* in which X and Y, in a certain variety of ways, induce responses from each other (68).
2. *Bargaining* (a form of negotiation), in which X and Y induce responses from each other by conditional threats and promises (71).
3. *Partisan discussion* (a form of negotiation), in which X and Y induce responses from each other by effecting a reappraisal of each other's assessment of the objective consequences of various courses of action (where bargaining alters the consequences, partisan discussion exchanges information about unaltered consequences [71]).
4. *Compensation,* in which X induces a response from Y by a conditional promise of benefit; and *bargained compensation* (a form of bargaining), in which X and Y make conditional promises to each other (74).
5. *Reciprocity,* in which X unilaterally, or X and Y symmetrically, in negotiation or otherwise, induce a response by calling in an existing obligation or acknowledging a new one (76).
6. *Authoritative prescription,* in which X prescribes a response to Y, who concedes X's authority (77f).
7. *Unconditional manipulation,* in which X induces a response from Y by unconditionally altering the advantages or disadvantages to Y of various responses (78f).
8. *Prior decision,* in which X takes a prior decision to induce Y to respond rather than forego the advantages of coordination with X (81).
9. *Indirect manipulation,* in which X uses any of the above forms of manipulation to induce a third decision maker to induce Y to make the desired response (83).

II. In actual democratic government (described in propositions 1–27 of Chapter 6) these processes of partisan mutual adjustment are combined in a variety of ways with central coordination, ranging from the only hypothetical possibility of a government in which centrality is dominant (Part I of Chapter 7) through real-world systems in which partisan mutual adjustment is either very strong or dominant (Part II of Chapter 7 and Chapter 8).

III. The contribution of partisan mutual adjustment to rational decision making can best be understood in the light of the fact that complex decision making is not synoptic (Part I of Chapter 9) but is fragmented, disjointed, and incremental (Parts II and III of Chapter 9) in such a way that multiplicity of "independent" decision makers is itself a source of rationality, as is also the form of their interaction (Chapter 10).

IV. A comparison of central coordination with partisan mutual adjustment throws great doubt on the validity of claims commonly made for central coordination.

    A. One claim is that in central coordination, the adjustment of relations among decisions or policies is made in the light of a survey and consideration of all important possible interrelationships among them (167f). For sufficiently complex problems, however, competence to accomplish an overview is lacking (Part II of Chapter 11); so also is motivation lacking (Part III of Chapter 11).

    B. A second claim is that the coordinating decisions are reasoned in the sense that there are criteria or guidelines of some sort for what the interrelationships should be, and these the coordinator employs (182). But a reasoned decision is impossible without adequate accepted criteria, and these are lacking where decision makers are, as often, partisan (Chapter 12).

    C. A third claim is that in central coordination decisions or policies to be coordinated are made more or less consistent with one another (192). But whether consistency can be achieved empirically is to be doubted for complex problems (Part I of Chapter 13).

    D. A fourth claim is that centrality imparts a consistent pattern to the decisions of the central coordinator so that coordination in one situation or at one time does not produce results at odds with those in other situations and other times (192). But a consistent pattern is not to be desired when, as is the case for complex problems, decision making is fragmented and disjointed (Parts II and III of Chapter 13).

V. Although superficially it would appear that partisan mutual adjustment would fail to achieve any defensible reconciliation of the conflicting values of partisans, in fact it moves partisans toward agreement on values and decisions (Chapter 14). Specifically:

    A. Many value conflicts that would in central systems constitute barriers to reaching agreed decisions do not constitute barriers in partisan mutual adjustment (207).

    B. Participants in partisan mutual adjustment have stronger

motives than do central coordinators to find an agreed decision or outcome (208).

C. The need for allies is an especially powerful motivation toward agreement in partisan mutual adjustment (210).

D. Agreement is also encouraged by the moderation imposed on demands in partisan mutual adjustment by reason of the tasks and other responsibilities attached to making a demand (213).

E. Because in partisan mutual adjustment, decisions or outcomes of adjustments are tentative and can easily be altered, participants will agree where otherwise they would not (215).

F. Participants find it to their advantage to make agreed concessions of specialized extralegal authority to each other, thus avoiding by prearrangement conflicts that would otherwise develop (217).

G. In partisan discussion, in contrast to cooperative discussion, is to be found an important potential for agreement (220).

H. Compensation, bargained compensation, and partisan discussion are available as a means of testing whether a given state of affairs is a Pareto optimum for the potential negotiators and, if it is not, of moving to such an optimum (222).

I. Lastly, many of the partisans in mutual adjustment pursue a version of the public interest (224).

VI. Moreover, where agreement is not obtained the reconciliation of values is marked, in partisan mutual adjustment, by important acceptable features (Chapter 15):

A. In the decisions and patterns of decisions reached through a system of partisan mutual adjustment the weight given to each of various conflicting values depends on and can systematically be made to depend on characteristics of that particular system, which is only one of many possible systems of partisan mutual adjustment; and even within a system the weight will vary and can be systematically varied to depend on factors to be specified in further propositions (228f).

B. In partisan mutual adjustment in the United States and in the Western democracies almost any value that any even relatively small number of citizens moderately or strongly wishes to see weighted into the policy-making process will be weighted at some value significantly above zero (229).

C. On some counts partisan mutual adjustment, compared to central coordination, reduces the possibility that a set of decisions are so arranged as to constitute a gain for no one and a loss for some (232).

D. In some large part the weight given to a value depends on the authority held by the participants in partisan mutual adjustment who pursue or protect it and by their adversaries (235).

E. Within very wide margins weights given to values can be systematically altered by systematic reallocations of authority (236).

F. By reason of the preceding two propositions and for other reasons as well, in any system of partisan mutual adjustment the weights given various values vary from one decision-making situation to another; and weights in one situation will often correct deficiencies in earlier weights (237).

G. In policy choices partisan mutual adjustment will often so weight values as to achieve after the decision a wide endorsement of the value weights implicit in the decision, despite the absence of any criteria that would call for such weights in advance of the decision and in the absence of prior agreement on weights (239).

H. Other things being equal, the more widely shared a value, interest, or preference the heavier its weight in partisan mutual adjustment (242).

I. Other things being equal, the more intensely held a value, interest, or preference the heavier its weight in partisan mutual adjustment (244).

VII. Although it might be objected that values are not equally weighted when reconciled or aggregated in partisan mutual adjustment, it is clear that they should not be (Chapter 16). For aside from internal contradictions and ambiguities in the criteria of equal weights, there are specific reservations about the majority–equality principle as a guide to policy:

A. To begin with, the view that at least in some cases the weight given preferences should be adjusted to take account of intensity of feeling about them contradicts the majority principle (255f).

B. Those who might wish to use such a criterion as equality for evaluating mutual adjustment will also disagree over how far to depart from the criterion in order to endorse the guarantee of certain minimum values to everyone (256).

C. There will be other departures from the equality–majority principle on the ground that some values, being more carefully considered, should be more heavily weighted than others (257).

D. As a practical recourse most of us also depart from equality in varying degrees to acknowledge the claims of special interest in a policy area (257).

E. Some observers will also justify departures from equal weighting because they want to motivate active participation in politics (258).

F. A final objection to the majority–equality criterion is that it conflicts with the criterion of consent (258ff).

VIII. In partisan mutual adjustment inequalities in weighting of values are of a kind usually sanctioned; in particular they meet the fundamental political requirement that values be weighted in ways that promote consent to democratic government (Chapter 17).

IX. Partisan mutual adjustment is not necessarily biased against widely shared values, nor against collective values, nor against values embraced in various concepts of "public interest" (Chapter 18).

X. The use of partisan mutual adjustment of various kinds for rational decision making is subject to control both through partisan mutual adjustment itself and through elements of central decision making; but the appraisal of partisan mutual adjustment for purposes of control must be carried on through fragmented, disjointed, and incremental analysis rather than through synopsis (Part II of Chapter 19).

XI. In considering when and how to use partisan mutual adjustment it is essential to take account of the way results will vary according to the distribution of power among participants, especially since the distribution can be remedied when defective (Part III of Chapter 19 and *passim*).

NOTES

Chapter 1
Rational Policy through Mutual Adjustment

1. Luther H. Gulick, "Notes on the Theory of Organization," in Gulick and L. Urwick (eds.), *Papers on The Science of Administration* (New York: Columbia University Press, 1937), p.6.

2. Victor A. Thompson, *Modern Organization* (New York: Knopf, 1961), pp.181–90.

3. William Yandell Elliott, *United States Foreign Policy,* a report of a study group for the Woodrow Wilson Foundation (New York: Columbia University Press, 1952), p.66.

4. Reinhold Niebuhr, *The Nature and Destiny of Man* (New York: Scribners, 1949) II, 266.

5. R. A. Dahl and Charles E. Lindblom, *Politics, Economics and Welfare* (New York: Harper, 1953), pp.171f., 238, 325, chap. xiii.

6. John M. Pfiffner and Robert V. Presthus, *Public Administration* (New York: Ronald Press, 1960), chap. ix, pp.149ff.

7. David Truman, *The Governmental Process* (New York: Knopf, 1951).

8. Arthur Bentley, *The Process of Government* (Evanston, Illinois: Principia Press, 1935).

9. Thomas Schelling, *The Strategy of Conflict* (Cambridge: Harvard University Press, 1960).

10. Michael Polanyi, "Manageability of Social Tasks," *The Logic of Liberty* (Chicago: University of Chicago Press, 1951); *Personal Knowledge* (Chicago: University of Chicago Press, 1958), p.217; and "Towards A Theory of Conspicuous Production," *Soviet Survey* (October–December, 1960), 90–99.

11. James G. March and Herbert A. Simon, *Organizations* (New York: Wiley, 1958), pp.129ff.

12. Henry M. Metcalf and L. Urwick, *Dynamic Administration: The Collected Papers of Mary Parker Follett* (New York: Harper, 1942), esp. pp.297–314.

13. Bentley, *op. cit.;* Truman, *op. cit.;* Earl Latham, *The Group Basis of Politics* (Ithaca: Cornell University Press, 1952); Pendleton Herring, *The Politics of Democracy* (New York: Rinehart, 1940).

14. Vincent Ostrom, Charles M. Tiebout, and Robert Warren, "The Organization of Government in Metropolitan Areas: A Theoretical Inquiry," *American Political Science Review,* LV (December, 1961), 831–42.

15. See Paul Lazarsfeld and Elihu Katz, *Personal Influence* (Glencoe, Illinois: Free Press, 1955); and V. O. Key, Jr., *Public Opinion and*

American Democracy (New York: Knopf, 1961), chaps. ii and iii, Sec. IV.

16. Such coordination can be found in the forest service, for example. See Luther H. Gulick, *American Forest Policy* (New York: Duell, Sloan, and Pearce, 1951), p.74.

17. For summaries, see Henry S. Kariel, *The Decline of American Pluralism* (Stanford: Stanford University Press, 1961), pp.142ff; Frederick Watkins, *The Political Tradition of the West* (Cambridge: Harvard University Press, 1957), pp.263ff.

18. Bentley, *op. cit.,* pp.204, 206.

19. I find only one possible hint of common interests and values in Bentley, *op. cit.,* p.454.

20. Latham, *op. cit.,* p.390.

21. Bentley, *op. cit.,* pp.264ff.

22. Truman, *op. cit.,* p.503.

23. Bentley, *op. cit.,* pp.283f., 458.

24. *Ibid.,* p.359.

25. *Ibid.,* pp.454f.

26. *Ibid.,* pp.448f.

27. Kariel, *op. cit.,* p.202.

28. Bentley, *op. cit.,* p.447.

29. Harold Lasswell, *Politics: Who Gets What, When, How* (Cleveland: World, 1958).

Chapter 3
Adaptive Adjustments

1. Jack Greenberg, *Race Relations and American Law* (New York: Columbia University Press, 1959), p.361.

2. *Ibid.,* pp.366ff.; and James C. Evans and David A. Lane, Jr., "Integration in the Armed Services," *Annals,* CCCIV (March, 1956), 82.

3. James R. Bell and Lynwood B. Steedman, *Personnel Problems in Converting to Automation,* The Inter-University Case Program No. 44 (University: University of Alabama Press, 1959), pp.2–5, 13.

4. Norman I. Wengert, *Valley of Tomorrow* (Knoxville: University of Tennessee, Bureau of Public Administration, 1952), p.79. That the pure types to be presented in this chapter are intertwined in actual practice is indicated by the reinforcement of the policy of deference through a Memorandum of Understanding in 1934 between TVA, the Department of Agriculture, and the colleges, the Memorandum presumably terminating a period of negotiation. (*Ibid.,* p.72.)

5. Robert A. Wallace, *Congressional Control of Federal Spending* (Detroit: Wayne State University Press, 1960), p.38.

6. Raymond H. Dawson, *The Decision to Aid Russia, 1941* (Chapel Hill: University of North Carolina Press, 1959), p.46.

7. Alvin W. Gouldner, "The Norm of Reciprocity: A Preliminary Statement," *American Sociological Review,* XXV (April, 1961), 171.

8. Wengert, *op. cit.,* p.114.

9. Herman Miles Somers, *Presidential Agency* (Cambridge: Harvard University Press, 1950), pp.76ff.

10. Dawson, *op. cit.,* pp.147ff., 230ff., esp. 235f.

Chapter 4
Manipulated Adjustments: Preliminary Survey

1. See, for example, Thomas Schelling, *The Strategy of Conflict* (Cambridge: Harvard University Press, 1960), p.5; Aaron Wildavsky, *Dixon-Yates* (New Haven: Yale University Press, 1962), p.311; Dahl and Lindblom, *op. cit.,* p.324; March and Simon, *op. cit.,* p.129f., but note qualifications; and Richard E. Neustadt, *Presidential Power* (New York: Wiley, 1960), p.36ff., 46, 187.

2. Somers, *op. cit.,* p.140ff.

3. This occurred, for example, in an early period in the history of the book and job printers of Chicago. See Emily Clark Brown, *Book and Job Printing in Chicago* (Chicago: University of Chicago Press, 1931), p.33.

4. Edward C. Banfield, *Political Influence* (New York: Free Press, 1961), pp.30f.

5. Wrote John Morton Blum, "The circumstantial evidence that there was some bargain or understanding is overwhelming." (*The Republican Roosevelt* [Cambridge: Harvard University Press, 1954], p.81.)

6. *Ibid.,* chap. vi, esp. pp.93–103.

7. *New York Times* (January 21, 1951), III:1:8; and (February 7, 1951), 20:4.

8. Richard T. Frost (ed.), *Cases in State and Local Government* (Englewood Cliffs, New Jersey: Prentice-Hall, 1961), chap. xxiv.

9. A quite similar classification, proposed as a classification of methods of control, is to be found in John C. Harsanyi, "Measurement of Social Power, Opportunity Costs, and the Theory of Two-Person Bargaining Games" (unpublished paper, 1961).

Chapter 5
Manipulated Adjustments: Specific Forms

1. Frank H. Knight, *Freedom and Reform* (New York: Harper, 1947), p.190.

2. Ernest Barker, *Reflections on Government* (London: Oxford University Press, 1942), p.40.

3. Ernest Barker (ed.), *The Politics of Aristotle* (New York: Oxford University Press, 1962), p.126.

4. Banfield, *op. cit.,* p.25.

5. Joseph Alsop and Turner Catledge, *The 168 Days* (Garden City, New York: Doubleday, Doran, 1938), pp.100, 116, 190, 198f., 250.

6. Banfield, *op. cit.,* p.193.

7. Quoted in Vernon Lee Fluharty, *Dance of the Millions* (Pittsburgh: University of Pittsburgh Press, 1957), pp.162f.

8. William J. Block, *The Separation of the Farm Bureau and the Extension Service* (Urbana: University of Illinois Press, Illinois Studies in the Social Sciences No. 47, 1960), p.39.

9. In Andrew M. Scott and Earle Wallace (eds.), *Politics, U.S.A.* (New York: Macmillan, 1961), p.36.

10. With more details and more complicated indirections, the story is told in Alan F. Westin (ed.), *The Uses of Power* (New York: Harcourt, Brace & World, 1962), pp.13ff.

Chapter 6
The Governmental Process

1. For the variety and subtlety of allocations of authority and function, see, for example, C. P. Cotter and J. M. Smith, "Administrative Responsibility: Congressional Prescription of Interagency Relationships," *Western Political Quarterly,* X (1957), 765–82.

2. Nicholas A. Masters, "Committee Assignments in the House of Representatives," *American Political Science Review,* LV (June, 1961), 352.

3. If this characterization of the role of the interest-group leader appears to be more speculative than the other propositions of this chapter, see, for corroboration, Gabriel Almond, *The American People and Foreign Policy* (New York: Harcourt Brace, 1950), pp.7, 139, 142, *passim.* Also Key, *op. cit., passim,* e.g., pp.77, 366ff.

4. That conventions are more powerful, for example, in negotiation between legislator and interest-group leader than is commonly believed is argued by *ibid.,* pp.526ff., 537ff.

5. It is not easy to do so on particular issues and, to some degree a threat to do so violates convention. See *ibid.,* pp.508–22; also E. E. Schattschneider, *The Semisovereign People* (New York: Holt, Rinehart and Winston, 1961), chap. iii.

Chapter 7
Mixed Systems: Emphasis on Centrality

1. Wallace S. Sayre and Herbert Kaufman, *Governing New York City* (New York: Russell Sage Foundation, 1960), p.511.

2. Block, *op. cit.,* pp.1, 22–32, *passim.*

3. *Ibid.,* p.270.

4. Neil W. Chamberlain, *Labor* (New York: McGraw-Hill, 1958), p.510.

5. Merle Fainsod, Lincoln Gordon, and Joseph C. Palamountain, Jr., *Government and the American Economy,* 3rd ed. (New York: Norton, 1958), pp.418ff.

6. R. A. Dahl, *Who Governs?* (New Haven: Yale University Press, 1961), pp.139f.

7. Grant McConnell, *The Steel Seizure of 1952* (University: University of Alabama Press, Inter-University Case Program, 1960), p.36.

8. Robert J. Morgan, "Pressure Politics and Resources Administration," *Journal of Politics,* XVIII (February, 1956), pp.50f.

9. Pendleton Herring, *Group Representation Before Congress* (Baltimore: Johns Hopkins Press, 1929), p.75.

10. J. L. Freeman, Jr., "The New Deal for Indians" (Ph.D. dissertation, Princeton University, 1952) pp.118–80.

11. Gus Tyler, *A Legislative Campaign for a Federal Minimum Wage* (New York: Henry Holt, 1959), p.2, *passim.*

Chapter 8
Mixed Systems: Mutual Adjustment Dominant

1. C. Vann Woodward, *Reunion and Reaction* (New York: Doubleday, 1956), p.265f.

2. Marshall E. Dimock, *The Executive in Action* (New York: Harper, 1945), pp.56–65.

3. S. E. Finer, *Anonymous Empire* (London: Pall Mall Press, 1958), p.66.

4. Heinz Eulau, in "The Party as a Reference Group in the Process of Legislative Consent" (presented at the Annual Meeting of the American Political Science Association in 1961), has appraised several alternative explanations of the phenomenon of unanimity in legislatures, all of which are consistent with the proposition given here that prior to the vote there are coordinating influences operating, among which a significant one is partisan mutual adjustment.

5. Arthur J. Vidich and Joseph Bensman, *Small Town in Mass Society* (Princeton: Princeton University Press, 1958), p.110.

6. Duane Lockard, *New England State Politics* (Princeton: Princeton University Press, 1959), p.281.

7. Richard F. Fenno, Jr., "The House Appropriations Committee as a Political System: The Problem of Integration," (presented at the Annual Meeting of the American Political Science Association in 1961), p.12.

8. *Ibid.,* p.24.

9. V. O. Key, Jr., Fritz Morstein Marx (ed.), *Elements of Public Administration* (New York: Prentice-Hall, 1946), p.342.

10. Marver H. Bernstein, *The Job of the Federal Executive* (Washington: Brookings Institution, 1958), pp.86f.

Chapter 9
Strategy in Problem Solving

1. The term, as well as the entire description of alternative views of problem solving in this chapter, is taken from David Braybrooke and Charles E. Lindblom, *A Strategy of Decision* (New York: Free Press, 1963).

2. For confirmation of the currency of such a conception of problem solving, see March and Simon, *op. cit.,* pp. 137f. For examples of acceptance of the method as an ideal in public policy making, see Arthur Smithies, *The Budgetary Process in the United States* (New York: McGraw-Hill, 1955), *passim,* esp. p.16), and Jan Tinbergen, *Economic Policy: Principles and Design* (Amsterdam: North Holland, 1956), pp.8–11, *passim.*

3. For a more extended discussion see Braybrooke and Lindblom, *op. cit.,* chap. v.

4. For a more precise definition of "incremental," see *ibid.,* chap. iv.

Chapter 11
Coordination by Overview

1. Bell and Steedman, *op. cit.,* pp.2–5, 13.

2. On the experiment with the consolidated appropriations bill, see Robert A. Wallace, *Congressional Control of Federal Spending* (Detroit: Wayne State University Press, 1960), pp.131–36.

3. On the history of the Court controversy, see Alsop and Catledge, *op. cit.,* pp.20, 27, 28, 36, *passim.*

4. Wildavsky, *op. cit.,* p.322. For the President's original decision, see p.20.

Chapter 12
Reasoned Coordination

1. Martin Meyerson and Edward C. Banfield, *Politics, Planning and the Public Interest* (Glencoe, Illinois: Free Press, 1955), pp.165f.
2. *Ibid.,* pp.166f.

Chapter 13
Consistency

1. For a brief explanation of a Pareto optimum, see Kenneth Boulding, "Welfare Economics" in Bernard F. Haley (ed.), *A Survey of Contemporary Economics,* (Homewood, Illinois: Irwin, 1952), II, 12ff.
2. For example, Lauren Soth, *Farm Trouble* (Princeton: Princeton University Press, 1957), pp.84–85.
3. Hans J. Morgenthau, "The Perils of Political Empiricism," *Commentary,* XXXIV (July, 1962), 60–63.
4. Victor A. Thompson, *The Regulatory Process in OPA Rationing* (New York: Columbia University Press, 1950), pp.292ff.
5. *Ibid.,* chap. iii.

Chapter 14
Social Agreement

1. For a more extended discussion of how strategic problem solvers maintain a high degree of flexibility in the search for agreement, see Braybrooke and Lindblom, *op. cit.,* chap. vii.
2. Metcalf and Urwick, *op. cit.,* pp.239ff; and M. P. Follett, *Freedom and Coordination* (London: Management Publications, 1949), pp.65f.
3. Truman, *op. cit.,* p.367.
4. Dimock, *op. cit.,* pp.56–65.
5. Jerome Rothenberg, *The Measurement of Social Welfare* (Englewood Cliffs, New Jersey: Prentice-Hall, 1961), chaps. iii and iv.
6. *New York Times* (May 19, 1962), 16:1:3.
7. Dimock, *op. cit.,* pp.285f.
8. Herbert Simon, Donald W. Smithburg, and Victor A. Thompson, *Public Administration* (New York: Knopf, 1959), p.90.
9. Thompson, *The Regulatory Process in OPA Rationing, op. cit.,* pp.318f.
10. For further discussion of these points see Braybrooke and Lindblom, *op. cit.,* chap. vii.
11. Schattschneider, *op. cit.,* p.26.

Chapter 15
Conflicting Values

1. H. Krabbe, *The Modern Idea of the State* (New York: Appleton, 1922), p.157.
2. John Dickinson, "Democratic Realities and Democratic Dogma," *American Political Science Review*, XXV (1930), 291f.
3. Truman, *op. cit.*, pp.264ff.
4. The veto in central systems is noted in Thompson, *op. cit.*, p.61.
5. For related comments on decision-maker subculture, see Key, *op. cit.*, pp.526ff.
6. *Ibid.*, p.233.
7. *Ibid.*, pp.208ff.
8. Robert E. Lane, *Political Life* (New York: Free Press, 1959), p.157.

Chapter 16
Equality as a Criterion

1. Thompson, *The Regulatory Process in OPA Rationing, op. cit.*, p.90.
2. For development of this point see R. A. Dahl, *A Preface to Democratic Theory* (Chicago: University of Chicago Press, 1956), chap. v.
3. *One Man—One Vote* (New York: The Twentieth Century Fund, 1962), pp.8f.
4. Carl J. Friedrich, *The New Image of the Common Man* (Boston: Beacon Press, 1950), chap. v.
5. For some interesting but inconclusive evidence from a sample of citizens see James W. Prothro and Charles M. Grigg, "Fundamental Principles of Democracy: Bases of Agreement and Disagreement," *Journal of Politics*, XXII (May, 1960), 276–94.

Chapter 18
Public Interest and Group Interests

1. For an insightful discussion of a distinction between "inflated" and "deflated" concepts of the public interest, see David Braybrooke, "The Public Interest," in Carl J. Friedrich (ed.), *The Public Interest*, Vol. V, *Nomos* (New York: Prentice-Hall, 1962), pp.129–54.
2. Harry Eckstein, *Pressure Group Politics* (Stanford: Stanford University Press, 1962), pp.162f.

Chapter 19
Choice Among Policy-Making Methods

1. Experimental work with small groups supports a common layman's view that participation in decision processes is a "good thing," although small group behavior is an inadequate guide to behavior in a complex political system. Small group studies on the point are summarized and evaluated in Sidney Verba, *Small Groups and Political Behavior* (Princeton: Princeton University Press, 1961), chaps. ix, x, esp. pp.227f.

2. This is described at greater length in Braybrooke and Lindblom, *op. cit.*

3. Cf. Bentley, *op. cit.:* Writing a book on or otherwise publicly analyzing a practical political issue is an act of "representation" that becomes part of the process of group representation in government (p.428).

4. Latham, *op. cit.,* pp.36f.

5. Ernest S. Griffith, *Congress: Its Contemporary Role* (New York: New York University Press, 1951), p.113.

6. Luther Gulick, *op. cit.,* p.6.

7. Carl J. Friedrich, *Constitutional Government and Democracy* (Boston: Ginn, 1950), p.47.

8. Joseph P. Harris, "The Future of Administrative Management," in L. D. White (ed.), *The Future of Government in the United States* (Chicago: University of Chicago Press, 1942), pp.175f.

9. Elliott, *op. cit.,* p.66.

10. Simon, Smithburg, and Thompson, *op. cit.,* pp.555ff.

11. Thompson, *Modern Organization, op. cit.,* pp.181, 183ff., 187f.

12. Luther Gulick, *Administrative Reflections from World War II* (University: University of Alabama Press, 1948), p.117.

13. Simon, Smithburg, and Thompson, *op. cit.,* pp.297, 309.

14. V. O. Key, Jr., *Politics, Parties, and Pressure Groups* (New York: Crowell, 1958), p.763.

15. Truman, *op. cit.,* p.13.

16. Latham, *op. cit.*

17. Joseph P. Harris, "The Reorganization of Congress," *Public Administration Review,* VI (Summer, 1946), 269.

18. *Ibid.,* p.280.

19. Paraphrased or summarized from Smithies, *op. cit.,* pp.16–28, 45, 164, 169, 175ff., 192f.

20. For an earlier development of the analysis of this book, applied to the budgetary process, see my "Decision-Making in Taxation and Expenditures," in Universities-National Bureau Committee for Economic Research, *Public Finances: Needs, Sources and Utilization* (Princeton: Princeton University Press, 1961), pp.295–329.

21. B. Klein, "The Decision-Making Problem in Development," Paper No. P-1916, The RAND Corporation, Santa Monica, California, February 19, 1960; B. Klein and W. Meckling, "Application of Operations Research to Development Decisions," *Operations Research,* VI (1958), 352–63.

Chapter 20
An Illustrative Application of the Analysis

1. American Political Science Association, *Toward A More Responsible Two-Party System* (New York: Rinehart, 1950).

2. Evidence on this point, offered in reply to the American Political Science Association Committee, is in Julius Turner, "Responsible Parties: A Dissent from the Floor," *American Political Science Review,* XLV (March, 1951), 143–49.

3. If points 14 and 15 are less obvious characteristics of party discipline than the others listed, see, for corroboration, Samuel H. Beer, "New Structures of Democracy: Britain and America," in W. N. Chambers and Robert H. Salisbury (eds.), *Democracy Today* (New York: Collier, 1962), p.65.

4. Harry Jaffa has called attention to the degree to which observers of party politics underplay, in their preoccupation with the party's function in offering alternatives, its function in building a consensus. (Public lecture, Yale University, May 2, 1963.)

5. American Political Science Association, *op. cit.;* Stephen K. Bailey, *The Condition of Our National Political Parties* (New York: Fund for the Republic, 1959).

6. The case for organization exclusively by *ad hoc* coalition rather than more stable party coalitions has been made by M. I. Ostrogorski in *Democracy and the Organization of Political Parties* (London: Macmillan, 1902), II, 658. A contemporary and less extreme position is in J. Roland Pennock, "Responsiveness, Responsibility, and Majority Rule," *American Political Science Review,* XLVI (September, 1952), p.801.

7. Beer, *op. cit.,* p.72.

8. American Political Science Association, *op. cit.;* Bailey, *op. cit.;* Fritz Morstein Marx in J. C. Wahlke and Heinz Eulau, (eds.) *Legislative Behavior* (New York: Free Press, 1959), pp.55–60.

9. ". . . parties claimed by theory and ideology to be responsive to local interests are in fact so responsive to national ones that the seeming triumph of the locality is the actual triumph of nationally organized, large-scale, well-incorporated private groups." (Kariel, *op. cit.,* p.285.)

10. For argument and evidence that the subversion goes far, see A. A. Rogow, *The Labour Government and British Industry, 1945–1951* (Ithaca: Cornell University Press, 1955).

11. Wallace S. Sayre and Herbert Kaufman find, for example, that in a political system marked by fragmentation of power, action will be inhibited because every innovation in policy is costly to some parties and will be resisted by them, because officials will hesitate to move against opposition, and because higher level decision makers to whom disputes are passed can always wait in the hope that agreement will later emerge or the problem will vanish. (*Op. cit.,* pp.716ff.) But these factors operate in nonfragmented systems, too, and in any case have to be evaluated by comparison with inhibitions characteristic of central decision making.

12. "Toward A More Responsible Two-Party System," *op. cit.,* p.495.

13. See, for example, Wilmoore Kendall, "The Two Majorities," *Midwest Journal of Political Science* IV (November, 1960), 317–45.

14. Pennock, *op. cit.,* p.799.

INDEX

See also Appendix: Summary of Analysis, pp. 330–5